RAGE™
WARRIORS OF THE APOCALYPSE

Into the Jaws of Ragnarok

Credits

Authors: Tim Byrd, Ken Cliffe, Ed Hall, Todd Mayville, Ethan Skemp, Mike Tinney, and Pocahontas Firestein van Elfinburg della Escondido, Esq.

Development: Ethan Skemp

Editing: Ed McKeogh

Vice President in Charge of Production: Richard Thomas

Art Directors: Aileen E. Miles & Lawrence Snelly

Layout & Typesetting: Robby Poore (with miniscule assistance from Aileen E. Miles)

Art: Barb Armata, Ash Arnett, Stuart Beel, John Bridges, Dennis Calero, Richard Case, Steve Casper, John Cobb, James Daly, Mike Danza, Tony DiTerlizzi, Mike Dringenburg, Jason Felix, Richard Kane Ferguson, Lee Fields, Scott Fischer, Rebecca Guay, Matt Haley, Tony Harris, Quinton Hoover, Mark Jackson, Brian LeBlanc, Larry MacDougall, Anson Maddocks, John Matson, Ken Meyer Jr., Jeff Miracola, Jesper Myrfors, Alan Pollack, William O'Conner, Jeff Rebner, SCAR (Steve Carter & Antoinette Ryder), Alex Sheikman, E. Allen Smith, Ron Spencer, Ron States, Joshua Gabriel Timbrook, Richard Thomas, Jamie Tolagson, Drew Tucker, Lawrence Allen Williams

Cover Design: Lawrence Snelly

Cover Art: Joshua Gabriel Timbrook

WHITE WOLF GAME STUDIO

SUITE 100
780 PARK NORTH BLVD.
CLARKSTON, GA 30021

Special Thanks

Pocahontas "Justin Achilli" **Firestein van Elfinburg della Escondido, Esq.,** for being strong enough to pull the ears off a Gundar.

Tim "Gone Postal" **Byrd,** for gritting his teeth and licking the envelopes.

Ed "Zip Code" **Hall,** for choosing the worst possible time to become an intern.

Paul "Slave Girls" **LePree,** for his heavily armored Blood Bowl team.

Todd "Misty Gum Remover" **Mayville,** for his vast reserves of gopher lore.

John "Orcish Scat" **Park,** for crooning over his Big Shiny Cup.

Richard "Necromancer King" **Thomas,** for acting the part with the silver-headed cane.

Mike "Field Trip" **Tinney,** for taking everybody out into the woods to accumulate chigger bites.

Extra Special Thanks

To all those writers who originally devised the characters that populate the **Werewolf** and **Rage** cosm, a heartfelt thank-you. Half the characters in here are your babies. Hope you appreciate the directions they're growing in; as for us, we're all very proud ourselves.

RAGE™
WARRIORS of the APOCALYPSE

Contents

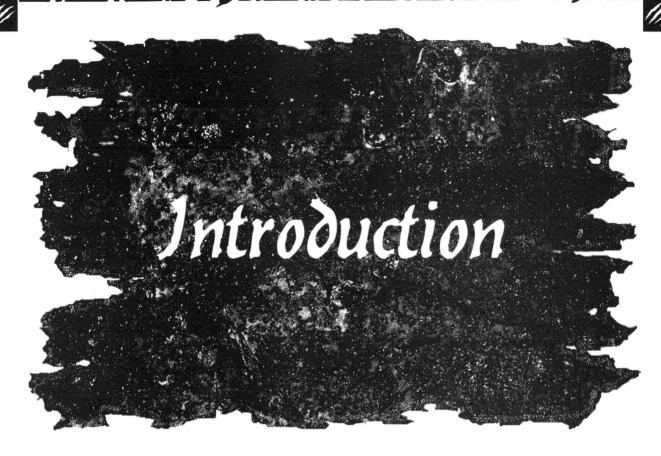

Introduction

During the **Rage** collectible card game development, everyone agreed that it had to accurately reflect its parent game, **Werewolf: The Apocalypse**. From that sprang the idea of character cards, based on the Garou that **Werewolf** players might run into or meet during their chronicles. It was pretty obvious to everybody involved that there were a lot of great characters lying around in various **Werewolf** supplements. So the developers hit the books, dragging a number of Garou and Wyrmspawn from various sources. Some got a facelift; others were adapted fairly whole-cloth. Many characters were invented on the fly. And lo and behold — the players liked them. Not just that; they wanted to know more about them.

That's where **Warriors of the Apocalypse** comes in. Herein are almost all of the character cards from **Rage**, presented for use with **Werewolf: The Apocalypse**. Not just **Rage**, either; there are also characters from the **Umbra**, **Wyrm**, and **War of the Amazon** supplements. You want to know how strong Anna Kliminski is? Or why Grimfang is so important? Now you can find out.

This book is also useful for Storytellers who don't play **Rage**. Any character within can be dropped with little modification into a **Werewolf** chronicle. For the first time, you can see statistics for Lord Albrecht, Mari Cabrah and Evan Heals-the-Past. You want enemies? We have more than a pack's worth of Black Spiral Dancers and a vanload of fomori, to say nothing of other threats. Several of these characters have gone out of print and deserve a second look.

You'll find the characters listed alphabetically by tribe; of course, this gets problematic with Garou and their diverse names. For simplicity's sake, we filed them according to the first letter in their name — Susan Anthony and Sister Judith Paws-of-Light are both under "S," for example.

Many of the characters presented here are brand-new, invented just for **Rage**. But many others have previously been published in other **Werewolf** supplements. For space's sake, we left out those published in the **Werewolf: The Apocalypse** rulebook and **The Werewolf Players Guide**. The others hail originally from **Caerns: Places of Power**, **Rage across Australia**, **Rage across the Amazon**, **Rage across New York**, **Rage across Russia**, **Umbra: The Velvet Shadow**, the tribebooks **Black Furies** and **Get of Fenris**, even **Under a Blood Red Moon** and **Dark Alliance: Vancouver**. The power level of these characters often varies significantly between the original source and the statistics presented here. This is not an oversight; this book simply presents the character at a different place along his journey. In addition, we've changed any first-edition characters to mesh with second-edition rules.

One distinct difference is that several characters shifted breed when translated to **Rage** statistics (Roshen One-Arm, for example). We've published them here with their original breed (the changes were made to balance the card game). Feel free to change them back to **Rage** information if that suits your chronicle.

Another difference: the Banes in **Rage** possess human bodies that they shed when pressed. In strict **Werewolf** terms, these Bane-possessed hosts would be fomori. However, there's a distinct difference between the Bane cards and the fomori cards in **Rage**. Assume that the Banes presented hereafter are not as attached to their host bodies and can destroy their meat vessels to free themselves when the situation demands. They are individuals, stronger players in the War of the Apocalypse.

Enough said. Here are the heroes of both sides of the War. Some are pure of heart and mind; others are traitors to everything they once valued. Some are filled with fury; others are just along for the ride. Whatever name they answer to, however, they're all fighters in one way or another. They are the Warriors of the Apocalypse.

Champions of Gaia

Black Furies

Alestro

Breed: Homid

Auspice: Ahroun

Physical: Strength 3 (5/7/6/4), Dexterity 4 (4/5/6/6), Stamina 4 (6/7/7/6)

Social: Charisma 3, Manipulation 2 (1/0/0/0), Appearance 3 (2/0/3/3)

Mental: Perception 3, Intelligence 3, Wits 4

Talents: Alertness 3, Athletics 4, Archery 5, Brawl 3, Dodge 4, Empathy 3, Expression 3, Intimidation 4, Leadership 2, Primal-Urge 4

Skills: Animal Ken 3, Etiquette 1, Melee (spears) 5, Stealth 2, Survival 4

Knowledges: Enigmas 3, Linguistics 1, Medicine 4, Occult 4, Rituals 3

Backgrounds: Past Life 3, Pure Breed 2, Resources 5

Gifts: (1) Persuasion, Razor Claws, Sense Wyrm; (2) Sense Silver, Staredown; (3) Coup de Grace

Rank: 3

Rage 6, Gnosis 5, Willpower 7

Alestro

Image: Alestro is a traditional Amazonian Black Fury. Even in Homid form she wears very little clothing. She seems to be of native South American descent; there is still a trace of her ancestral Greek heritage in her face, but it is hardly obvious. She appears to be about 18. Her Crinos and Lupus forms are large, lean and black.

Roleplaying Notes: You are typically not very outgoing. You appreciate help when it's offered, but cannot tolerate idiots who overestimate their own capabilities. You have no love for the outsider Garou and trust only Uktena and other Black Furies. You keep quiet and keep your own counsel; only those who grew up fighting this war have any idea what is really at stake.

History: The Black Furies of the Sept of Gold have been living in the Dorado Realm for centuries, leaving only when low on good breeding stock to mate with. If the natives of the closest villages could be convinced to talk, they would tell stories of the demons that came in the night and stole their men or simply forced themselves on them before leaving. The Kinfolk in El Dorado are almost entirely the victims of pillaging in local villages and are — or were — quite content with their lives. They have been treated very well, although they are still second-class citizens. These Furies are the basis for the legendary Amazon warriors of lore, and their ancestors were responsible for the deaths of many conquistadors.

Alestro, like the rest of her sept, has pledged to defend the ancient mage El Dorado from outsiders. To this end, she carries silver-tipped arrows and spears aplenty, ever ready to sink them in a Black Spiral Dancer's fetid hide. The war for the Amazon hardened her very quickly, giving her plenty of opportunity to practice her skills while fueling her mistrust. She has met with Mokolé and Bastet before and can properly and politely deal with them. Many non-native Garou would be grateful to have her as a guide, but her distrust of their motives keeps her distant.

Amari Howls-from-Soul

Breed: Lupus

Auspice: Galliard

Nature/Demeanor: Competitor/Fanatic

Physical: Strength 3 (5/7/6/4), Dexterity 3 (3/4/5/5), Stamina 2 (4/5/5/4)

Social: Charisma 4 , Manipulation 4 (3/1/1/1), Appearance 2 (1/0/2/2)

Mental: Perception 2, Intelligence 2, Wits 2

Talents: Alertness 2, Empathy 2, Expression 3, Primal-Urge 2

Amari Howls-from-Soul

While the rest of her pack was content to accept their traditional and survivalist ways, Amari found herself questioning established facets of life. Alone among her pack, Amari began to manifest the traits of her auspice at a point at which she had nowhere else to turn, she howled all through the night with her unanswered questions to a mute moon. Her First Change lifted a veil from her vision, allowing her to experience the greater depth of the world as it truly is, and the Black Furies have gladly accepted her into their tribal structure during these days of dwindling lupus populations.

Cassandra Shadow-Walker

Breed: Homid
Auspice: Theurge
Nature/Demeanor: Survivor/Loner
Physical: Strength 4 (6/8/7/5), Dexterity 4 (4/5/6/6), Stamina 3 (5/6/6/5)
Social: Charisma 4, Manipulation 3 (2/0/0/0), Appearance 4 (3/0/4/4)
Mental: Perception 5, Intelligence 4, Wits 4
Talents: Alertness 4, Athletics 3, Brawl 4, Dodge 3, Empathy 2, Expression 3, Intimidation 2, Primal-Urge 4, Subterfuge 1
Skills: Animal Ken 2, Etiquette 2, Instruction 3, Meditation 5, Leadership 1, Melee 3, Performance 3, Stealth 3, Survival 3
Knowledges: Enigmas 5, Linguistics 2, Medicine 3, Occult 4, Rituals 5
Backgrounds: Past Life 2, Pure Breed 3
Gifts: (1) Heightened Senses, Mother's Touch, Sense Wyrm, Spirit Speech; (2) Command Spirit, Sense of the Prey; (3) Pulse of the Invisible, Tongues, Visceral Agony; (4) Grasp of the Beyond, Wasp Talons
Rank: 4
Rage 7, Gnosis 10, Willpower 9
Rites: All (yes, all!)
Fetishes: Moonsilver Whip, Key to the Umbra, Phoebe's Veil, Faerie Armor

Image: In Homid form, Cassandra is a striking woman with black hair, blue eyes and the body of an aerobics instructor. Her coat in Crinos, Hispo and Lupus form is shiny black with silver fur covering her chest. She wears pieces of ancient Greek-style faerie armor in her Homid, Glabro and Crinos forms, which add to her Amazonian appearance.

Roleplaying Notes: You project an aura of confidence and don't back away from challenges. You're a prophetess and wanderer, open to new ideas and unencumbered by many of the prejudices of your tribe. However, you hate the Get with a passion matched by few others. You are friendly to young Garou in the Umbra, and you cherish friends.

Skills: Animal Ken 1, Leadership 2, Performance 3, Stealth 3, Survival 3
Knowledges: Enigmas 1, Investigation 2, Occult 1, Rituals 1
Backgrounds: Allies 1, Kinfolk 1, Mentor 1, Pure Breed 1, Rites 1
Gifts: (1) Beast Speech, Heightened Senses, Sense Wyrm
Rank: 1
Rage 4, Gnosis 5, Willpower 3
Rites: (Mystic) Rite of the Questing Stone
Fetishes: None

Image: In her Lupus form, Amari is a lithe black wolf with a piercing stare that betrays her intellect. In Homid form, she retains her grace and tends to wear comfortable and casual clothing, but rarely wears jewelry.

Roleplaying Notes: You are a valuable member of the Black Furies, howling the wolf-songs that bring your packmates into battle. Though inexperienced, your will is strong and your motives are still pure. You enjoy singing and spinning tales, although you are generally reserved in social interactions and concerned with observing the world around you.

History: Amari experienced her First Change relatively late in her lupus life. Before her true nature became apparent, she felt that something inexplicable was... missing.

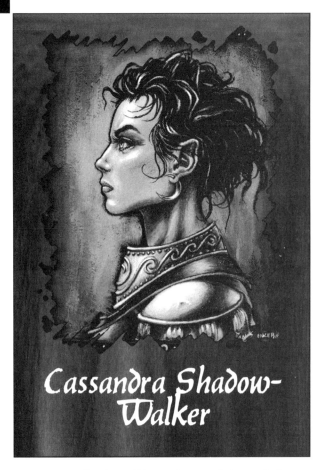

Cassandra Shadow-Walker

History: The Get of Fenris destroyed Cassandra's sept and conquered its caern when she was a cub, and she escaped the attack by fleeing into the Umbra. She was forced to quickly learn the Umbra's ways. She would travel when the moon was high and find a realm or domain to hide in after the moon set. She has spoken to Phoebe and possesses a fetish whip made of Moonsilver. Cassandra has now been in the Umbra for some time and is well on her way to gaining great power and the Fifth Rank.

Cassandra makes certain to return to Gaia after each journey so that she doesn't lose herself in the spiritual wonder of the Umbra. She has visited all of the Near Realms, and will give instructions and guidance to any who would follow her. She is currently on a quest for Pegasus, who has promised her the aid of a Gaffling if she succeeds.

Cassandra believes that the Silver Fang understanding of the Triat and reality is the closest to the truth about the Umbra. She still loathes all Get of Fenris, and woe to the unhappy Get who dares to challenge her in the Umbra.

Julisha of the Thousand Masks

Breed: Homid
Auspice: Ragabash
Nature/Demeanor: Autist/Gallant
Physical: Strength 3 (5/7/6/4), Dexterity 5 (5/6/7/7), Stamina 4 (6/7/7/6)

Social: Charisma 4, Manipulation 3 (2/0/0/0), Appearance 4 (3/0/4/4)
Mental: Perception 4, Intelligence 3, Wits 5
Talents: Alertness 4, Athletics 4, Brawl 3, Dodge 4, Expression 3, Primal-Urge 3, Streetwise 3, Subterfuge 5
Skills: Demolitions 4, Disguise 5, Drive 2, Etiquette 3, Firearms 2, Melee 3, Performance 3, Repair 3, Stealth 5, Survival 2
Knowledges: Computer 4, Enigmas 4, Investigation 3, Linguistics 3, Occult 1, Politics 2, Rituals 2
Backgrounds: Contacts 3, Past Life 3, Pure Breed 2
Gifts: (1) Blur of the Milky Eye, Open Seal, Persuasion, Sense Wyrm; (2) Alter Scent, Blissful Ignorance, Jam Technology, Taking the Forgotten; (3) Fly Feet, Reshape Object, Silence; (4) Wasp Talons; (5) Assimilation, The Thousand Forms
Rank: 5
Rage 6, Gnosis 8, Willpower 7
Rites: (Accord) Rite of Cleansing, (Mystic) Rite of Summoning, Rite of Talisman Dedication
Fetishes: Baneskin, Fang Dagger, Monkey Puzzle

Image: Julisha is quite lovely and has a fetching smile when she feels like smiling. Her braided hair reaches her shoulders, and her form is limber and strong. In Crinos, Hispo and Lupus form, her coat is a velvety brown, dark to the point of being almost black. Of course, most who encounter Julisha see someone entirely different....

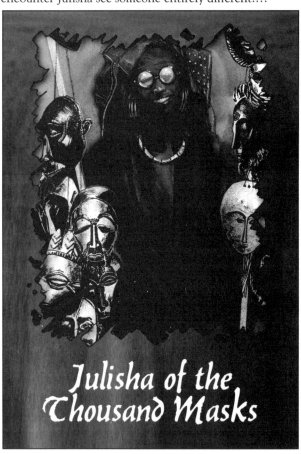

Julisha of the Thousand Masks

Roleplaying Notes: Laugh a little, but mostly to yourself. You don't typically feel like sharing your agenda, even if you're currently running with a clever pack. Wait and watch your targets, then pull the rug out from under them. After all, the best way to treat the Wyrm-tainted is by making sure they're humiliated and shocked in the last few seconds of their lives.

History: This African Fury is rumored to belong to the Inner Calyx, the highest circle of the tribe, but no one (except the Calyx themselves) knows for sure. She is a mistress of disguise and infiltration. Ragabash to the core, Julisha's deadly pranks are known the world over.

Julisha's past is a closed book. Many assume she was born into the Zulu or Masai and received a first-rate education in England or elsewhere. Somewhere along the way she picked up her impressive technical training, as well as her subversive skills of disguise and infiltration. Some Glass Walkers nod knowingly and say she undoubtedly received MI6 training, but this is usually dismissed as hopeless James Bond fans' fantasizing. Speculation abounds.

Julisha herself has been quite active in the war for Gaia, and more than one Black Spiral Hive has gone up in purifying flames as she drifts through town. She sometimes assembles temporary packs around herself when a job calls for it, but runs alone for the most part. Her calling card, a miniature Zulu war mask, is said to have greeted Robert Allred himself as he fluffed his pillow one night. The explosion killed six Pentex employees, but not, regrettably, Allred.

Mari Cabrah

Breed: Homid

Auspice: Theurge

Nature/Demeanor: Survivor/Competitor

Physical: Strength 3 (5/7/6/4), Dexterity 4 (4/5/6/6), Stamina 4 (6/7/7/6)

Social: Charisma 2, Manipulation 3 (2/0/0/0), Appearance 3 (2/0/3/3)

Mental: Perception 3, Intelligence 3, Wits 3

Talents: Alertness 3, Athletics 3, Brawl 4, Dodge 3, Intimidation 2, Primal-Urge 3, Streetwise 2

Skills: Drive 3, Firearms 3, Melee 3, Stealth 4, Survival 2

Knowledges: Computer 1, Enigmas 3, Investigation 1, Law 1, Linguistics 2, Medicine 1, Occult 3, Rituals 3

Backgrounds: Contacts 2, Pure Breed 2, Resources 1

Gifts: (1) Heightened Senses, Persuasion, Razor Claws, Sense Wyrm, Spirit Speech; (2) Command Spirit, Sense of the Prey, Staredown; (3) Coup de Grace, Exorcism

Rank: 3

Rage 6, Gnosis 7, Willpower 7

Rites: (Accord) Rite of Cleansing; (Mystic) Rite of Binding, Rite of Spirit Awakening, Rite of Summoning, Rite of Talisman Dedication

Fetishes: None

Mari Cabrah

Image: Mari is an intense, wiry, powerful young Hispanic-Italian woman. She tends to wear practical, loose-fitting clothing like tank tops and fatigues. In Crinos form, she is massive and sleek, with white markings on her face and torso. Multiple earrings and a studded collar are her only concessions to fashion.

Roleplaying Notes: Work out as often and as hard as you can. Resist attempts to boss you around, especially from non-Furies. You're hard as nails around most people, although you soften up a little around kids. You can be a lost cub's best friend and a pushy Garou's worst nightmare. A lot of people say you'd make a great Ahroun; maybe so, but you're an excellent Theurge. We all must do as Gaia wills.

History: An urban Amazon, Mari stalks the neon-drenched maze of New York, hunting Bane and corrupt human alike. Abused as a teenager, Mari swore to protect other girls from the pain she suffered. She runs a self-defense dojo, teaching martial arts to any women who want to learn. Though she prefers to live alone, she has taken more than a few young runaways under her wing, teaching them to stand on their own before sending them back into the world.

Mari has a soft spot for kids and a special hatred for urban predators. Among the Garou she is known for her sharp tongue, fighting prowess and keen familiarity with the Weaver's jungle. She is currently running with an intertribal pack called the Guardian Rage. This pack has begun to fray at the edges, and the tension is aggravating Mari.

(These statistics represent Mari before she met Lord Albrecht for the first time. By the time the two clash, they are roughly equal in power. Their battle and eventual reconciliation, as well as the story of her current pack, are detailed in the **Werewolf** rulebook (pages 206-239), its comic "Legacy Rite" and *The Silver Crown*.)

Sister Judith Paws-of-Light

Breed: Metis
Auspice: Theurge
Nature/Demeanor: Maker/Visionary
Physical: Strength 2 (4/6/5/3), Dexterity 3 (3/4/5/5), Stamina 4 (6/7/7/6)
Social: Charisma 3, Manipulation 2 (1/0/0/0), Appearance 2 (1/0/2/2)
Mental: Perception 3, Intelligence 4, Wits 4
Talents: Alertness 3, Athletics 1, Brawl 4, Dodge 4, Empathy 2, Intimidation 2, Primal-Urge 3
Skills: Animal Ken 1, Drive 1, Firearms 3, Melee 3, Leadership 2, Stealth 4, Survival 4
Knowledges: Enigmas 3, Investigation 3, Linguistics 2, Medicine 5, Occult 2, Rituals 3
Backgrounds: Allies 3, Past Life 2, Resources 3, Rites 1
Gifts: (1) Heightened Senses, Mother's Touch, Sense Wyrm, Spirit Speech; (2) Command Spirit, Curse of Aeolus, Grandmother's Touch (same as Mother's Touch,

but Judith can heal herself), Sight from Beyond; (3) Eyes of the Cat, Tongues; (4) Bacchanantes' Rage, Wasp Talons
Rank: 4
Rage 4, Gnosis 8, Willpower 8
Rites: (Accord) Rite of Cleansing, Rite of Contrition; (Mystic) Rite of the Fetish, Rite of the Questing Stone
Fetishes: Tongue of the Leech

Image: Sister Judith's Homid form is that of a weathered Mediterranean woman in her late 30s. Her Lupus form is a lean, rock-hard black wolf with snowy paws. Her natural Crinos form is tall and powerful, and her white paws fit neatly around a large man's head.

Roleplaying Notes: Keep to yourself. You're busy enough with your duty; there's no need for you to get mired in local Garou politics. You're a healer first, a warrior second, and those two keep you so occupied that there isn't time for a third duty. When you have to get involved in squabbles to prevent your goals from being delayed, speak decisively and firmly. Unless you're dealing with an elder, your word should be final.

History: Sister Judith displays eerily accurate foresight and has a powerful bond with the living land. Rumors tell of Sister Judith raising new saplings from desert dust and healing advanced cases of leprosy. Light blazes from her snow-white paws as she works her potent Gifts; some even say she can banish Banes with a command. Such stories are doubtless wishful thinking, but most Furies concede that Sister Judith holds special favor with the Mother.

She is reputed to have skinned Iraqi soldiers alive during the occupation of Kuwait and slaughtered Israeli and PLO fighters alike to save innocents caught in a crossfire. Fury gossips claim that Sister Judith has gone into Bosnia to put an end to ethnic cleansing.

Although Sister Judith primarily concerns herself with stopping human evils, she gladly attacks any Wyrmspawn she happens across, occasionally gathering a pack around her for extra muscle. She has recently learned of the Seventh Generation and their evils, and woe to those defilers who stray into her path.

Susan Anthony

Breed: Homid
Auspice: Philodox
Nature/Demeanor: Gallant/Reveler
Physical: Strength 3 (5/7/3/4), Dexterity 3 (3/4/5/5), Stamina 2 (4/5/5/4)
Social: Charisma 4, Manipulation 3 (2/0/0/0), Appearance 4 (3/0/4/4)
Mental: Perception 2, Intelligence 2, Wits 2
Talents: Alertness 1, Brawl 1, Dodge 1, Empathy 3, Streetwise 2, Subterfuge 3
Skills: Drive 1, Etiquette 1, Firearms 2, Performance 2, Stealth 1

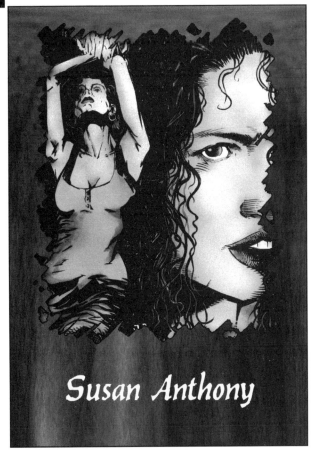

Susan Anthony

Knowledges: Computer 2, Investigation 2, Law 2, Linguistics (Greek, Latin) 2, Medicine 2, Politics 2, Rituals 1, Science 1

Backgrounds: Allies 2, Kinfolk 3

Gifts: (1) Heightened Senses, Persuasion, Truth of Gaia; (2) Curse of Aeolus, Staredown

Rank: 2

Rage 3, Gnosis 3, Willpower 4

Rites: (Caern) Moot Rite; (Punishment) Rite of Ostracism

Fetishes: None

Image: Susan is a very attractive woman in her mid-20s, and she knows it. Form-fitting and otherwise flattering city clothes are her favorites, though she looks spectacular in whatever she wears. In Crinos form, she is savagely beautiful, combining graceful proportions with functional deadliness.

Roleplaying Notes: Most men are weak enough to succumb to your feminine wiles, and that's the way you like it. Besides, you enjoy their company, at least until they grow uninteresting. Vamp your way in and out of social situations, but never let your true agenda suffer. You are Garou, after all, and though you want to enjoy every moment before the imminent Apocalypse, you do have responsibilities to fulfill.

History: As a child, Susan knew she was different from the other girls. Luckily, she was pretty enough to be popular and never had to suffer through the loneliness most homid Garou experience before they learn of their true nature. In junior high and high school, Susan always had a boyfriend, if not several. She developed a somewhat sullied reputation during her high school years, and when a date with one of the school's baseball players went sour as he forced his affections on her, Susan underwent her First Change. There wasn't enough left of the boy to fill his baseball cap.

Even after her Change, she kept many lovers. Some Black Furies frown upon her amorousness, accusing her of being a plaything for men, but more than once Susan has garnered vital information for the Black Furies through her network of contacts and relations and her effective methods of extracting the facts from men. Susan comes from an extended family and seems to have a knack for getting involved with the Kinfolk of other Garou. Naturally, none of these Kinfolk complain, though Susan has earned an enemy or two among other Garou.

She has recently earned the appreciation of her tribe by "befriending" an employee of a Pentex importing company that doubled as a smuggling ring. Through her relationship with the night watchman, she led a group of Black Furies and Glass Walkers into a warehouse stocked to the roof with firearms and supplies for the Pentex efforts in the Amazon; the Garou seized the supplies and burned the warehouse and its fomor laborers to the ground.

Volcheka Jbarruri

Breed: Lupus

Auspice: Ahroun

Nature/Demeanor: Fanatic/Predator

Physical: Strength 3 (5/7/6/4), Dexterity 3 (3/4/5/6), Stamina 4 (6/7/7/6)

Social: Charisma 3, Manipulation 2 (1/0/0/0), Appearance 3 (2/0/3/3)

Mental: Perception 3, Intelligence 2, Wits 4

Talents: Alertness 3, Athletics 1, Brawl 3, Dodge 2, Intimidation 2, Primal-Urge 4

Skills: Animal Ken 2, Stealth 3, Survival 5

Knowledges: Enigmas 2, Linguistics 2, Medicine 1, Rituals 1

Backgrounds: Kinfolk 3, Pure Breed 3, Rites 1

Gifts: (1) Heightened Senses, Leap of the Kangaroo, Razor Claws, Sense Wyrm; (2) Scent of Sight, Sense of the Prey, Spirit of the Fray

Rank: 2

Rage 5, Gnosis 5, Willpower 7

Rites: (Accord) Rite of Contrition; (Minor) Hunting Prayer, Prayer for the Prey

Fetishes: None

Image: Volcheka's breed form is that of a healthy dark-gray wolf. When she shifts to Crinos, there is an almost silvery cast to her coat. Her Homid form is thin and attractive, although very feral-seeming. Her hair is a mane of black streaked with white, and she sometimes paints the Fury glyph on her forehead when hunting. Her eyes remain yellow in every form.

Volcheka Jbarruri

Roleplaying Notes: Speak slowly and carefully, in a rich, raw voice. You're always careful around humans; although some seem to have a touch of unexpected compassion, most seem completely self-interested.

History: Volcheka was born to an Alaskan pack of Kinfolk wolves, and the Furies expectantly watched her and her littermates from afar. She was among Garou almost immediately after her First Change, and there she learned why the humans hunted her and her kin. Once done with her Rite of Passage, she left the Furies to return to the woods.

Her first name means "wolf-lover"; her last is a tribute to a Spanish revolutionary. This up-and-coming young Fury wages a personal war against the wolf-hunters of Alaska. She rarely kills her prey; she prefers to maim them and leave them bleeding on the outskirts of a nearby town. Her psychological warfare has already taken a toll on the hunting trade....

The Alaskan authorities fear a band of radicals has taken up terrorism in the forests, but Volcheka wages a lone crusade, even disdaining the help of other Garou. Her immunity to the Arctic cold and seeming ability to control winter storms leads some to believe she serves the Wendigo totem. Wendigo Garou in fact refuse to work against Volcheka, preferring to aid her efforts from afar. Volcheka already seems to be a legend; more Furies know of her by reputation than can ever claim to have met her.

To date, Volcheka hasn't met any fomori, Black Spiral Dancers, or other obvious minions of the Wyrm. If any come after the wolves and territory under her protection, they will have a hard fight on their hands.

Bone Gnawers

Banana Split

Breed: Metis

Auspice: Ahroun

Nature/Demeanor: Rebel/Jester

Physical: Strength 2 (4/6/5/3), Dexterity 3 (3/4/5/5), Stamina 3 (5/6/6/5)

Social: Charisma 2, Manipulation 4 (3/1/1/1), Appearance 2 (1/0/2/2)

Mental: Perception 3, Intelligence 2, Wits 5

Talents: Alertness 2, Brawl 3, Dodge 2, Primal-Urge 2, Streetwise 3, Subterfuge 1

Skills: Animal Ken 2, Cooking 1, Leadership 2, Melee 2, Stealth 2, Survival 2

Knowledges: Enigmas 1, Occult 3, Rituals 1

Backgrounds: Contacts 2, Mentor 2, Rites 1

Gifts: (1) Create Element, Razor Claws, Scent of Sweet Honey

Rank: 1

Rage 5, Gnosis 3, Willpower 5

Rites: (Minor) Breath of Gaia, Greet the Moon

Fetishes: None

Image: Banana Split is a tall hermaphrodite with reddish hair, pointed ears, and blue eyes. To disconcert opponents, "it" has been known to dress in body suits, veils and bandanas. In wolf or Crinos form, it has shaggy reddish fur.

Roleplaying Notes: Even among the tolerant Bone Gnawers you are something of an outsider. However, your cunning in battle has begun to earn you respect. You are the eternal jester, leading some to remark that you are more Ragabash than Ahroun, yet those remarks are said with respect, given your cunning use of humor in combat.

History: Banana Split was fortunate enough to be born into the Bone Gnawers tribe, which, while regarding him as an outsider due to his metis heritage, treated him better than other tribes would have. His mentor, an old Bone Gnawer named Wyrm Eater, took Banana Split in when the young Garou's parents were killed while fighting the Wyrm. The youth proved to be very intelligent and cunning and possessed of a natural wit that proved to be as effective a weapon as his claws. In spite of being metis, Banana Split became well liked by the members of his sept and was expected to do well in his Rite of Passage.

When puberty struck, and Banana Split began to develop breasts, more than a few jokes were made at his expense. In fact, he initiated many, unsettling those who sought to mock his metis nature. Similar jokes also proved effective in combat. More than one opponent has been caught off guard or distracted by Banana Split's self-deprecating remarks.

Banana Split

Banana Split performed even better than expected in his Rite of Passage and assumed a vital role in his mixed-tribe pack. He returned a wiser, more cunning Garou, and the elders of his sept now watch him closely, expecting that he may someday lead a pack, if not an entire sept, in battle against the Wyrm. When asked about Banana Split, Mother Larissa merely laughs softly and says, "Yes, yes; he is one to be watched now, isn't he?"

Buggerhead

Breed: Lupus

Auspice: Ragabash

Nature/Demeanor: Caregiver/Jester

Physical: Strength 3 (5/7/6/4), Dexterity 3 (3/4/5/5), Stamina 3 (5/6/6/5)

Social: Charisma 4, Manipulation 5 (4/2/2/2), Appearance 4 (3/0/4/4)

Mental: Perception 3, Intelligence 3, Wits 4

Talents: Alertness 3, Brawl 2, Dodge 2, Primal-Urge 4, Streetwise 1, Subterfuge 1

Skills: Leadership 2, Stealth 3, Survival 2

Knowledges: Enigmas 1, Occult 2, Rituals 2
Backgrounds: Kinfolk 1, Rites 2
Gifts: (1) Blur of the Milky Eye, Heightened Senses, Scent of Sweet Honey; (2) Sense the Unnatural, Taking the Forgotten, Odious Aroma; (3) Catfeet
Rank: 3
Rage 5, Gnosis 6, Willpower 5
Rites: (Mystic) Rite of Summoning
Fetishes: None

Image: In Homid form, Buggerhead is a small, thin, young man with dark hair and eyes, wearing a perpetual smile. Buggerhead's Lupus form is a small black wolf with brown markings.

Buggerhead

Roleplaying Notes: You miss your brothers and sisters a great deal and are constantly in search of them, but not to a degree that your hunt has distracted you from your true mission: the destruction of the Wyrm. You've been through a lot in life, but in spite of it all you remain optimistic and see humor in nearly everything.

History: Buggerhead was born in the suburbs of Denver, Colorado, into a pack of "mixed breed" wolves owned by a wealthy couple. Unwanted, the young cubs were driven out into the mountains and left to their own devices. Buggerhead and his littermates, frightened and unaccustomed to the wilderness, made their way back to Denver, where they were confused for a pack of stray dogs. The local animal control service eventually caught them and put them in a shelter for adoption. Weeks passed as individuals were adopted, until only Buggerhead and one of his brothers remained.

One night Buggerhead's cage was opened by a man from the shelter who smelled of strange chemicals and death. The two cubs shied away as the human reached for Buggerhead's young brother. Ever protective, Buggerhead attacked. As the fight progressed, Buggerhead was surprised to find himself growing larger than the man, who promptly fainted. Buggerhead took advantage of the situation and his new shape to escape from the shelter, taking his brother with him. The two wandered the streets of Denver once again, this time searching for their brothers and sisters. They were soon found by members of a Bone Gnawers pack, which took them in and taught Buggerhead the ways of the Garou.

Buggerhead has proven to be a resourceful Garou, finding or improvising things in desperate situations to save his packmates' lives. That and his good humor have made him one of the best-liked and most respected Garou in his sept.

Crick Rumwrangler

Breed: Lupus
Auspice: Philodox
Physical: Strength 2 (4/6/5/3), Dexterity 3 (3/4/5/5), Stamina 3 (5/6/6/5)
Social: Charisma 3, Manipulation 3 (2/0/0/0), Appearance 2 (1/0/2/2)
Mental: Perception 3, Intelligence 3, Wits 5
Talents: Alertness 4, Brawl 3, Dodge 4, Empathy 2, Expression 1, Primal-Urge 3, Streetwise 3, Subterfuge 2
Skills: Animal Ken 2, Drive 3, Firearms 3, Melee 1, Leadership 1, Repair 2
Knowledges: Computer 2, Enigmas 1, Politics 2, Rituals 1
Backgrounds: Contacts 3, Kinfolk (Pack of Dogs) 2
Gifts: (1) Cooking, Heightened Senses, Scent of the True Form; (2) Call to Duty
Merits/Flaws: Luck
Rank: 2
Rage 3, Gnosis 4, Willpower 6
Rites: Talisman Dedication
Fetishes: Blanket of Peaceful Dreams, Friendship Ring

Image: Crick is a lanky wolf with mottled dark spots over his fur, giving him the look of an ugly mongrel. He keeps his fur trim and is well-groomed in Homid form. He feels he has to keep up appearances so that others will like him. As a human, he is half-Caucasian and half-Spanish, a *meztico*. He stands five feet tall and weighs about 115 pounds. He appears to be in his 30s.

Roleplaying Notes: Take things easy and slow. Rushing things never got anyone anywhere except into trouble. Smile and nod a lot when your superiors talk to you. Be friendly with those under you. You never know when they'll be goin' up the ladder and you'll be goin' down.

Crick Rumwrangler

Social: Charisma 2, Manipulation 2 (1/0/0/0), Appearance 2 (1/0/2/2)

Mental: Perception 4, Intelligence 2, Wits 4

Talents: Alertness 2, Athletics 1, Brawl 2, Dodge 2, Expression 2, Intimidation 1, Streetwise 3

Skills: Drive 2, Firearms 2, Melee 1, Performance 3, Stealth 1

Knowledges: Computer 1, Law 2, Medicine 1, Science 1

Backgrounds: Allies 1, Contacts 3, Resources 1

Gifts: (1) Mindspeak, Persuasion, Scent of Sweet Honey

Rank: 1

Rage 4, Gnosis 1, Willpower 4

Rites: None

Fetishes: None

Image: Dharma Bum is a wiry man of average build with kinky black hair and the thousand-yard stare. He wears the latest street fashions popular with his young black crowd and is almost never found without a complement of flashy but trashy rings and necklaces. In Lupus form, he is a short-haired and very doglike wolf, often mistaken for a German shepherd.

Roleplaying Notes: You better show these clowns what time it is. Yeah, you're young, but still, man, you're a damn werewolf, and you'll beat some fool's ass if he gives you any lip. Not only that, but your record career's on the rise, and these chumps don't know they have a celebrity in the house.

History: Crick wasn't born in the city like most Bone Gnawers. He was part of a litter born to a 75% wolf kept by Mississippi Kinfolk. They were delighted when he underwent his First Change and promptly called in the tribe to take care of him. The scraggly lupus took quickly to Garou life and began traveling from city to city, making good with the Gnawer and Glass Walker elders. When the call came from the Amazon for reinforcements, Crick obligingly headed south.

Crick is one of the few Bone Gnawers in the Amazon and is not widely respected because of it. He performs his duties with a sense of caution because he always seems to be the object of criticism from somewhere, either from the Amazonian War Council or from his peers. He is cleaner than most of his tribe, due in part to his need to impress those in the chain of command. His good luck and cagey tactics have served him well so far and will probably give him an edge in climbing up the ranks. He's a quiet type, but doesn't allow himself to be pushed too far.

Dharma Bum

Breed: Homid

Auspice: Galliard

Nature/Demeanor: Autist/Show-Off

Physical: Strength 2 (4/6/5/3), Dexterity 3 (3/4/5/5), Stamina 3 (2/6/6/5)

Dharma Bum

History: Dharma Bum, born Lester Grimes, was in and out of foster homes by the time he was 7. Soon thereafter, when nobody else wanted him, he went AWOL from his boys' home and took up penny-ante hustling to put food in his mouth. The ability to become eight feet tall and 600 pounds helped out a bit, but the streets are hardly a charming place, and Dharma soon found himself on a first-name basis with local cops, with an arrest record that rivaled the length of *War and Peace*. In his spare time, he spun lascivious rap tales at a hip-hop club and managed to catch the eye of a major-label producer, for whom he cuts records when he's not out with his boys.

Scratches-at-Fleas

Breed: Lupus

Auspice: Ahroun

Nature/Demeanor: Caregiver/Jester

Physical: Strength 4 (6/8/7/5), Dexterity 4 (4/5/6/6), Stamina 4 (6/7/7/6)

Social: Charisma 3, Manipulation 2 (1/0/0/0), Appearance 1 (0/0/1/1)

Mental: Perception 3, Intelligence 3, Wits 3

Talents: Alertness 4, Athletics 3, Brawl 3, Dodge 3, Primal-Urge 5, Streetwise 4

Skills: Animal Ken 2, Leadership 3, Melee 4

Knowledges: Investigation 3, Law 1, Linguistics 2

Backgrounds: Allies 2, Kinfolk 3

Scratches-at-Fleas

Gifts: (1) Heightened Senses, Inspiration, Leap of the Kangaroo; (2) True Fear; (3) Catfeet, Heart of Fury

Rank: 3

Rage 6, Gnosis 6, Willpower 7

Rites: None

Fetishes: None

Image: In Lupus form, which he favors, Scratches-at-Fleas is a small but muscular beast of indeterminate heritage: part wolf, part dog, part dingo. Despite his ragged appearance, his brown eyes are sharp and alert. In Homid form, Scratches is a short, stocky man in his late 20s, with sandy hair and bright eyes. Regardless of his form, he is forever absentmindedly scratching himself for fleas, often at inappropriate moments.

Roleplaying Notes: You are a Bone Gnawer hero, albeit a modest one. Grin disarmingly, defer to others and always ask people for advice. Treat everything as a joke, except for the topic of the homeless and the dispossessed, which you take extremely seriously.

History: Scratches-at-Fleas spent the first two years of his life scrounging from garbage bins and dumpsters behind Australian restaurants. Even before his First Change he was a social animal, always sharing his scraps with the weaker scavengers of his pack. When cornered by dogcatchers he would snarl and bark threateningly, making sure others were clear before he made his escape.

It was during one such confrontation that Scratches-at-Fleas experienced his first transformation. As he stood barking at a fat, greedy dogcatcher, he felt Rage boiling up inside him. Before he understood what was happening, Scratches-at-Fleas found himself standing on his hind paws. One great claw tossed the dogcatcher aside; the other ripped open the man's truck and released the dogs within.

Since that day Scratches-at-Fleas has made it his duty to serve Gaia's weakest children. A member of the Sept of the Mother and the Sacred King, he is also part of the 'Hood. He takes special care of those humans who cannot fend for themselves: the homeless and the helpless, schizophrenic streetkids, prostitutes raped by police, tramps and derelicts. He brings them food and protects them from further harm. Scratches-at-Fleas is one of the greatest warriors of his sept and has often sprung new cubs from hospitals, prisons and insane asylums. These actions have won him much acclaim, but he is a modest Garou, much happier telling jokes around the fire than listening to praise.

Stories of Scratches-at-Fleas' exploits have perhaps had greater impact on the War of the Apocalypse than he himself. Scratches-at-Fleas has made efforts to keep himself out of the War, not that he has no love for Gaia or his kind, but because the War tends to come to him rather than him going to it. Legends of his victories are widespread and have grown in the telling. They have inspired many Garou to help weaker brethren, septs and tribes against the Wyrm. Even enemies have stood side-by-side when Scratches-at-Fleas' name has been invoked.

Shakey Mac

Breed: Homid
Auspice: Theurge
Tribe: Bone Gnawer
Nature/Demeanor: Bravo/Judge
Physical: Strength 2 (4/6/5/3), Dexterity 3 (3/4/5/5), Stamina 3 (5/6/6/5)
Social: Charisma 1, Manipulation 4 (3/1/1/1), Appearance 1 (0/0/1/1)
Mental: Perception 4, Intelligence 4, Wits 3
Talents: Alertness 4, Brawl 2, Dodge 1, Empathy 2, Expression 2, Intimidation 3, Streetwise 4, Subterfuge 1
Skills: Drive 1, Repair 1, Stealth 2, Survival (City/Street) 4
Knowledges: Enigmas 3, Law 2, Linguistics 2, Occult 3, Politics 1, Rituals 3
Backgrounds: Contacts 2, Fetish 4, Rites 2
Gifts: (1) Mother's Touch, Persuasion, Spirit Speech; (2) Blissful Ignorance, Command Spirit, Jam Technology, Staredown; (3) Call the Flame Spirit, Gift of the Skunk; (4) Spirit Drain
Rank: 4
Rage 5, Gnosis 10, Willpower 6
Rites: (Caern) Moot Rite; (Mystic) Rite of Binding, Rite of the Questing Stone, Rite of Spirit Awakening, Rite of Summoning, Rite of the Fetish; (Seasonal) Rite of the Winter Winds
Fetishes: Bottlecap of Shakey Mac (Level 4, Gnosis 7. By spending a Gnosis point, the cap's wielder can invoke an instant Rite of Binding, with the target spirit's Gnosis reduced by four. The fetish's Gnosis may be substituted for the Garou's Willpower.)

Image: In Homid form, Shakey Mac is a tired, bitter old man. His receding white hair is unwashed and ragged. His face and hands have been hardened by the elements. His Crinos form is pale and lean, with ketchup stains here and there. In Lupus form he's all ribs.

Roleplaying Notes: You hate everyone. You're bitter and angry at the world. You feel your rightful place within Garou society has been usurped and now take your anger out on everybody around you, particularly spirits or other bums; most others avoid you.

Shakey Mac

History: Shakey Mac has lived on the streets of New York for as long as he can remember. He grew accustomed to taking the things he needed to survive, often not caring who got hurt in the process.

He entrenched himself in Bone Gnawer society and prepared to take Shecky Lindburg's place as tribal elder when Shecky passed away. Shakey Mac had a rival for the role, though: Mother Larissa. Unfortunately for Shakey Mac, the best woman won.

Now Shakey lives on the periphery of human and Garou society. His only real pleasure, if it can be called that, comes from subduing and binding spirits. He has built himself an entourage of unwilling helpers. He has also fashioned a powerful fetish to help him in his spirit-binding tasks. Too bad for Shakey that a Ragabash gaffled his bottlecap.

Children of Gaia

Cernonous, Arm of the Goddess

Breed: Metis

Auspice: Theurge

Nature/Demeanor: Fanatic/Curmudgeon

Physical: Strength 4 (6/8/7/5), Dexterity 3 (3/4/5/5), Stamina 5 (7/8/8/7)

Social: Charisma 2, Manipulation 2, Appearance 1 (0/0/1/1)

Mental: Perception 3, Intelligence 3, Wits 2

Talents: Athletics 3, Brawl 3, Dodge 3, Expression 3

Skills: Animal Ken 3, Leadership 1, Stealth 1

Knowledges: Computer 2, Enigmas 2, Investigation 4, Medicine 3, Rituals 3, Science 5

Backgrounds: Contacts 3

Gifts: (1) Create Element, Mother's Touch, Resist Pain, Sense Wyrm; (2) Curse of Hatred; (3) Reshape Object

Rank: 3

Rage 4, Gnosis 4, Willpower 5

Rites: (Accord) Rite of Contrition; (Mystic) Rite of the Totem; (Punishment) Rite of Ostracism

Fetishes: Shard of Despair, Vulcan's Interface

Image: In Homid form, Cernonous is a thick-set man of late middle age. In Lupus form he is a gaunt, gray wolf with small horns protruding from his forehead. These horns, his metis deformity, are evident in all of his forms save Homid. It is because of this disfigurement that he bears the name Cernonous, after the Horned God of Celtic myth, consort of the Goddess. When dealing with humans he calls himself Professor Curwen Nostrum.

Roleplaying Notes: You are a serious Garou, bearing the weight of the world on your broad shoulders. Although capable of mirth, you are more inclined to be grave. Speak slowly, consider every word, and smile only rarely.

History: Cernonous was born of two Children of Gaia. His mother was of Serbian descent, his father Filipino. They believed that their love was not unnatural, for surely it came from Gaia, not the Wyrm. Cernonous was raised without guilt, and it came as a shock to him when he first experienced the prejudice and scorn most metis experience. For many years he lived bewildered and frightened, gradually coming to know shame. Cernonous perceived that his horns were what marked him to other Garou as unnatural, and so he swore to enter human society and learn all he could about genetics in order to free himself of his metis taint.

Years of study taught Cernonous much, and under the name Curwen Nostrum he became one of the rising stars in Australian genetic research. The answer to his quest still eluded him, however, and Cernonous began shunning humans and Garou alike in favor of furious research and heavy drinking. Late one night, while staggering along Bondi Beach singing drunkenly to the stars, Cernonous received a vision of Gaia. He saw the Goddess dancing down a path of moonlight reflected across the waves, a thylacine fawning at her feet.

Since that day Cernonous has devoted himself to the task of bringing back the Bunyip, a now-extinct Garou tribe from Australia's past. He believes that he might find the Bunyip gene in a thylacine, if any of the creatures still live in Tasmania's wilderness, or, failing that, in viable cells in bones or hair from museum specimens. With his knowledge, Cernonous hopes to extract DNA and clone the Bunyip, reintroducing them to the world. To date he has had no success, but Cernonous perseveres. He keeps his research secret from other Garou. Were the Red Talons to discover that he sought to return the Bunyip to the world, Cernonous believes that Mamu and his tribe would not hesitate to kill him. The only Garou Cernonous has entrusted with his secret is Darius Winchester, the Silver Fang king, who has funded his research. Unknown to all,

Cernonous, Arm of the Goddess

Cernonous' research is monitored by the Progenitor Convention of Technocracy mages; modern wizards of technology. The Progenitors have not yet acted to prevent his discoveries, hoping to claim the results as their own.

Cernonous' dedication to the Goddess and his strength of spirit are respected by his tribe, which is considering him for possible election as Arm of the Goddess for Australia's Nimbin Protectorate. How Cernonous will receive this honor is uncertain, but acceptance would certainly curtail his research time. Yet leadership would bring Cernonous into a prominent role in the War of the Apocalypse; any successes he might have in restoring the Bunyip would be well received by loyal followers. The return of the Bunyip would certainly strike a blow against the Wyrm.

Diem

Breed: Homid

Auspice: Ragabash

Nature/Demeanor: Survivor/Lone Wolf

Physical: Strength 2 (4/6/5/3), Dexterity 3 (3/4/5/5), Stamina 2 (4/5/5/4)

Social: Charisma 2, Manipulation 3 (2/0/0/0), Appearance 2 (1/0/2/2)

Mental: Perception 4, Intelligence 4, Wits 3

Talents: Alertness 2, Expression 3, Primal-Urge 2

Skills: Animal Ken 2, Performance (Photography) 4, Survival 3

Knowledges: Enigmas 3, Investigation 3, Rituals 2, Science 3

Backgrounds: Mentor 1, Past Life 2

Gifts: (1) Mother's Touch, Open Seal, Persuasion, Scent of Running Water

Rank: 1

Rage 2, Gnosis 5, Willpower 6

Rites: (Mystic) Rite of Talisman Dedication, Rite of the Questing Stone

Fetishes: Dream Trap

Image: Diem is a middle-aged Cambodian, small in stature with a light build. Diem is going bald on his crown, but gray hair sweeps down his shoulders; this is often tied back with a colorful ribbon. He always appears balanced, relaxed and comfortable and is extremely patient. His lined face is more often smiling than frowning, and he peers with penetrating eyes from behind delicate, gold-rimmed glasses.

Roleplaying Notes: You are a man who knows how to wait. Unfailingly polite, you always listen to what people have to say and respond with a few carefully chosen words. You are a great believer in beauty and a voracious devourer of stories; you pay special attention to anyone who provides you with either of these. Although quiet and serene, you always scrutinize people and can detect lies with uncanny accuracy.

History: Diem was born in Cambodia, which he fled at age 13 with his family during the reign of Pol Pot and the

Diem

Khmer Rouge, just before undergoing his First Change. Diem had been contacted by a mysterious group of Cambodian Garou who had claimed him as their own. Diem, however, chose to leave Cambodia with his family, and to this day he does not know who these Garou were or whether he will ever meet one of them again.

Upon his arrival in a refugee camp on the Australian coast, the young and frightened Diem was found by Michelle Moonrise, a Child of Gaia from the Nimbin Protectorate. The Children of Gaia taught Diem the lore of the Garou and made him one of their own. Years later, Diem is still unsure of who he really is and is torn between the Children's kindness and a nagging feeling that he does not belong in Australia.

Diem is an accomplished photographer. He often travels to the outback, where, using a combination of his skills and Garou abilities, he takes spectacular photographs. Diem serves Gaia by printing these photographs and showing humanity the beauty of Her creations. He is responsible for many of the pictures, whether of whales or desert landscapes, that hang in suburban homes, schools and corporate offices around the world. It is a private joke of Diem's that the picture hanging in Pentex's Sydney reception room is a photo of Mamu, leader of the Red Talons, sleeping in Lupus form beneath a boab tree.

In the War of the Apocalypse, Diem hopes to accomplish more with his camera than with his claws. He believes that by educating mortals about the beauty of nature, they will better respect Gaia and turn from the Wyrm. The efforts of mundane preservation societies are an indication that Diem's efforts are succeeding; his photographs have been used in numerous fund-raising campaigns and have increased human awareness of his subjects.

Jennifer Moon-Wizened

Breed: Homid
Auspice: Galliard
Tribe: Children of Gaia
Nature/Demeanor: Visionary/Survivor
Physical: Strength 2 (4/6/5/3), Dexterity 1 (1/2/3/3), Stamina 2 (4/5/5/4)
Social: Charisma 2 , Manipulation 1 (0/0/0/0), Appearance 2 (1/0/2/2)
Mental: Perception 3, Intelligence 2, Wits 2
Talents: Alertness 1, Athletics 2, Brawl 1, Dodge 2, Empathy 1, Expression 2, Instruction 2
Skills: Animal Ken 1, Drive 1, Meditation 2, Performance 1, Survival 2
Knowledges: Enigmas 1, Herbalism 2, Linguistics 1, Medicine 1, Occult 2, Philosophy 3, Rites 2

Jennifer Moon-Wizened

Backgrounds: Allies 3, Rites 2
Gifts: (1) Smell of Man, Mindspeak, Mother's Touch; (2) Calm, Distractions, Song of Rage, Staredown; (3) Reshape Object, Spirit Friend
Rank: 3
Rage 5, Gnosis 5, Willpower 5
Rites: (Death) Gathering for the Departed; (Renown) Rite of Accomplishment
Fetishes: None

Image: Jennifer is an average-looking woman in her late 20s. She dresses in soft colors and jeans — generally comfortable clothing. She often wears necklaces made from crystals and pewter. Her Lupus form is a slim, gray wolf.

Roleplaying Notes: In many ways, you are the stereotypical Child of Gaia. You are introspective and a highly spiritual philosopher and seek to maintain a balance within yourself in hopes of restoring balance in the world. You don't speak much; you are reluctant to give advice, preferring that others find their own answers from within. When you do speak, you are usually listened to, for your encouragement is always sincere. In battle, you are a vicious warrior, almost but not quite to the point of being cruel.

History: Jennifer was raised by her mother in a middle-class home in the western United States. Her mother was aware of her heritage and feared that Jennifer would manifest Garou blood. Those fears proved justified when Jennifer underwent her First Change while on a hiking trip in the Rocky Mountains. Jennifer's mother awoke to find her daughter sitting in a clearing, growling and assuming Crinos form. Other Garou in various forms materialized out of the shadows and escorted Jennifer away. Jennifer's mother never said a word, knowing that her daughter's destiny lay elsewhere.

Jennifer returned to her mother several months later and resumed her former life, though she was not the same young, naive girl. From time to time Jennifer would disappear, and this became accepted between mother and daughter. Ultimately Jennifer graduated high school and college and began teaching philosophy at a private school in the Colorado mountains. She also pursued studies in Tai Chi and meditation techniques.

Jennifer doesn't speak much of her Rite of Passage, but her spirituality and connection to Luna were infinitely intensified by the rite. She often stares at the moon when contemplating difficult problems and frequently awakens from these "trances" with answers to dilemmas. Her Garou name stems from the way that the moon seems to have aged her beyond her years. When not seeking advice for her pack, Jennifer tends to be found in the Umbra, seeking paths to Luna herself.

Pearl River

Breed: Homid

Auspice: Theurge

Tribe: Children of Gaia

Nature/Demeanor: Caregiver/Confidant

Physical: Strength 3 (5/7/6/4), Dexterity 3 (3/4/5/5), Stamina 3 (5/6/6/5)

Social: Charisma 5, Manipulation 3 (2/0/0/0), Appearance 4 (3/0/4/4)

Mental: Perception 3, Intelligence 4, Wits 4

Talents: Brawl 4, Dodge 4, Empathy 5, Expression 3, Primal-Urge 3, Streetwise 1, Subterfuge 2

Skills: Animal Ken 2, Leadership 5, Survival 3

Knowledges: Enigmas 3, Occult 4, Rituals 5

Backgrounds: Allies 4, Contacts 2, Kinfolk 4, Past Life 3

Gifts: (1) Persuasion, Spirit Speech, Mother's Touch; (2) Calm, Sight From the Beyond; (3) Dazzle, Pulse of the Invisible, Spirit Friend; (4) Serenity, Spirit Ward, Ultimate Argument of Logic; (5) The Living Wood

Rank: 5

Rage 3, Gnosis 8, Willpower 6

Rites: (Accord) Rite of Cleansing; (Caern) Rite of Caern Building, Rite of the Opened Bridge; (Mystic) Rite of Binding, Rite of Talsiman Dedication, Rite of Spirit Awakening, Rite of Summoning, Rite of the Fetish

Fetishes: Spirit Tracer, Sanctuary Chimes, Sacred Soil (Talen, Gnosis: 4. This is earth that was carefully tended and purified before it was removed from its Umbral Glen. When placed carefully into a plot on the ground, it sprouts any seed, instantly growing the plant or tree by one year's reckoning for each success on the Soil's Gnosis roll, difficulty 8.)

Image: Pearl is a white-gold wolf with a gentle-sloping muzzle and a graceful walk. In Homid form, she is a middle-aged, mixed-race woman with long, lightly curled, pale-brown hair. She wears sensible clothes. She has a serene, youthful face that radiates concern.

Roleplaying Notes: Smile and listen patiently. Sigh occasionally.

History: The ruler of New York's Children of Gaia is the wise shaman Pearl of the River, who presides from the Sept of the Hand of Gaia. She listens carefully to the council of her followers and institutes policies enforced by True Silverheels. Because of this unique co-leadership arrangement, emissaries from other tribes often believe that True is the real leader and Pearl his advisor.

Pearl is faced with the challenge of trying to unify 12 tribes that often want to tear each other to bits. She seeks

Pearl River

to focus their energies in one direction: to help and heal, not only other Garou but mankind and the living world. At times she fears she will not be able to accomplish even the first step in this plan and despairs for the tremendous power squandered by Garou in reckless in-fighting and short-sighted vanity. Yet she perseveres and searches for a clear purpose to unify her people.

In the polygamous society that New York's Children of Gaia have created, Pearl has taken several Kinfolk as lovers and has continued her own line of Kinfolk through several litters.

As the War of the Apocalypse escalates, Pearl must reconsider her position as leader of her tribe. Already perceived as an advisor, other tribes probably won't acknowledge her as the true facilitator of a Garou union. To save face with the other tribes, she may have to step down and allow True Silverheels to assume total authority, whether as a willing puppet or genuine tribal leader. Can such a reversal of tradition be accomplished without disruption, or will any jealousy or bitterness become the soil in which the Wyrm can plant its seed? The fate of New York's Childen of Gaia and perhaps all of its Garou would hang in the balance.

Questor Treetalker

Breed: Lupus
Auspice: Galliard
Nature/Demeanor: Caregiver/Confidant
Physical: Strength 4 (6/8/7/5), Dexterity 3 (3/4/5/5), Stamina 4 (6/7/7/6)
Social: Charisma 3, Manipulation 3 (2/0/0/0), Appearance 2 (1/0/2/2)
Mental: Perception 3, Intelligence 3, Wits 3
Talents: Alertness 2, Brawl 3, Dodge 3, Empathy 2, Primal-Urge 3
Skills: Animal Ken 2, Leadership 3, Stealth 3, Survival 4
Knowledges: Enigmas 2, Rituals 3
Backgrounds: Allies 2, Kinfolk 2, Rites 3
Gifts: (1) Call of the Wyld, Heightened Senses, Leap of the Kangaroo, Resist Pain; (2) Distractions, Sense the Unnatural, Luna's Armor; (3) Catfeet, Eye of the Cobra
Rank: 3
Rage 4, Gnosis 6, Willpower 6
Rites: (Death) Gathering for the Departed; (Mystic) Rite of Summoning; (Renown) Rite of Accomplishment, Rite of Wounding
Fetishes: None

Questor Treetalker

Image: Questor's Homid form is a well-muscled man of above-average height, with dark blond hair and jade-green eyes. Questor's Lupus form is a large, sturdy gray wolf with green eyes.

Roleplaying Notes: You are a fairly quiet individual; you rarely initiate conversations. Your relationship with the Inuit family back home has tempered your judgment of humans; you otherwise find them to be bewildering and frequently frustrating. Yet, you realize that humans play a role in Gaia's plan, and feel strongly against exterminating them. You are thought of as levelheaded, and you generally think carefully before responding to questions put before you.

History: Questor was born in the forests of northern Canada, where his first contact with humanity was an Inuit family with whom his pack shared territory and an understanding of sorts. Questor was the largest member of his litter, but was also the most mild-mannered.

His First Change occurred while hunting. He and his packmates were pursuing a herd of caribou when a large, foul-smelling, tentacled creature burst from the ground. Questor's sister was gored. As he watched his sister's body tumble through the air, Questor felt an anger rise within him such as he had never known before. His body began to change and grow, and he tore into the creature. This was his first encounter with a Wyrm creature, and he was both horrified and furious that such an abomination could exist. Upon returning to his den, Questor found a small pack of wolves awaiting him. They spoke to him of the Garou and told him that he was to go with them and learn of his true nature. Realizing that his path lay with these creatures, Questor obeyed.

Questor's mild temperament and balanced thinking enabled him to form lasting bonds with the members of his new pack. He also found his new friends eager to help him wage war against the Wyrm, for which, remembering his sister's death, he developed a deep hatred.

Tim Rowantree

Breed: Homid
Auspice: Ahroun
Nature/Demeanor: Director/Traditionalist
Physical: Strength 4 (6/8/7/5), Dexterity 3 (3/4/5/5), Stamina 3 (5/6/6/5)
Social: Charisma 4, Manipulation 3 (2/0/0/0), Appearance 2 (1/0/2/2)
Mental: Perception 3, Intelligence 2, Wits 2
Talents: Alertness 3, Brawl 2, Dodge 3, Intimidation 4, Primal-Urge 3
Skills: Drive 2, Leadership 3, Melee 3, Stealth 3, Survival 3
Knowledges: Rituals 1

The complete serenity of a caern is something that Tim prizes more highly than anything else. When one of Gaia's caerns is attacked, Tim leaps headfirst into battle with a ferocity that seems startlingly out of character. He is currently trying to find a Garou to tutor him in the secret knowledges so that he will be better prepared for the wars ahead.

True Silverheels

Breed: Homid
Auspice: Ahroun
Nature/Demeanor: Confidant/Alpha
Physical: Strength 4 (6/8/7/5), Dexterity 4 (4/5/6/6), Stamina 3 (5/6/6/5)
Social: Charisma 4, Manipulation 3 (3/0/0/0), Appearance 4 (3/0/4/4)
Mental: Perception 3, Intelligence 3, Wits 3
Talents: Alertness 3, Athletics 3, Brawl 4, Dodge 5, Empathy 3, Expression 3, Primal-Urge 4
Skills: Animal-Ken 2, Leadership 4, Melee 3, Stealth 2, Survival 3
Knowledges: Rituals 3
Backgrounds: Allies 3, Contacts 4, Kinfolk 3, Pure Breed 1
Gifts: (1) Inspiration, Persuasion, Resist Pain; (2) Luna's Armor, Staredown; (3) Reshape Object, Silver Claws; (4) Cocoon, Serenity, Stoking Fury's Furnace
Rank: 4
Rage 4, Gnosis 6, Willpower 7
Rites: (Accord) Rite of Cleansing, Rite of Contrition; (Mystic) Rite of the Totem, Talisman Dedication
Fetishes: Silver Sword, Clay Pact (Level: 5, Gnosis: 7. This is a small ceramic plate with the paw imprints of all the members of True Silverheels' old pack. By activating it, True can create a Mindspeak [the Galliard Gift] with any of his pack, no matter how far away they are, even if they are in the Deep Umbra.)

Image: In Lupus form, True is a shaggy brown wolf with collie markings. He looks like a friendly dog. In Homid form, he is a white man in his early 40s with dark hair and chiseled good looks.

Roleplaying Notes: You are eager and have an assertive interest in everyone. You genuinely like others, even the most annoying and unpleasant.

History: True Silverheels is a Child of Gaia belonging to New York's Sept of the Hand of Gaia. He is a ruggedly handsome, vigorous man. He has boundless reserves of energy and often applies them to the hedonistic pleasures that New York's Children of Gaia are tolerant of.

True Silverheels is the advisor and assistant of Pearl River, leader of New York's Children of Gaia. True confers with Pearl River and then carries out the tribal policies that she institutes. Because he is the most visible symbol of tribal

Tim Rowantree

Backgrounds: Allies 2, Familiar Spirit 3
Gifts: (1) Inspiration, Persuasion, Resist Pain; (2) Jam Technology, Staredown
Rank: 2
Rage 5, Gnosis 4, Willpower 5
Rites: (Renown) Rite of Wounding
Fetishes: Spirit Whistle, seven Pine Daggers
Merits/Flaws: Calm Heart; Uneducated (illiterate)

Image: Tim is a large, gentle man with heavily calloused hands, long sandy blond hair and blue eyes. He normally wears jeans and a tie-dyed T-shirt. He puts his hair in a ponytail. In Lupus form, he has light brown, slightly shaggy fur. Tim's spirit ally is always around him, hovering in the Umbra. His spirit friend is a Jaggling from a grove of rowan trees near Tim's birthplace.

Roleplaying Notes: Be somewhat shy, but not overly so. Always look around and keep tabs on who is present. Be very supportive of your pack leader; after all, unity is the key to success.

History: Tim grew up in remote eastern Quebec among illiterate, simple homesteaders who had no place in the busy modern world. He always loved the deep forests that surrounded his home, and as a boy, he learned to survive in the deep woods. When the Change came, Tim gladly accepted his role as a defender of the forests. He traveled broadly before settling down at a caern.

True Silverheels

power, many Garou of other tribes think he is in charge, just as white settlers of what became New York thought that native tribes had only male chiefs; they only saw men carrying out policy.

True is well connected in local towns and helped Rochester institute its ground-breaking health care plan. He also helps Loba Carcassone, Silver Fang protectress, find safe places for human children through the Heaven network — an underground railroad that assists children escaping abusive families.

In the War of the Apocalypse, True seeks to unify the tribes so that they may fight the Wyrm together. Because many outsiders perceive him to be the leader of New York's Children of Gaia, it will fall to him to act as moderator in reconciling the tribes' differences. If unification is to succeed, the Childen of Gaia may have to change their traditions of leadership and place True above Pearl River. Certainly the Children would understand the necessity of such an action, but that might mean the Wyrm has ultimately won by undoing Garou traditions.

Rage: Warriors of the Apocalypse

Fianna

Bron Mac Fionn

Breed: Homid

Auspice: Galliard

Nature/Demeanor: Visionary/Judge

Physical: Strength 4 (6/8/7/5), Dexterity 4 (4/5/6/6), Stamina 4 (6/7/7/7)

Social: Charisma 5, Manipulation 4 (3/1/1/1), Appearance 3 (2/0/3/3)

Mental: Perception 3, Intelligence 3, Wits 4

Talents: Alertness 3, Athletics 4, Brawl 5, Dodge 3, Empathy 2, Expression 4, Intimidation 3, Primal-Urge 4, Subterfuge 3

Skills: Animal Ken 3, Drive 2, Etiquette 1, Firearms 1, Leadership 5, Melee 4, Performance 5, Stealth 2, Survival 2

Knowledges: Enigmas 3, Linguistics 1, Medicine 2, Occult 2, Rituals 4

Backgrounds: Mentor 5, Totem 4, Contacts 1

Gifts: (1) Beast Speech, Call of the Wyld, Persuasion, Resist Toxin; (2) Brew, Distractions, Howl of the Banshee; (3) Faerie Kin, Ley Lines, Song of Rage; (4) Balor's Gaze, Faerie Blood; (5) Call the Hunt

Rank: 5

Rage 7, Gnosis 10, Willpower 9

Rites: (Accord) Rite of Cleansing, Rite of Contrition; (Caern) Moot Rite, Rite of the Opened Bridge, Rite of the Opened Caern, Rite of the Shrouded Glen, The Badger's Burrow; (Death) Gathering for the Departed; (Mystic) Baptism of Fire, Rite of Binding, Rite of Talisman Dedication, Rite of the Fetish; (Punishment) The Hunt, Voice of the Jackal; (Renown) Rite of Passage

Fetishes: Fang Dagger, Gae Bolg (Level 4, Gnosis 7. This massive ancient spear has a difficulty of 5 and does Strength + 5 damage due to powerful spirit energies within it. When the spear impales an opponent, the shaft splits in a hundred different directions. When removed, the spear joins itself together instantly.)

Image: Bron is a large black wolf with bright green eyes. He wears his many battle scars proudly. The most noticeable of them run across his left cheek. In Homid form, he is a tall, burly man (about 6'1") with a red beard and mustache. He appears to be in his late 40s. He is the type of man who looks either extremely friendly or intimidating, depending on whether he smiles or scowls.

Bron Mac Fionn

Roleplaying Notes: You are the Righ of Brugh Na Boinne. You are responsible for defending your sept, the caern and all of Ireland. The High Righ of all the Fianna in Tara is your mentor, and the position may one day be yours. You listen to all advice and pretend to consider it, but only your own inner counsel truly matters in the end. You would sacrifice your life to defend the land. You believe that your inner song holds the key to surviving the Apocalypse. Trust only those strangers who share your brew.

History: Through great effort, Bron climbed through Garou society. Always defending Ireland, he has fought Get of Fenris, crazed Red Talons, members of the Fianna Brotherhood of Hern camp and minions of the Wyrm. The current High Righ of the Fianna was Bron's mentor when he was a cub. As he has risen through the ranks of the Fianna, Bron has also risen. Bron took the name Mac Fionn after becoming Righ. It means "son of Fionn," and every Righ at Brugh Na Boinne takes the name.

Bron has a vision of utopia that he keeps to himself. He wants a world in which werewolves, faeries and humans live together in harmony. He laments the loss of myth and magic in the world. He follows Dana as his totem, and she has never guided him falsely. All other members of the sept share her granted ability to entrance listeners. He may also use his background points of Totem as the Past Life background.

Goll Mac Mourna

Breed: Homid
Auspice: Galliard
Nature/Demeanor: Traditionalist/Curmudgeon
Physical: Strength 3 (5/7/6/4), Dexterity 3 (3/4/5/5), Stamina 3 (5/6/6/5)
Social: Charisma 4, Manipulation 3 (2/0/0/0), Appearance 2 (1/0/2/2)
Mental: Perception 4, Intelligence 3, Wits 3
Talents: Alertness 2, Athletics 1, Brawl 3, Empathy 2, Expression 3, Intimidation 2, Streetwise 2, Subterfuge 2
Skills: Etiquette 3, Leadership 3, Melee 2, Performance 3, Stealth 1
Knowledges: Enigmas 3, Linguistics 1, Occult 2, Rituals 2
Backgrounds: Kinfolk 4, Pure Breed 2
Gifts: (1) Call of the Wyld, Persuasion, Resist Toxin; (2) Dreamspeak, Glib Tongue, Staredown; (3) Disquiet, Song of Rage

Goll Mac Mourna

Rank: 3
Rage 6, Gnosis 4, Willpower 5
Rites: (Caern) Moot Rite; (Death) Gathering for the Departed; (Mystic) Baptism of Fire, Rite of Talisman Dedication; (Punishment) Rite of Ostracism; (Renown) Rite of Accomplishment, Rite of Passage
Fetishes: Sanctuary Chimes, Spirit Whistle

Image: Grouchy but with a cutting wit, Goll Mac Mourna is the fire in the heart of his community. His rough, deep voice resonates with authority and wisdom. He wears the mantle of wise one well, but all remember that not so long ago this elder-in-the-making was a young brawler with a temper as quick as his tongue. A bard of great skill, Goll is still a strong and ready warrior.

Roleplaying Notes: Tell stories, especially of great Fianna heroes. Sing loudly. Drink much. Act as the heart and conscience of your community. Try to be grandfatherly, though you reckon yourself still young. Work hard to prove yourself worthy of the great trust you have been given. Watch your temper.

History: Born 35 years ago into a village of Fianna and their kin in the hills of Northern Ireland, Goll Mac Mourna grew to manhood largely untouched by the modern world. In spite of television and the comings and goings of various Irish militants, his community clung tenaciously to its traditions, guided largely by strong Garou leaders who saw beyond the petty religious bickering of their countrymen to the larger threat of the Wyrm. One of these leaders was a Galliard named MacManus, who held the Chair of Stories for the local sept. MacManus was beloved and kept spirits high, for his tales and songs kept everyone's eyes on the higher goal of harmony with the earth herself and on the honor of sacrifice made in her name.

Goll worked odd jobs and sang rock songs with his friends in the local pub. He was known more for his brawls than his songs, however, and many assumed he would die in battle, hopefully against the Wyrm's minions and not against his own kin in a drunken row.

One morning, he was called to MacManus's house, where he was led to the great Galliard's bedside. MacManus was dying of Wyrm-inflicted wounds from a mission to Belfast, and MacManus told the young brawler that he was to take MacManus' place in the community. Filled with doubt but honored at being chosen, Goll spent the next few days at the dying Garou's side, learning all he could of the path ahead of him. At MacManus's wake, it was Goll who sang his dirge, in a voice full of sorrow and greatness, the voice of a Galliard born. From that day, he bore his responsibility solemnly, and has tried to live up to the memory of the Garou elder he replaced. All but he feel that he has succeeded.

Morgan the Unworthy

forms, his eyes are murky green with almost no visible pupils.

Roleplaying Notes: You love attention. You draw it to yourself whenever possible. You know you're insane, but that doesn't bother you — from madness comes insight. You always waffle in moments of decision, uncertain whether to fight or flee.

History: Like all metis, Morgan lives with the consequences of his parents' actions. Once shunned and hopelessly insane, Morgan came under the watchful eye of an old Fianna named Patrick McDougal. It was under McDougal that Morgan began to understand and work within Garou society. Morgan overcame many of his handicaps and learned to make the best of others; he has offset many would-be tormentors with unpredictable and bizarre acts.

Morgan lives for the moment and cannot be relied upon to accomplish goals. However, he has an uncanny knack for being in the right place at the right time. There have also been a few occasions when he has invoked powerful Gifts and rites that would normally have been beyond his ability. McDougal's patronage and Morgan's unmistakable luck keep the leaders of his sept from casting him out.

Now with the War of the Apocalypse at hand, Morgan, like all other Garou, is drawn into the conflict. He discovers new allies and enemies at every turn — Morgan's remarkable talents and notoriety keep him in the War — but few packs suffer his companionship for long.

Morgan the Unworthy

Breed: Metis
Auspice: Philodox
Nature/Demeanor: Rebel/Showoff
Physical: Strength 2 (4/6/5/3), Dexterity 2 (2/3/4/4), Stamina 4 (6/7/7/6)
Social: Charisma 1, Manipulation 4 (3/1/1/1), Appearance 1 (0/0/1/1)
Mental: Perception 3, Intelligence 5, Wits 1
Talents: Alertness 1, Brawl 4, Dodge 2, Expression 1, Intimidation 1, Primal-Urge 2, Subterfuge 2
Skills: Etiquette 1, Performance 2, Repair 1, Survival 1
Knowledges: Enigmas 3, Medicine 1, Politics 3, Rituals 2
Backgrounds: Mentor 4, Rites 1
Gifts: (1) Resist Toxin, Sense Wyrm, Truth of Gaia; (2) Burrow, Curse of Hatred
Rank: 2
Rage 4, Gnosis 6, Willpower 3
Rites: (Death) Gathering for the Departed
Fetishes: Bane Arrow

Image: Morgan usually remains in Crinos form. His fur and hair are matted and unwashed. He walks — or lumbers — with stooped shoulders and dangling arms. Regardless of

No'iri'n Ni' Dhonaill

Breed: Homid
Auspice: Ahroun
Nature/Demeanor: Rebel/Gallant
Physical: Strength 3 (5/7/6/4), Dexterity 3 (3/4/5/5), Stamina 4 (6/7/7/6)
Social: Charisma 4, Manipulation 3 (2/0/0/0), Appearance 4 (3/0/4/4)
Mental: Perception 3, Intelligence 3, Wits 4
Talents: Alertness 2, Brawl 4, Dodge 3, Empathy 3, Expression 4, Primal-Urge 4
Skills: Animal Ken 1, Leadership 2, Performance (Dance) 2, Stealth 1
Knowledges: Enigmas 2, Linguistics 3, Medicine 2, Politics 2
Backgrounds: Allies 2, Kinfolk 2, Pure Breed 2
Gifts: (1) Inspiration, Persuasion, Razor Claws, Resist Toxin; (2) Glib Tongue
Rank: 2
Rage 5, Gnosis 4, Willpower 6
Rites: None
Fetishes: None

Image: Despite her homid heritage, No'iri'n prefers her Lupus form, in which she appears as a dainty wolf with

No'iri'n Ni' Dhonaill

No'iri'n believes that the ongoing feud between her tribe and the Silver Fangs diverts Rage from the Wyrm. She also believes that the Garou should cease wallowing in grief and self-pity over the genocide of Australia's ancient Bunyip tribe. Rather than mourn that which is lost, No'iri'n believes that the Garou must make amends for what they have done. To this end, she argues constantly for Garou support of Aboriginal land rights and similar issues, in the process earning the hatred of the Red Talons and Get of Fenris.

Whether she realizes it or not, No'iri'n possesses the skills and charisma to become a compelling leader in the War of the Apocalypse. Her tendency to question the assumed and established blesses her with new perspectives on long-standing problems. That insight might be what it takes to unite Australia's tribes and strike back at the Wyrm. Energetic and conscientious, No'iri'n speaks her mind at all Fianna moots and has slowly begun to gain followers among the young of her kind. Perhaps that youth can be led to ensure a future for all Garou.

Son-of-Moonlight

Breed: Lupus
Auspice: Theurge
Nature/Demeanor: Fanatic/Alpha
Physical: Strength 2 (4/6/5/3), Dexterity 4 (4/5/6/6), Stamina 4 (6/7/7/6)
Social: Charisma 3, Manipulation 2 (1/0/0/0), Appearance 2 (1/0/2/2)
Mental: Perception 5, Intelligence 4, Wits 4
Talents: Alertness 5, Athletics 3, Brawl 4, Dodge 2, Expression 1, Intimidation 3, Primal-Urge 5, Subterfuge 2
Skills: Animal Ken 5, Melee 2, Leadership 2, Performance 3, Stealth 4, Survival 4
Knowledges: Enigmas 2, Linguistics 1, Occult 3, Rituals 3
Backgrounds: Allies 3, Totem 2
Gifts: (1) Leap of the Kangaroo, Mother's Touch, Persuasion, Sense Wyrm; (2) Command Spirit, Glib Tongue, Name the Spirit; (3) Exorcism, Ley Lines; (4) Beast Life, Song of the Dire
Rank: 4
Rage 7, Gnosis 7, Willpower 7
Rites: (Accord) Rite of Cleansing, Rite of Contrition; (Caern) Rite of the Opened Caern; (Mystic) Rite of Binding, (Punishment) Rite of Ostracism, The Hunt; (Renown) Rite of Wounding
Fetishes: None

Image: Son-of-Moonlight has a crimson (almost blood-red) coat in Lupus form. In Homid form, he has dark hair and green eyes. He is 28 years old and stands at 5'11". Son-of-Moonlight has a feral appearance in all of his forms.

reddish, white-tipped fur. Her tongue lolls, and her head is invariably cocked inquisitively to one side. When in Homid form, No'iri'n has a permanent grin on her fine-boned face. Freckles dot her nose and cheeks, and her auburn hair is cut short and ragged. She has green, dancing eyes. She wears whatever clothes are at hand, from baggy tracksuits to ballgowns.

Roleplaying Notes: You are never content with the way things are and believe there is a better way to achieve any goal. You think that the Fianna are in a rut and that someone has to lead them out of it, even if they have to be dragged by the ears.

History: No'iri'n was always a troublemaker. Even when carried off by Garou, she did not fit in, questioning assumptions and beliefs held for millennia. Returning to human society after her Rite of Passage, No'iri'n discovered that Melbourne, Australia, no longer held any attraction for her. Thus she set off once more into the country.

Today No'iri'n is a member of Australia's Tower Hill Sept. Unlike most Ahroun, she is not a mindless killer, although when angered she is a deadly fighter. Unlike most Fianna, she does not despise the Silver Fangs. Despite her flamboyance, her roguish, devil-may-care behavior and her desire for attention, No'iri'n is a serious candidate for the Righ of Australia, although as yet none knows it save herself.

Son-of-Moonlight

Roleplaying Notes: You want wolves to reclaim Ireland for their own. For now, you conduct secret raids against the people of Ireland with groups of others. The others do not suspect you, blaming your savage attacks on Red Talons, Ronin or Black Spiral Dancers. The wildlife around your caern aids you in your righteous cause, including a wolf pack that you have brought to the area. You save your greatest hatred for Irish wolfhounds, mercilessly slaughtering any you find.

History: Son-of-Moonlight was born in a zoo in Leinster. The first and largest of his litter, Son-of-Moonlight dominated his brothers and sisters. When he got older, a zookeeper accidentally placed him in a pen with one of the other male wolves. During a fight for dominance, Son-of-Moonlight experienced the Change. He tore through the bars of the pen and fled into the night.

The Fianna found him and brought him to the caern of Brugh Na Boinne. After learning about his true nature, Son-of-Moonlight devoted himself to the sept and defending his fellow animals.

Son-of-Moonlight spent many of his early days with the Fianna, protecting the wildlife of Ireland from hunters and polluters. The humans' actions appalled Son-of-Moonlight. Also, as he recalled his past lives, he remembered Irish wolfhounds and men hunting and eradicating the wolves of Ireland. His soul cried out for vengeance.

Son-of-Moonlight serves as warder for the Tri-Spiral Sept. He hates letting humans travel into the caern, no matter what healing effects it may have on them. Son-of-Moonlight secretly aids the Eire Fundamentalist camp of the Fianna tribe. He constantly looks for potential recruits. With time, Son-of-Moonlight grows bold. He knows that Bron Mac Fionn will not be Righ forever and has grown careless about his antihuman sentiments. Thankfully, his first priority is still defending his wolf brothers and not genocide.

Wind-across-the-Hills

Breed: Homid
Auspice: Ragabash
Nature/Demeanor: Gallant/Jester
Physical: Strength 2 (4/6/5/3), Dexterity 4 (4/5/6/6), Stamina 2 (4/5/5/4)
Social: Charisma 3, Manipulation 3 (2/0/0/0), Appearance 4 (3/0/4/4)
Mental: Perception 2, Intelligence 3, Wits 2
Talents: Alertness 1, Athletics 3, Brawl 2, Dodge 3, Empathy 2, Primal-Urge 2, Streetwise 1, Subterfuge 2
Skills: Drive 1, Performance 2, Stealth 3
Knowledges: Enigmas 3, Investigation 1, Linguistics 1, Occult 2, Rituals 2
Backgrounds: Contacts 2, Rites 1, Totem 2
Gifts: (1) Blur of the Milky Eye, Heightened Senses, Persuasion
Rank: 1
Rage 2, Gnosis 3, Willpower 5
Rites: (Mystic) Rite of Talisman Dedication
Fetishes: None

Image: Wind-across-the-Hills is a lanky chap with long, dirty-blond hair that constantly falls in front of his face. He is about 5'9", but seems taller. In Lupus form, he is a black-and-red wolf with telltale Fianna-green eyes. Wind-across-the-Hills has a perpetual smile on his face. He is 23.

Roleplaying Notes: You are confident, witty, good-looking and fast. Everything you do is fast. You like beautiful women, and you love good drink. You exist to enjoy life to the fullest, and you try to help everyone else do the same.

History: Wind-across-the-Hills lives a life blessed by the luck of the Irish. Extreme convenience follows him everywhere. He didn't undergo the Change until well past puberty. He was kidnapped by Garou as a teenager while leaving a bank, mere moments before Protestants bombed it. During his Rite of Passage, his pack invaded a Black

Wind-across-the-Hills

Spiral Hive and discovered that all the Black Spiral Dancers had recently killed each other.

Wind-across-the-Hills is increasingly proving his ability to extricate himself from scrapes, and he makes his stories sound absolutely thrilling. Bron Mac Fionn likes the potential of the young Garou.

He loves to run in all of his forms. When he meets most Garou, he challenges them to a quick race. If they take losing well, he likes them. If they beat him, he gains instant admiration for them. Wind-across-the-Hills also loves to flirt. He nearly got hurt badly when a Black Fury took his playfulness the wrong way.

Wind-across-the-Hills has many human and wolf acquaintances in the Leinster area. He loves the nightlife of Irish cities. Although still a cub when compared to the likes of Bron, he has the potential to achieve much more in the War of the Apocalypse.

Get of Fenris

Bjorn-Blood-from-Stone

Breed: Metis

Auspice: Ahroun

Nature/Demeanor: Martyr/Lone Wolf

Physical: Strength 3 (5/7/6/4), Dexterity 4 (4/5/6/6), Stamina 3 (5/6/6/5)

Social: Charisma 4, Manipulation 2 (1/0/0/0), Appearance 1 (0/0/1/1)

Mental: Perception 4, Intelligence 3, Wits 4

Talents: Alertness 5, Athletics 1, Brawl 2, Dodge 2, Empathy 5, Intimidation 2

Skills: Animal Ken 2, Melee 2, Leadership 1, Stealth 1, Survival 2

Knowledges: Enigmas 5, Occult 3, Rituals 2

Backgrounds: Allies 5

Gifts: (1) Create Element, Resist Pain, Sense Wyrm, The Falling Touch; (2) True Fear; (3) Eyes of the Cat, Might of Thor

Rank: 3

Rage 6, Gnosis 6, Willpower 9

Rites: (Accord) Rite of Cleansing; (Mystic) Rite of Summoning

Fetishes: None

Image: A fearsome giant of a man, Bjorn-Blood-from-Stone is something lifted directly from tales of Ragnarok. Standing over seven feet tall in Homid form, he is an immense portrait of solid muscle; in Crinos, he is a boogie man. His metis disfigurement is recognizable immediately in the form of a right arm and hand swollen with veins and muscle, fully four times the size of their left-side counterparts. Those encountering Bjorn get a mixed sense of wisdom and madness, focused through an intensity of scorching strength.

Roleplaying Notes: You treat others with formality and respect, determined to be better than those who raised you. The freedom to find one's own destiny, unhindered by the limitations imposed (for whatever reasons) by others, is sacred to you. You will not limit the freedom of others, not even of your enemies. It is better to kill something outright and let it die free, than to imprison it and steal from it all self-respect and dignity.

History: The product of a drunken union between two low-ranked Get of Fenris, Bjorn-Blood-from-Stone was born into a world of cruelty and pain. While the Get did not kill or banish him, they also did nothing to support him in any way, except provide sustenance. They would rarely speak to him, and when they did it was always in a demeaning, cruel way. They wouldn't allow him to participate in social affairs,

except occasionally as an errand boy. In their eyes he was a freakish aberration, impure and misbegotten, and it was enough that he was suffered to live, that he had his life to do something with if he proved resourceful enough.

Bjorn did. Filled with great strength of spirit, he channeled his pain and rage, and as he grew and his body swelled with muscle, it was almost as if that repressed emotion was taking physical form. His fierce gaze penetrated his tormentors as if they had ceased to exist, and in time he began to respond to their belittlements and commands with a gruff "Leave me be."

During his Rite of Passage, Bjorn and his fellow pups traveled to the Umbra, and the others returned properly bound together as packmates. Bjorn remained in the spirit world. He had an epiphany there: in the realm of spirits, he would find the end to his own pain and that of Gaia. He has rarely returned to the physical world, the world of his pain; it is said that getting Bjorn out of the Umbra is like getting blood from a stone.

Now he travels the Umbral world, seeking knowledge and wisdom, ever willing to sacrifice for Gaia's well-being, for he grew accustomed to pain long ago and it means nothing to

Bjorn-Blood-from-Stone

him. Many a Bane has met its destruction at his hands, many an Umbral traveler has found him a sudden, unexpected ally against spiritual horrors, and many tales have already been told of his sullen wisdom and great strength.

Bladetooth

Breed: Lupus

Auspice: Theurge

Nature/Demeanor: Caregiver/Rebel

Physical: Strength 4 (6/8/7/5), Dexterity 4 (4/5/6/6), Stamina 3 (5/6/6/5)

Social: Charisma 3, Manipulation 2 (1/0/0/0), Appearance 2 (1/0/2/2)

Mental: Perception 2, Intelligence 3, Wits 2

Talents: Alertness 2, Athletics 4, Brawl 4, Dodge 3, Intimidation 3, Primal-Urge 4

Skills: Melee 3, Survival 2

Knowledges: Occult 3, Rituals 2

Backgrounds: Enigmas 2, Fetishes 4, Occult 1, Rites 2

Gifts: (1) Heightened Senses, Resist Pain, Sense Wyrm, (2) Scent of Sight

Rank: 2

Rage 8, Gnosis 5, Willpower 4

Rites: (Accord) Rite of Cleansing; (Mystic) Rite of Binding

Fetishes: Basket of Bones, Fang Dagger, Moon Sign

Bladetooth

Image: Bladetooth is a great, gray wolf with tawny striping down her head and back. Her jaws are huge and can snap entire Garou heads in a single bite. Her face is filled with sadness. In Homid form she is a stout, middle-aged blonde woman. She wears gray, unadorned clothes.

Roleplaying Notes: You feel sorrow, regret and shame. Though you still bear a strong maternal instinct, you cannot help but feel that a suicidal death is more fitting for you than nuturing other Garou.

History: Bladetooth was a great warrior among New York's Get of Fenris. Her undoing occurred when she fell in love with the tribal leader, Arn Guth Stormbright. He spurned her love but she was resolute; love won in the end. Their secret affair exacted its price though. Pregnant, Bladetooth had a vision of bearing metis twins, and she fled the tribe.

Arn Guth Stormbright did not suspect the real reasons for Bladetooth's apparent betrayal until years later, when he encountered his look-alike son, the leader of a skinhead pack: New York's Bastards of Fenris. Bladetooth's daughter disappeared altogether. A self-proclaimed outcast and held to be a traitor by the Get, Bladetooth fell in with the Black Furies and became a devoted guardian of the Caern of the Hand of Gaia.

Today, Bladetooth's spirit remains broken. She hurls herself headlong into every battle against the Wyrm. Though she seeks her own death as punishment for her perceived betrayals and failures as a pack mother, she cannot seem to succeed in her suicidal efforts. Perhaps Gaia has Her own plans for Bladetooth, or so Antonine Teardrop, a Stargazer, has told her. Those plans might involve an epic sacrifice in the War of the Apocalypse, or so Bladetooth hopes.

Carla Grimsson

Breed: Homid

Auspice: Philodox

Nature/Demeanor: Fanatic/Martyr

Physical: Strength 3 (5/7/6/4), Dexterity 4 (4/5/7/7), Stamina 4 (6/7/7/6)

Social: Charisma 4, Manipulation 4 (3/0/0/0), Appearance 3 (2/0/3/3)

Mental: Perception 4, Intelligence 5, Wits 4

Talents: Athletics 4, Brawl 4, Dodge 3, Empathy 3, Expression 5, Intimidation 4, Streetwise 3

Skills: Etiquette 3, Leadership 5

Knowledges: Law 3, Rituals 3, Science 3

Backgrounds: Pure Breed 3, Resources 3

Gifts: (1) Persuasion, Resist Pain, Razor Claws, Scent of the True Form, Truth of Gaia; (2) Call to Duty, Staredown, Strength of Purpose; (3) Disquiet, Might of Thor, Weak Arm; (4) Scream of Gaia

Rank: 4

Rage 7, Gnosis 8, Willpower 9

Carla Grimsson

Protectorate, she initially argued for the controlled growth of mortal civilization and then for its outright cessation. Her fears were not only for the spread of the Wyrm throughout Australia, but for the rights and protection of the Aboriginals, whom she believed had as much right to the land as anyone. Unfortunately, her words were largely misinterpreted as racist, and her arguments against further immigration into Australia were deemed a purity movement. Indeed, even skinhead groups formed by Get and their Kinfolk believed her sympathetic to their cause.

With the escalation of the War of the Apocalypse, Carla has determined to make her true intentions clear. She has begun a personal war on the Wyrm made manifest in the urbanization of wildlands, has staged acts of terrorism to reduce Australian tourism and immigration, and has attacked Get — verbally in council and physically outside it — whom she believes have embraced the Wyrm by following a code of bigotry.

Not surprisingly, Carla is quickly losing the support of her tribe and sept. Even those she presumes to defend are beginning to question her ways. It cannot be long before Carla is alone in her convictions, not only against the Wyrm but against mortal authorities and rival Garou.

Fang Jumper

Breed: Lupus
Auspice: Ragabash
Nature/Demeanor: Competitor/Jester
Physical: Strength 2 (4/6/5/3), Dexterity 4 (4/5/6/6), Stamina 2 (4/5/5/4)
Social: Charisma 2, Manipulation 4 (3/1/1/1), Appearance 2 (1/0/2/2)
Mental: Perception 4, Intelligence 2, Wits 5
Talents: Alertness 3, Brawl 2, Dodge 4, Primal-Urge 5, Streetwise 2
Skills: Animal Ken 2, Stealth 5, Survival 2
Knowledges: Enigmas 3, Occult 2, Rituals 1
Backgrounds: Resources 1
Gifts: (1) Blur of the Milky Eye, Leap of the Kangaroo, Open Seal, Resist Pain
Rank: 1
Rage 3, Gnosis 8, Willpower 6
Rites: (Minor) Greet the Moon, Prayer for the Prey
Fetishes: Collar of Innocence (Level 4, Gnosis 8. A small leather collar that, when activated in Lupus form, makes the wearer appear to be a small, harmless puppy.)

Image: In Homid form, Fang Jumper is an unimpressive, bald man. His only remarkable feature is his constant, curious expression. In Lupus form, he usually appears as a puppy.

Roleplaying Notes: You are a prankster among Garou who cannot even fathom the term. Life is pure entertainment to you, even in this time of war.

History: Fang Jumper has an unusual history with the Get of Fenris. He wandered into a Get caern as a pup and

Rites: (Death) Gathering for the Departed, Rite of the Winter Wolf; (Punishment) Rite of Ostracism, Stone of Scorn; (Renown) Rite of Wounding
Fetishes: Pine Dagger

Image: Carla is a tall woman of obvious Nordic ancestry. Even among other Get of Fenris, she stands out as a leader. Carla has short, platinum-blond hair and ice-blue eyes. She is not arrogant, though she is certainly confident. Her intelligence is betrayed by her expression, and she seems to anticipate any question asked of her. Carla's Lupus form, which she proudly displays, is an arctic wolf — pure white, lean and fierce.

Roleplaying Notes: You have always been confident and proud. You've had your convictions and have stayed true to them, no matter how misunderstood they or you have been. Lately, however, you sense an immediacy to your beliefs, that if they are not acted upon, and boldly, Australia will be lost. You're not sure when you realized all this, but it was sometime after you defeated a Wyrm creature that had inflicted a wound that healed very slowly.

History: Despite her appearance, Carla has been an Australian all her life. She was born in rural New South Wales, though what was her childhood home is now a suburb of Sydney.

For years Carla was concerned about the industrialization and development of Australian wildlands. When she became Jarl of the Get of Fenris and leader of the Flinders

Fang Jumper

Skills: Animal Ken 2, Drive 2, Firearms 3, Melee 2, Repair 3, Stealth 2, Survival 4

Knowledges: Enigmas 1, Investigation 3, Linguistics 1, Medicine 3, Occult 2, Rituals 2

Backgrounds: Allies 2, Past Life 2, Pure Breed 3, Resources 1

Gifts: (1) Persuasion, Razor Claws, Resist Pain, Smell of Man; (2) Halt the Coward's Flight, Spirit of the Fray, True Fear; (3) Might of Thor, Reshape Object; (4) Scream of Gaia

Rank: 4

Rage 7, Gnosis 4, Willpower 8

Rites: (Accord) Rite of Cleansing; (Renown) Rite of Wounding

Fetishes: Scar Fetish (granting him two extra Hurt Health Levels)

Image: Gere in Homid form is a burly man with blond hair and a mustache, dressed like any other hunter or trapper. He has a low, gruff voice and speaks tersely. In Crinos form, he becomes a huge, dark-gray brute. The faint smell of blood often follows Gere.

Roleplaying Notes: You don't socialize much, even with other Garou. You're a loyal son of Fenris, but hold even greater reverence for Gaia. Would Great Fenris want his earthly cousins trapped and shot from helicopters? Hell, no. Someone needs to do something about these Alaskan bastards, and pretty little words just don't get the point

was taken in, no doubt because the Garou sensed a kinship. Within days, Fang Jumper underwent his First Change.

Thereafter he remained with the tribe, much to its members' regret: Fang Jumper quickly proved to be an annoying joker, especially during times of crisis when other Get prepared themselves for hardship, suffering and death.

Fortunately, Gaia seems to smile upon Fang Jumper for he has escaped, dodged and eluded misfortune his entire life. That blessing comes in handy as the Get frequently send Fang Jumper on quests that keep him out of their fur.

Fang Jumper brings his irreverence even to the War of the Apocalypse. He has joked in battle against the deadliest of Wyrm creatures and has chuckled over corpses of fallen comrades, not out of disrespect but in memory of what was best about his friends.

Gere-Hunts-the-Hunters

Breed: Homid

Auspice: Ahroun

Nature/Demeanor: Fanatic/Bravo

Physical: Strength 3 (5/7/6/4), Dexterity 3 (3/4/5/5), Stamina 5 (7/8/8/7)

Social: Charisma 2, Manipulation 2 (1/0/0/0), Appearance 2 (1/0/2/2)

Mental: Perception 4, Intelligence 3, Wits 3

Talents: Alertness 3, Brawl 4, Dodge 2, Intimidation 4, Primal-Urge 3, Streetwise 1

Gere-Hunts-the-Hunters

across like spilling blood does. You don't even particularly care if your prey survives to learn their lesson or not — you'd just as soon see them dead and good luck to them in the hereafter.

History: Not all those who hunt humans are Red Talons. Gere has declared open season on the wolf hunters of Alaska. Gere believes in teaching his prey lessons: He has recently taken to stripping the hunters he catches of all of their weapons and leaving them to survive alone on the frozen tundra. If the hunters have actually killed any wolves, he slices their hamstrings and dresses them in the fur of the animal they slaughtered — after removing their tongues. Those who do not bleed to death either starve or are shot by other hunters.

If they have not actually killed any wolves, he takes their shoes and clothing and leaves them to fend for themselves as they walk back across the tundra. One has survived to tell of his experiences, and he has sworn never again to hunt wolves.

Nobody knows precisely where Gere developed his anger against wolf hunters; he obviously isn't lupus and seems fairly new to Alaska. He doesn't discuss his past, and few are willing to push the issue.

Gere's savagery shocks and dismays many gentler Garou, but just as many werewolves nod, agreeing that something indeed needs to be done. His tribemates are particularly proud of his actions and have honored him with a powerful scar fetish. He is rarely willing to leave Alaska. Gere has met the Black Fury Volcheka Ibarruri on one occasion; despite the enmity between their tribes, the two parted as friends.

Golgol Fangs-First

Breed: Homid

Auspice: Ahroun

Physical: Strength 5 (7/9/8/6), Dexterity 4 (4/5/6/6), Stamina 5 (7/8/8/7)

Social: Charisma 4, Manipulation 3 (2/0/0/0), Appearance 2 (1/0/2/2)

Mental: Perception 4, Intelligence 4, Wits 4

Talents: Alertness 4, Athletics 5, Brawl 5, Dodge 5, Intimidation 5, Primal-Urge 4

Skills: Animal Ken 2, Firearms 2, Leadership 5, Melee 4, Stealth 2, Survival 3

Knowledges: Enigmas 1, Medicine 2, Rituals 3

Backgrounds: Pure Breed 2, Contacts (Septs outside the Amazon) 2, Allies (the Amazon War Force) 5

Gifts: (1) Inspiration, Smell of Man, Razor Claws, Resist Pain; (2) Spirit of the Fray, Staredown; (3) Combat Healing, Might of Thor, Silver Claws; (4) Body Shift, Hero's Stand; (5) Horde of Valhalla, Strength of Will; (6) Unstoppable Warrior (Ahroun) — A Garou who uses this potent Gift can regenerate aggravated damage. This works against all attacks except those from silver weapons. Each turn, roll Stamina + Primal-Urge against a difficulty 8; if successful, then spend one point of Rage

Golgol Fangs-First

per Health Level healed (much like a vampiric Blood Pool).

Rank: 6

Rage 8, Gnosis 7, Willpower 10

Merits/Flaws: Overconfident, Untamable

Rites: (Punishment) Rite of Ostracism, Stone of Scorn, The Hunt; (Renown) Rite of Wounding

Fetishes: Fist of Thor, Battle Harness (Level 5, Gnosis 6. This regal iron vest adds two to the wearer's Strength and adds three armor dice. It must be activated before it can even be lifted. It becomes weightless after successful activation.)

Image: Golgol is a huge Garou, over seven feet tall in Homid form and 13 feet tall in Crinos. He is almost 65 years old and is getting gray hairs, even in Lupus form, but is still in incredibly trim-and-fit fighting shape. He wears an impressive battle harness (see above), and his body is laced with battle scars and ritual pictograms.

Roleplaying Notes: You are quite level-headed for a Get of Fenris. You have seen so many battles that you remain completely calm during a fight, even with bombs dropping on all sides. Through your life, you have grown from a fierce, excitable pup to a disciplined and introspective tactician.

History: Golgol was born on a World War II battlefield. On that day, his Garou mother stopped fighting only long enough give birth before going back into battle. She died in glory before he could suck at her teat, but her pack adopted him, ensuring his survival. His human father never knew that he — or the Garou — existed.

As the war ended, his mother's pack achieved a position of honor. They had been among the Get of Fenris packs who had fought against Germany. When Germany lost, the Garou considered Golgol to be a good omen, a symbol of a new generation fated to succeed. As Golgol grew, he worked to live up to his reputation. In Vietnam, he fought for the fun of it and learned about jungle tactics. Now he is using this hard-won knowledge in the Amazon War.

Many of the young Fenris fear him, for they have grown up hearing legends of his exploits. This causes the other tribes, who haven't heard all the tales, to wonder just what he does to them for disciplinary action. All he really has to do is dart a scowling glance at a Fenris to stop any problem behavior. He fully intends to meet the wars for the Amazon (and ultimately the Apocalypse) in the same manner — fangs first.

Scar Throat Leech-Killer

Breed: Lupus

Auspice: Galliard

Nature/Demeanor: Bravo/Fanatic

Physical: Strength 5 (7/9/8/6), Dexterity 4 (4/5/6/6), Stamina 4 (6/7/7/6)

Social: Charisma 2, Manipulation 2 (1/0/0/0), Appearance 3 (2/0/3/3)

Mental: Perception 4, Intelligence 3, Wits 2

Talents: Alertness 4, Athletics 4, Brawl 3, Dodge 3, Empathy 4, Expression 5, Intimidation 5, Primal-Urge 5

Skills: Animal Ken 4, Leadership 3, Melee 2, Stealth 5, Survival 4

Knowledges: Enigmas 3, Law 2, Linguistics 1, Politics 1, Rituals 4

Backgrounds: Allies 3, Pack Totem 1, Past Life 4

Gifts: (1) Call of the Wyld, Heightened Senses, Leap of the Kangaroo, Razor Claws, Sense the Unnatural; (2) Call of the Wyrm, Distractions

Rank: 2

Rage 6, Gnosis 8, Willpower 7

Rites: (Accord) Rite of Cleansing, Rite of Contrition; (Mystic) Ritual of the Questing Stone

Fetishes: Phoebe's Veil, Baneskin

Image: Scar Throat Leech-Killer is lean and gray, with a large bald patch on his throat, a permanent reminder of his survival of his first encounter with the Sabbat. He bears markings on his fur like those of a tiger and is almost never seen in Homid form. When forced to become Homid, his hair is blond, and his face has sharp features.

Roleplaying Notes: You take your duty as warder of Germany's Caern of the Blood Fist very seriously and challenge anyone who comes within the protective bawn

Scar Throat Leech-Killer

that surrounds it. In issues involving humans, your opinions are very similar to those of the Red Talons; you even consider Homid-breed Garou inferior.

History: Scar Throat earned his name before he went through his Rite of Passage. His First Change came about as a result of an attack by a Gangrel *antitribu* in the woods. The Sabbat vampire never knew what hit him — one moment he was sinking his fangs into the throat of his prey; the next he was losing his head. Fortunately, Scar Throat's father, Raven Corpse-Killer, was nearby when the Change occurred.

Scar Throat developed no permanent lunacy from the attack, save perhaps for a passionate hatred of Leeches. He consistently goes out of his way to attack any vampire he encounters and has even been known to use his Gift: Call of the Wyrm to ambush the bloodsucking undead.

Scar Throat's father was, until recently, Jarl of Caern of the Blood Fist. Corpse-Killer was killed by a successor who feared that his leader had been corrupted by the Wyrm. Scar Throat understands the reasons why his father was killed, but has yet to fully come to terms with the loss.

In the War of the Apocalypse, Scar Throat set himself on a personal mission to destroy all the vampires he can. He does so not only to avenge his childhood assault, but to avenge his father whom he believes was tainted by the Sabbat.

Glass Walkers

Dr. Stephen "Mindbender" Garrison

Breed: Homid

Auspice: Theurge

Nature/Demeanor: Director/Visionary

Physical: Strength 2 (4/6/5/3), Dexterity 4 (4/5/6/6), Stamina 3 (5/6/6/5)

Social: Charisma 3, Manipulation 4 (3/1/1/1), Appearance 2 (1/0/2/2)

Mental: Perception 4, Intelligence 4, Wits 3

Talents: Alertness 3, Athletics 1, Brawl 2, Dodge 3, Instruction 3, Primal-Urge 2, Streetwise 1, Subterfuge 3

Skills: Drive 1, Meditation 2, Melee 1, Leadership 2, Repair 4, Stealth 2

Knowledges: Computer 3, Enigmas 4, Hypnotism 2, Investigation 1, Linguistics 1, Medicine 1, Occult 2, Rituals 3, Science 4

Backgrounds: Contacts 2, Familiar Spirit 2, Resources 2

Gifts: (1) Control Simple Machine, Spirit Speech, Sense Weaver; (2) Command Spirit, Cybersenses, Jam Technology, Name the Spirit; (3) Control Complex Machine, Invent, Pulse of the Invisible, Web Walker

Rank: 3

Rage 4, Gnosis 7, Willpower 7

Rites: (Accord) Rite of Contrition, Rite of Cleansing; (Caern) Rite of the Opened Bridge; (Mystic) Rite of Becoming, Rite of Binding, Rite of Spirit Awakening, Rite of Summoning, Rite of Talisman Dedication, Rite of the Fetish, Rite of the Totem

Fetishes: Key to the Umbra, Vulcan's Interface, Klaive of Electricity (Level 4, Gnosis 5. This is a blade of steel with an electricity elemental trapped within it. It may be used to fire lightning bolts that do five dice of damage.)

Image: In his wolf forms, Mindbender has steel-colored fur with neon-yellow circuit patterns. In Homid form, he has long brown hair, wears glasses (although he doesn't need them) and consistently dresses in blue jeans and unusual T-shirts.

Roleplaying Notes: You're completely brilliant. You create theories on everything from the nature of the Abyss to the most efficient manner for brewing coffee. You see yourself as a man in wolf's clothing and have almost a superhero mindset about your ability to transform. You love nothing more than knowledge.

History: Dr. Garrison has spent his many years researching and exploring the Umbra. He has even visited Malfeas in the Deep Umbra. Dr. Garrison has performed experiments in the Umbra with various Gifts and rites, and he is still interested in gathering data about the Umbra.

Despite the spiritual nature of the Umbra, Dr. Garrison believes that theories can be formed regarding its nature. In Dr. Garrison's view, the Weaver has to be the base point when studying the Umbra. The Pattern Web underlies the structure of reality. Dr. Garrison believes that Zones are pieces of the Pattern Web. He also believes that the abstract nature and illogic of some sections of the Umbra are signs of their decay. The Wyrm spends most of its time attacking the Wyld, and the Wyld has no organization to its minions. It is slowly being driven from the system. However, Dr. Garrison is pleased to cite the Computer Web as evidence that the Weaver cannot be part of change.

Dr. Garrison is an intelligent Garou who labors to support his conclusions with evidence. He has bound a number of Net-spiders to himself and also keeps a Malleon, who has come to agree with his ideas. Dr. Garrison is zealous about exploration, and he is always interested in obtaining new information about the Umbra, even if it contradicts his current theories.

Dr. Stephen "Mindbender" Garrison

Roger Daly

Breed: Homid

Auspice: Theurge

Nature/Demeanor: Alpha/Director

Physical: Strength 4 (6/8/7/5), Dexterity 4 (4/5/6/6), Stamina 5 (7/8/8/7)

Social: Charisma 4, Manipulation 3 (2/0/0/0), Appearance 4 (3/0/4/4)

Mental: Perception 4, Intelligence 4, Wits 5

Talents: Alertness 1, Brawl 3, Dodge 3, Empathy 3, Expression 4, Primal-Urge 5, Streetwise 4, Subterfuge 2

Skills: Drive 3, Etiquette 4, Firearms 3, Leadership 5, Performance 3, Repair 1, Stealth 2, Survival 1

Knowledges: Computers 3, Investigation 2, Law 3, Linguistics 1, Politics 4, Rituals 4, Science 2

Backgrounds: Allies 4, Contacts 4, Resources 5

Gifts: (1) Control Simple Machine, Persuasion, Sense Wyrm; (2) Jam Technology, Power Surge, Sight from Beyond; (3) Pulse of the Invisible; (4) Attunement, Ultimate Argument of Logic

Rank: 4

Rage 3, Gnosis 3, Willpower 4

Rites: (Caern) Moot Rite, Rite of the Opened Caern, Rite of the Shrouded Glen; (Punishment) Voice of the Jackal

Roger Daly

Fetishes: Protected Assets (Level 3, Gnosis 5. This expensive looking business suit has protective spirits woven into it. It acts as three dice of armor against all forms of attack.)

Image: In his vastly preferred Homid form, Roger Daly appears to be in his late 50s or early 60s — an elegant-looking man of average height. His short, thinning hair is silver and always perfectly arranged. He wears gunmetal-framed Dunhill glasses. This is more for show than anything else, some observers note. His eyes are ice-gray and are reminiscent of a hired killer's. In his Lupus form, Daly is a silver-hackled black wolf with white markings that resemble glasses around his eyes.

Roleplaying Notes: You are the perfect image of the high-powered businessman: intelligent, well-read and erudite. You aren't egotistical, even though you have plenty of reason to be.

History: Daly was born and raised in the Shaugnessy region of Vancouver, the only child of an affluent family. His father, Graham Daly, was leader of the Vancouver Glass Walkers and a successful businessman. Roger's mother knew her husband's true nature; she wasn't subject to the Delirium. Both of Roger's parents died in the '70s — his father was killed in a fight with a vampire, who was later hunted down and extinguished by his own kind. Roger was left with an estate worth several million dollars — enough to support him in comfort, but he couldn't operate that way. He had inherited more than the "Garou gene" from his father.

Roger established Daly & Associates, a management consulting firm. The successful business has provided him with important business contacts throughout the city, allowing him to influence business policy in a way that benefits Gaia and the Garou. Daly also followed in his father's footsteps by becoming leader of the Corporate Raiders Sept.

Few individuals human, Garou or Kindred really know Roger Daly. Many of his junior septmates consider him to be stolid and unimaginative. Those few who know better realize that he has a sharp sense of humor and an inner sadness.

In the War of the Apocalypse, Daly realizes that it's the job of the Glass Walkers (and Bone Gnawers) to protect Vancouver from invasion. While other tribes make sure nothing approaches the city over land, the Glass Walkers stand guard at the airport and watch the marinas.

Daly lives in a sprawling house in the British Properties overlooking the Lions Gate Bridge. He also owns the Smiling Buddha, the location of Vancouver's Glass Walker caern. He has his fingers in countless business "pies" that frequently involve him in business dealings and conflicts with the Kindred. There are unsubstantiated rumors that Daly and an influential vampire are locked in a vicious, no-holds-barred proxy battle that might ruin them both.

Song Chiang, "Welcome Rain"

Breed: Homid

Auspice: Galliard

Nature/Demeanor: Curmudgeon/Caregiver

Physical: Strength 2 (4/6/5/3), Dexterity 2 (2/3/4/4), Stamina 2 (4/5/5/4)

Social: Charisma 4, Manipulation 4 (4/1/1/1), Appearance 3 (2/0/3/3)

Mental: Perception 3, Intelligence 4, Wits 5

Talents: Alertness 2, Brawl 1, Dodge 2, Empathy 3, Expression 3, Intimidation 1, Primal-Urge 4, Streetwise 2, Subterfuge 1

Skills: Animal Ken 4, Etiquette 3, Leadership 4, Performance 3 (Drum), Survival 1, Herbalism 2, Kailindo 1, Meditation 2

Knowledges: Computer 3 (Robotics), Enigmas 4, Linguistics 4, Medicine 3, Occult 1, Politics 1, Rituals 3, Science (Hydroponics) 4

Backgrounds: Allies 4, Contacts 4, Kinfolk 2, Resources 4

Gifts: (1) Beast Speech, Control Simple Machines, Mindspeak; (2) Dreamspeak; (3) Control Complex Machines, Cybersenses, Invent, Tongues; (4) Attunement, Bridge Walker, Shadows by the Fire Light

Rank: 4

Rage 4, Gnosis 7, Willpower 9

Rites: (Accord) Rite of Contrition, Rite of Cleansing; (Caern) Moot Rite, Rite of the Opened Bridge, Rite of the Opened Caern; (Mystic) Baptism of Fire, Rite of Binding, Rite of Spirit Awakening, Rite of Summoning, Rite of Talisman Dedication, Rite of the Questing Stone, Rite of the Totem

Fetishes: Bells of Rain, Lagomorph's Boon, Spirit Drum, Sacred Soil

Merits/Flaws: Longevity, Park Department Ties, Judicial Ties/Soft-Hearted

Image: Bristling with an air of dignity, Song Chiang's long silky beard cannot be missed in a crowd. In Lupus form, a black mask of fur covers his face, and fur of bark brown covers his body.

Roleplaying Notes: A very sincere and gentle man, you live by your word. Nothing is more important than honor and justice. You link your artistic ability directly to Awen and tend to fight your battles on an emotional level, rather than leaping into physical combat.

History: As a young adult, Song Chiang was prone to fits of Harano when inebriated. He lost great renown by scribbling on the walls of Hong Kong bars, especially when he wrote poetry about the Garou. As he aged, his character grew stronger, and the strength of his soul forged the way for him to become leader of the Hong Kong City Farmers and Warder of the Mother of Peach Trees Caern.

Song Chiang is respected for his level-headed forethought. He not only relies upon his own intuition about

threats to the caern, but also uses the combined sensory powers of all the Garou on the island (through his Galliard Gifts).

Song Chiang has befriended both the Junk Junk King (leader of the Bone Gnawer pack known as Broken Junk City) and All-Seeing-Eye (leader of the Bone Gnawer pack known as the Watchers of the Streets), and they visit him often. Easygoing Song Chiang hates only injustice.

Syntax

Breed: Homid

Auspice: Ragabash

Nature/Demeanor: Visionary/Lone Wolf

Physical: Strength 2 (4/6/5/3), Dexterity 4 (4/5/6/6), Stamina 2 (4/5/5/4)

Social: Charisma 3, Manipulation 2 (1/0/0/0), Appearance 4 (3/0/4/4)

Mental: Perception 4, Intelligence 3, Wits 4

Talents: Alertness 2, Athletics 2, Brawl 2, Dodge 2, Streetwise 2, Subterfuge 4

Skills: Drive 1, Firearms 2, Melee 2, Stealth 4

Knowledges: Computer 3, Investigation 1, Rituals 1

Backgrounds: Allies 1, Contacts 3, Resources 1

Gifts: (1) Blur of the Milky Eye, Control Simple Machine, Open Seal, Smell of Man

Rank: 1

Syntax

Then her father left academia, taking a position with a growing computer design firm, and he was no longer able to devote much time to Susanna's education. She was sent to a private school, where her complete lack of socialization made her the butt of her classmates' cruelties. She retreated into her mind, into the logic and science that had been her bedrock for years, and though she was a natural beauty, she learned to avoid attention, to steal through life like a shadow at night.

A year ago, at 19, Susanna was kidnapped by the Glass Walkers of Seattle. It was revealed to her that her mother had been Kinfolk and that she herself was Garou. Though Susanna refused to accept the story as truth, during her Rite of Passage she was the first of her pack to change, exploding into Crinos, releasing years of pent-up anger on a Pentex security squad. Thereafter, she realized this was her place — this was the community that had been denied her so long, and this mission — to save Gaia from Her despoilers — was *hers*. Though wilderness terrified her, she knew she could fight for it in the cities with her tribe and took to the war with a patriot's zeal.

No record remains, anywhere, of Susanna Willingham's identity or past. Now the girl who learned the way that things fit together is using that knowledge to pull things apart... and the name of Syntax is on its way to becoming legend.

Rage 2, Gnosis 3, Willpower 4

Rites: (Mystic) Rite of the Questing Stone, Rite of Talisman Dedication

Fetishes: None

Image: Syntax comes across like a winter wind: cold and intense and impossible to ignore. She only speaks when she has to and dislikes attention, yet her beauty draws the eye like a single star in a black sky.

Roleplaying Notes: Don't speak. Don't flirt. Don't smile or laugh. You're aware of everything going on around you; react with immediacy and precision. You are steel and ice to the public eye, and only when alone do you relax and allow yourself to feel the full force of your emotions, which are very strong indeed. The truth is, you fear others, and stay away from them as much as you are able. You live alone, and even your packmates know little about you.

History: An only child whose mother died of cancer a year after her birth, Susanna Willingham was raised by her father, a theoretical mathematician at the University of Washington. Professor Willingham was a logical, exact man, distrustful of emotion and dedicated to precision in every area of his life, including the rearing of his daughter. Until she was 10, Susanna lived mostly within their condominium in Seattle, where her father spent hours a day "home-schooling" her in facts and figures and logic. She learned a lot about the worlds of science, but next to nothing about the world beyond the door.

Teeth-of-Titanium

Breed: Lupus
Auspice: Ahroun
Nature/Demeanor: Masochist/Alpha
Physical: Strength 5 (7/9/8/6), Dexterity 3 (3/4/5/5), Stamina 4 (7/8/8/6)*
Social: Charisma 2, Manipulation 3 (3/3/0/0)*, Appearance 1 (0/0/1/1)
Mental: Perception 4, Intelligence 4, Wits 3
* While in Glabro, Crinos and Hispo forms, Teeth-of-Titanium gains additional Stamina because of his technological nature. Furthermore, he is capable of perfect, if mechanical, human speech in his Glabro and Crinos forms.
Talents: Alertness 3, Athletics 3, Brawl 4, Dodge 3, Intimidation 5, Primal-Urge 1, Streetwise 3
Skills: Animal Ken 2, Melee 3, Repair 2, Stealth 3, Survival 2
Knowledges: Computer 1, Occult 3, Rituals 3, Science 3
Backgrounds: Pure Breed 2, Resources 1
Gifts: (1) Control Simple Machine, The Falling Touch, Heightened Senses, Leap of the Kangaroo; (2) Cybersenses; (3) Control Complex Machine, Elemental Favor
Rank: 3
Rage 5,† Gnosis 3, Willpower 8

† Because of his quasimechanical nature, Teeth-of-Titanium needs five successes on a Rage roll to frenzy.

Rites: (Accord) Rite of Cleansing, Rite of Contrition; (Caern) Moot Rite, (Mystic) Rite of Talisman Dedication; (Renown) Rite of Passage, Rite of Wounding

Fetishes: The Technomantic device implanted in him allows Teeth-of-Titanium to use the following Gifts automatically: Control Simple Machine, Control Complex Machine and Summon Net-Spider.

Image: In Homid form, Teeth-of-Titanium is a well-dressed man of middle age. He is fit and trim, his gray hair is slicked back, his nails are manicured and his expensive suits are spotless. Astute observers note a cold gleam in his eyes. Teeth-of-Titanium's dingo Lupus form is similarly slick, though his glossy pelt smells faintly of machine oil. In his Crinos form, which he favors, Teeth-of-Titanium is most startling. The entire left side of his hulking body is sheathed in metal, with numerous exposed wires, hydraulic pistons, gears and circuitry. His Hispo and Glabro forms are similarly cybernetic.

Roleplaying Notes: You are a doer, not a thinker, and prefer to act instead of talk. Your speech is cold and mechanical.

History: Teeth-of-Titanium was born Bloody Teeth, a Red Talon. On a raid against Australia's Technomancers — technology-wielding mages located in Perth — he was captured and subjected to a series of experiments. After months of agony, the hideously disfigured Bloody Teeth escaped. However, the Technomancers had implanted a living mechanical entity in his body, and over the next few months Bloody Teeth was transformed into a cybernetic mockery of a Garou.

Bloody Teeth returned to his tribe, but after almost being slain, he fled to Perth where he was found by the Glass Walkers. Fascinated by his condition, the Glass Walkers adopted Bloody Teeth, renaming him Teeth-of-Titanium. Grateful to his new tribe, Teeth-of-Titanium has served the Glass Walkers faithfully and learned to master his new body. With the passing years he has risen to become the Lord of Perth, holding a seat on the Glass Walker Board.

Teeth-of-Titanium's long struggle to master the machine he has become has left him bereft of emotion. He finds it difficult to understand the motivations of fleshy creatures. Because of his lack of emotion, he rarely frenzies.

In the War of the Apocalypse, Teeth-of-Titanium is as dangerous to Gaia as he is outwardly protective of her. His corruption by the Technocracy has implanted him with the seed of the Wyrm; the Glass Walkers have simply refused to acknowledge it, once because they were blinded by curiosity and concern for his condition and now because he is a powerful and feared member of the tribe. As the War escalates, the machine within Teeth-of-Titanium will do more than stifle his emotions; it will take control of his body and mind. Australian Garou of other tribes are begin-

Teeth-of-Titanium

ning to realize the threat that Teeth-of-Titanium poses, but anyone trying to free him from Wyrm taint or more simply to destroy him must go through his Glass Walker brethren, who refuse to admit their mistake.

Virus-to-Wyrm

Breed: Homid

Auspice: Ahroun

Tribe: Glass Walkers

Nature/Demeanor: Predator/Rebel

Physical: Strength 2 (4/6/5/3), Dexterity 3 (2/3/4/4), Stamina 2 (4/5/5/4)

Social: Charisma 2, Manipulation 2 (1/0/0/0), Appearance 4 (3/0/4/4)

Mental: Perception 3, Intelligence 5, Wits 2

Talents: Alertness 2, Brawl 1, Dodge 2, Intimidation 3, Primal-Urge 1, Streetwise 3

Skills: Drive 3, Melee 2, Leadership 2, Stealth 2

Knowledges: Computer 4, Enigmas 2

Backgrounds: Allies 2, Contacts 2, Resources 2

Gifts: (1) Control Simple Machine, Persuasion, Razor Claws; (2) Power Surge, Spirit of the Fray, Staredown

Rank: 2

Rage 5, Gnosis 4, Willpower 6

Rites: None

Fetishes: None

Virus-to-Wyrm

Image: Virus-to-Wyrm is a tall, attractive, dark-haired woman of about 24 years with steel-blue eyes and black hair. She generally dresses in casual shirts and jeans. Her Lupus form is a silver-white wolf with a long mane.

Roleplaying Notes: You come across as someone who should not be taken lightly in a fight, and you cultivate that image. You will often pretend to be less intelligent than you really are, letting others underestimate you, but when it's time to get down to business, you let your true self show, especially if the situation at hand involves a computer. You are quiet and strong-willed; if anyone is going to push you around, they'd better be able to back up their words. Physical combat is not your strength, so you will instead goad the other into issuing the challenge so that you can choose the type of challenge. You prefer gamecraft, though you are not above selecting whatever appears to be the challenger's greatest weakness.

History: Virus-to-Wyrm, born Sarah Whitman, never really fit in with her peers, and often chose to ostracize others before they could ostracize her. This social isolation only increased after her First Change, when Virus-to-Wyrm realized she truly was different from her peers. She did not blame her isolation on being Garou; instead, it reinforced her attitude that she was superior to many people around her, including her own family.

In high school, she demonstrated a strong aptitude for computers and soon knew more than her instructors. She entered college with intentions of majoring in computer science, but quit after her first semester, finding it too "elementary" for her. Her skills managed to get her a job in a prestigious software production company, where she creates a wide range of computer viruses and then introduces those viruses into various Wyrm-tainted computers via cyberspace, earning the name Virus-to-Wyrm.

Virus-To-Wyrm is aware of the suspicions the other Garou have about her tribe and deeply resents those accusations. Being a Garou means everything to her, and has given Virus-to-Wyrm a sense of belonging. In seeming response to those accusations, Virus-to-Wyrm is especially cruel in combat with Wyrm creatures, be it in physical combat or in what she views as the "new" combat arena — the combat of cyberspace.

Red Talons

Eater-of-Bears

Breed: Lupus
Auspice: Ragabash
Nature/Demeanor: Predator/Alpha
Physical: Strength 3 (5/7/6/4), Dexterity 4 (4/5/6/6), Stamina 3 (5/6/6/5)
Social: Charisma 1, Manipulation 2 (1/0/0/0), Appearance 3 (2/0/3/3)
Mental: Perception 3, Intelligence 2, Wits3
Talents: Alertness 2, Athletics 2, Brawl 3, Dodge 3, Primal-Urge 4
Skills: Animal Ken 3, Stealth 3, Survival 4
Knowledges: Enigmas 3, Rituals 2
Backgrounds: Allies 3, Kinfolk 4, Past Life 1
Gifts: (1) Beast Speech, Blur of the Milky Eye, Leap of the Kangaroo
Rank: 1
Rage 4, Gnosis 5, Willpower 6
Rites: (Accord) Rite of Contrition; (Caern) Rite of the Opened Caern
Fetishes: Amulet of Good Cheer (Level 2, Gnosis 6. This fetish renders the owner immune to Harano as long as it is worn. However, when the amulet is initially removed, the owner suffers Harano for an indefinite period of time.)

Image: Eater-of-Bears is a sleek, muscular wolf of medium-brown and black coloration. She is unusually graceful when she moves. Her Homid form is that of an attractive 5'9" woman in her mid-20s. She has long black hair that falls to her waist.

Roleplaying Notes: You are a very aggressive Garou and a true Ragabash. Your loathing of humans surpasses that of most of your tribemates. You're the one member of the Red Talons in your area who constantly harasses townsfolk and kills travelers. You run with a large number of wolves and enjoy taking your huge pack through the local small towns at night. You love the hunt and especially the kill; you'd be as good an Ahroun as you are a Ragabash.

History: Eater-of-Bears was a whelp when she was taken, along with two others, for her Rite of Passage. She was the only one to survive; the other two were killed by a Bane-infested grizzly bear. She would have been killed had she not run away to seek the aid of her former wolf pack, made up of Kinfolk. With their aid, she slew the bear and feasted upon it, thus becoming Eater-of-Bears. She is working on devouring all the bears within close range of the sept.

She enjoys pretending to be a human hitchhiker. Once she is picked up, she slays the driver and takes his valuables.

Eater-of-Bears

She often leaves her name in blood on one of the windows so that humans will know the killing was not a wolf attack.

She patronizes Storm-Chaser and tries intimidating him subtly whenever she can get away with it. She sees Stands-Like-Mountain as a potential rival, but puts up with her from a sense of companionship. She wants her sept to turn from their ways of solitude to join the Red Talon fight against the Wyrm and the humans. To this extent, she is considering approaching other lupus and metis Garou to join her cause. To date, she has not been very successful, but she is young yet. With persistence, she may be able to gather plenty of allies and cull the humans in force before the Apocalypse strikes once and for all.

Fireclaw

Breed: Lupus
Auspice: Theurge
Nature/Demeanor: Predator/Traditionalist
Physical: Strength 3 (5/7/6/4), Dexterity 3 (3/4/5/5), Stamina 3 (5/6/6/5)

Fireclaw

ralled so that they can be monitored. You are quite proud of your leather coat. When asked about it, you only smile.

History: Fireclaw was born in Alaska, far from civilization. His father was a Garou, and Fireclaw was underwent the Baptism of Fire a short time after birth. Upon his First Change, his father took him from his pack, brought him to a moot and sent him on his Rite of Passage.

Fireclaw's first contact with humanity came sometime after his initiation into Garou society. He and his pack were tracking a herd of caribou when a strange buzzing creature dropped out of the sky. A man leaned out of it, and a sharp crack was heard over the roaring buzz of the frightening bird. The snow kicked up in Fireclaw's face, startling and angering the young Garou. He and his pack began running toward a stand of trees, hoping to hide from the strange beast. Another crack came from above, and one of Fireclaw's packmates fell, its blood coloring the snow.

Enraged, Fireclaw raced to a nearby stream. Gazing into a pool of water, he stepped into the Umbra. Calling the spirits of the air to his aid, he brought the helicoptor crashing to the ground.

Returning to the material world, Fireclaw found two bodies. Both were clad in the skins of animals. In retribution, Fireclaw decided to make an example of his attackers, to warn off any other strangers who might come to his homeland. To this day, when Fireclaw stands on two legs, he wears his coat like a badge of courage.

Growls-at-Moon

Breed: Lupus
Auspice: Galliard
Nature/Demeanor: Alpha/Bravo
Physical: Strength 4 (6/8/7/5), Dexterity 2 (2/3/4/4), Stamina 4 (6/7/7/6)
Social: Charisma 1, Manipulation 2 (1/0/0/0), Appearance 3 (2/0/3/3)
Mental: Perception 4, Intelligence 2, Wits 2
Talents: Alertness 5, Athletics 1, Brawl 3, Dodge 2, Intimidation 3, Primal-Urge 2
Skills: Animal Ken 2, Melee 1, Survival 4
Knowledges: Linguistics 1, Occult 2, Rituals 3, Genealogy 3
Backgrounds: Pure Breed 3, Rites 2
Gifts: (1) Beast Speech, Call of the Wyld, Heightened Senses, Mindspeak, Razor Claws; (2) Beastmind
Rank: 2
Rage 4, Gnosis 5, Willpower 7
Rites: (Mystic) Rite of Talisman Dedication; (Renown) Rite of Wounding; (Seasonal) The Great Hunt
Fetishes: None

Image: When Growls-at-Moon deigns to take Homid form she attracts lumberjacks of both genders. New England's finest treekillers all stand the same chance with her, though: none. She's a pre-Raphaelite woman of iron, complete with a heart of stone. Her most insistent human admirers are

Social: Charisma 3, Manipulation 5 (4/2/2/2), Appearance 3 (2/0/3/3)
Mental: Perception 4, Intelligence 3, Wits 3
Talents: Alertness 2, Brawl 2, Dodge 2, Primal-Urge 3, Subterfuge 1
Skills: Animal Ken 2, Leadership 1, Stealth 2, Survival 4
Knowledges: Enigmas 1, Occult 2, Rituals 2
Backgrounds: Kinfolk 3, Rites 2
Gifts: (1) Beast Speech, Leap of the Kangaroo, Spirit Speech; (2) Command Spirit, Scent of Sight; (3) Elemental Favor, Trackless Waste
Rank: 3
Rage 4, Gnosis 7, Willpower 5
Rites: (Caern) Rite of the Opened Caern; (Minor) Hunting Prayer, Prayer for the Prey; (Mystic) Rite of Talisman Dedication
Fetishes: None

Image: In Homid form, Fireclaw is of average height and build. He wears a large leather coat, dedicated to him, made from human skin. He has bright red hair and light brown eyes. In Lupus form, Fireclaw's fur is blue-black with gray markings, with the exception of markings on his forehead, which are bright red.

Roleplaying Notes: You have never interacted with humans on friendly terms. While you don't necessarily believe in the total extermination of humanity, you do feel that people should be kept under strict population control, perhaps cor-

Growls-at-Moon

growl. (This is how she comments on *everything*). Her name was meant as hyperbole: "Bet she even growls at the moon!").

Though still not her pack's alpha, Growls she feels she deserves to be. Growls-at-Moon is respected in her sept as the sternest of warriors. She is dismissive of weapons and fetishes (sometimes at her peril), invoking her own adage, "We are our own best weapons."

Mamu

Breed: Lupus
Auspice: Ahroun
Nature/Demeanor: Bravo/Alpha
Physical: Strength 5 (7/9/8/6), Dexterity 3 (4/5/6/6), Stamina 4 (6/7/7/6)
Social: Charisma 3, Manipulation 1 (0/0/0/0), Appearance 2 (1/0/2/2)
Mental: Perception 4, Intelligence 3, Wits 4
Talents: Alertness 4, Athletics 4, Brawl 5, Dodge 3, Intimidation 5, Primal-Urge 5, Subterfuge 1
Skills: Animal Ken 4, Leadership 3, Stealth 4, Survival 5
Knowledges: Rituals 2
Backgrounds: Allies 2, Kinfolk 4, Past Life 3
Gifts: (1) Heightened Senses, Inspiration, Leap of the Kangaroo, Scent of Running Water; (2) Sense of the Prey, Sense the Unnatural; (3) Trackless Waste, True Fear; (4) Stoking Fury's Furnace; (5) Song of the Great Beast
Rank: 5

sometimes gruesomely dismembered in the forest by the imposing, dun-colored she-wolf.

Roleplaying Notes: Humanity repulses you. You assume "that form" only in the direst emergencies. People describe you as haughty, but never within earshot (so they believe). In Lupus form, your manner is, in a word, gruff.

History: Once Growls-at-Moon understood her Garou nature, she became obsessed with her lineage. Indeed, she traced her forebears back to Red Talon legend.

She joined a sept outside Rutland, Vermont, not far from her birthplace. There she earned a reputation as a fierce protector of Gaia. She delighted in stalking the area's loggers, but chafed at her subordinate role in pack attacks. While storming a sawmill one night, she ignored her pack leader's order to zigzag. A squabble ensued among the packmates, and the assault was aborted. Growls-at-Moon's alpha, Races-with-Fire, accused her of having violated the Litany. The sept divided over this matter for a time, as both Garou were thought to be headstrong and both had partisans.

Ultimately, Growls-at-Moon was censured, but she was never repentant. She was resentful for a time, but later saved Races-with-Fire's life in a Pentex ambush. He returned the favor, but sacrificed himself in the process. She swore then never to allow another packmate to die at her side.

It is said that Growls once rescued two fellow Garou simultaneously, though they were on opposite sides of a lake. Her only comment on this episode was a low, dismissive

Mamu

Rage 9, Gnosis 7, Willpower 6

Rites: (Caern) Moot Rite; (Punishment) Rite of Ostracism; (Renown) Rite of Wounding

Fetishes: None

Image: On the rare occasions that Mamu appears in Homid form, he has the appearance of a shaggy-haired, sullen Aboriginal giant. His build is solid and rippling with muscle; his skin is a glossy black. In Lupus form, Mamu is a calf-sized dingo. His jet-black hair is shot through with red highlights. His red-rimmed eyes mark him as a dangerous predator, regardless of his form.

Roleplaying Notes: Rarely speak, only grunt and snarl. When you must speak, your voice is hoarse and guttural. Stare down all who would threaten you or tear out their throats.

History: For the first two years of his life Mamu ran with his dingo pack in Australia. As he grew, none could withstand him except the pack leader, who soon became Mamu's hated enemy. When his Change approached, only the pack leader sensed the difference in Mamu, and he united the pack to drive Mamu out.

Alone in the desert, Mamu knew fear for the first time. He heard voices in the wind and saw shadows flicker across the ground. Unknown to Mamu, he was seeing the spirit world for the first time. With the rising of the full moon, Mamu howled in agony as his body began to stretch and change. In terror he ran back to the pack that had exiled him. The pack leader snarled as Mamu returned, and an irresistible, bloody tide of Rage flooded the young Garou's mind. In seconds Mamu stood on his hind legs in Crinos form, the tattered body of the elder dingo hanging from his jaws. No longer did Mamu have a rival. He led the dingo pack for another year before encountering other Red Talons. Although he left his pack for his new tribe, in times of need Mamu can still call upon his old followers and their descendants.

Mamu is without a doubt the largest and strongest Red Talon in Australia, although his strength is of no consequence where the council is concerned. More than once Mamu has had to restrain himself from tearing out the throats of his fellow council members, who bewilder him with their webs of words. Mamu is a fighter, not a thinker.

In the War of the Apocalypse, Mamu has his own agenda. He plans to use the chaos of warfare to pursue the priorities of the Red Talons. Specifically, he intends to use the opportunity to eliminate as many humans as possible and to destroy their spreading "civilization." If other tribal leaders don't recognize the value of his work, they might also fall under his claw, for being as Wyrm-tainted as he perceives humanity.

Old Storm-Chaser

Breed: Lupus

Auspice: Theurge

Nature/Demeanor: Judge/Confidant

Physical: Strength 2 (4/6/5/3), Dexterity 2 (2/3/4/4), Stamina 3 (5/6/6/5)

Social: Charisma 3, Manipulation 3 (2/0/0/0), Appearance 2 (1/0/2/2)

Old Storm-Chaser

Mental: Perception 3, Intelligence 4, Wits 3

Talents: Alertness 1, Brawl 4, Dodge 2, Intimidation 2, Primal-Urge 5

Skills: Animal Ken 4, Leadership 4, Performance 5, Stealth 3, Survival 5

Knowledges: Enigmas 4, Occult 2, Rituals 4

Backgrounds: Past Life 4, Pure Breed 2

Gifts: (1) Mother's Touch, Sense the Unnatural, Sense Wyrm, Spirit Speech; (2) Beastmind, Command Spirit, Name the Spirit, Scent of Sight; (3) Pulse of the Invisible; (4) Beast Life, Spirit Drain

Rank: 4

Rage 2, Gnosis 10, Willpower 8

Rites: (Caern) Rite of the Opened Bridge, Rite of the Opened Caern; (Mystic) Rite of Binding, Rite of Spirit Awakening, Rite of Summoning, Rite of Talisman Dedication, Rite of the Fetish; (Renown) Rite of Passage

Fetishes: Spirit Whistle and various talens, including a good supply of Ghost-Tobacco (Gnosis 6. When smoked by a Garou, all spirits in a 50-yard radius will become intoxicated. Prolonged exposure will make spirits so drunk that they might play pranks or "pass out." Some spirits can become addicted to the smoke and will serve the smoker to get more.)

Image: In Lupus form, Old Storm-Chaser has ruddy-brown fur and is slightly larger than other wolves. In Homid form, he is a white-haired old man in his late 60s, 5' 6" and 130 pounds. He has a beard and keeps a pair of bifocals.

Roleplaying Notes: You have fought many battles and survived. Now you enjoy telling your companions about your escapades. You are quite clever; if asked for advice, ask questions and lead the conversation so that the questioner will answer the question for herself. You love to have fun and have a great sense of humor; sometimes this is the only thing holding Harano at bay.

History: Old Storm-Chaser is the last of his generation. He was once almost a Ragabash, rejoicing in his love of tricks and defiance of the sept. However, this cost him his best friend in battle. He has never forgiven himself. He sometimes suffers Harano, and often goes off into the woods to be alone. When he is not depressed, he is a very lively fellow who delights in storytelling.

He is very kind to all members of his sept, helping teach them all he knows. He knows his time is coming soon, and he wants to leave them prepared. He dislikes Eater-of-Bears, seeing her as a threat to the others. Even for a Ragabash, she is unhinged, and she reminds him of himself when he was young. He has taken a special interest in Stands-Like-Mountain. He sees wisdom in her, as well as a heart filled with bravery. He knows her courage will be a useful weapon against the Wyrm one day. He also knows she will one day leave the sept behind to fulfill a greater destiny. As for himself, Old Storm-Chaser is content to wait and see what fate Gaia brings him in the War of the Apocalypse.

Stands-Like-Mountain

Breed: Lupus

Auspice: Philodox

Nature/Demeanor: Confidant/Conformist

Physical: Strength 4 (6/8/7/5), Dexterity 2 (2/3/4/4), Stamina 4 (6/7/7/6)

Social: Charisma 2, Manipulation 2 (1/0/0/0), Appearance 2 (1/0/2/2)

Mental: Perception 2, Intelligence 3, Wits 3

Talents: Alertness 2, Athletics 3, Brawl 4, Dodge 3, Intimidation 2, Primal-Urge 4

Skills: Animal Ken 2, Repair 2, Stealth 2, Survival 3

Knowledges: Enigmas 3, Rituals 2

Backgrounds: Contacts 2, Pure Breed 1, Kinfolk 2

Gifts: (1) Beast Speech, Heightened Senses, Resist Pain; (2) Call to Duty, King of the Beasts

Rank: 1

Rage 6, Gnosis 4, Willpower 5

Rites: (Accord) Rite of Contrition; (Caern) Moot Rite; (Mystic) Baptism of Fire; (Punishment) Rite of Ostracism; (Renown) Rite of Passage

Fetishes: Fang Dagger

Image: Stands-Like-Mountain is a stocky, dark-brown wolf. Her ears are a little large, and the tips of her paws are white, as is the underside of her neck. Her Homid form is that of a 5'6", 135-pound woman with medium-length, curly brown hair. She appears to be in her mid-20s.

Roleplaying Notes: You are very friendly and love to meet Garou from outside your sept. You travel a great deal and spend about as much time away from the sept as you do in the sept. You are occasionally kind to humans, though you're readily cruel to them in the presence of other Red Talons. You are secretly considering moving to a large city, but you know this is next to impossible. Still, you haven't yet ruled out the possibility.

History: Stands-Like-Mountain was born to a wolf pack in the Northern Territories. She was found by a pack of Red Talons. Shortly afterwards, all but one were killed by a Pentex First Team. The remaining Talon, Mighty Jaws, turned her over to Storm-Chaser, an old ally. Mighty Jaws knew he was going to seek vengeance, and he figured he might not return. He didn't. Stands-Like-Mountain became part of the Weeping Daughter's Sept, Storm-Chaser's domain. She has since been a firm supporter of taking the fight to the Wyrm, but unlike Eater-of-Bears, she does not favor murdering humans unnecessarily.

Stands-Like-Mountain loves Storm-Chaser as the father she never had, and she looks to him for advice and training. She gets along with Eater-of-Bears and is the closest thing to a friend that the rebellious Garou has. She is always willing to join a multitribal pack for a foray against the Wyrm's minions, in part because she relishes learning more from the homids among them. If Stands gains enough rank in the coming war, she just might be able to convince her tribemates that not all humans are innately wicked—quite a task for a young Garou. Although this is unlikely in the extreme, only time will tell.

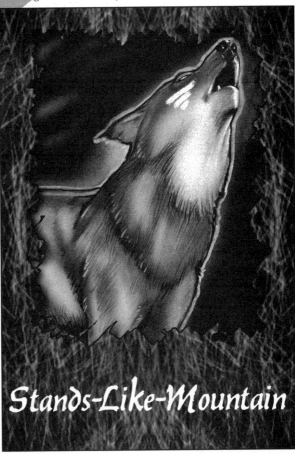

Stands-Like-Mountain

Shadow Lords

Anna Kliminski

Breed: Homid

Auspice: Ahroun

Nature/Demeanor: Alpha/Predator

Physical: Strength 4 (6/8/7/5), Dexterity 4 (4/5/6/6), Stamina 5 (7/8/8/7)

Social: Charisma 3, Manipulation 4 (3/1/1/1), Appearance 4 (3/0/4/4)

Mental: Perception 3, Intelligence 3, Wits 4

Talents: Alertness 3, Athletics 4, Brawl 4, Intimidation 4, Primal-Urge 3, Streetwise 2, Subterfuge 3

Skills: Drive 2, Leadership 5, Melee 4, Stealth 2, Survival 2

Knowledges: Enigmas 1, Investigation 2, Law 3, Linguistics 2, Occult 2, Politics 3, Rituals 1

Backgrounds: Fetish 3, Kinfolk 2, Pure Breed 4, Resources 4

Gifts: (1) Aura of Confidence, Inspiration, Razor Claws; (2) Spirit of the Fray, Staredown, True Fear; (3) Disquiet, Heart of Fury, Icy Chill of Despair; (4) Strength of the Dominator; (5) Kiss of Helios

Anna Kliminski

Rank: 5

Rage 9, Gnosis 8, Willpower 8

Rites: (Death) Gathering for the Departed, Rite of the Winter Wolf; (Punishment) Gaia's Vengeful Teeth, Rite of Ostracism, Stone of Scorn, The Hunt

Fetishes: Klaive

Image: Dark, deadly and mysterious, Anna epitomizes the image of the Shadow Lords. Her unmistakable presence helps her dominate Garou in any gathering and intimidate the weak at heart. She often wears the pelts of her victims, Garou or otherwise, as trophies.

Roleplaying Notes: There is no doubt that Anna is a powerful Garou — anyone who meets her can sense that. She uses physical power and intimidation to get what she wants. Anna is as cunning as she is dangerous. Although famous for defeating Garou in single combat, Anna never seeks to kill her kind. She doesn't hesitate to kill Garou who cross her, though.

History: Anna's mother died during labor, and her father raised her within the strict confines of Garou society. Anna resented the fact that she didn't have a normal childhood; the entirety of her formative years were spent in training. From the time she could walk, she was taught the martial arts and the ins and outs of Garou society. Although she could not yet change shape, she could already walk taller than most Garou. Her father, a highly respected Shadow Lord, would have it no other way. There was no love in the relationship, only respect and discipline.

On her 13th birthday, during a moot, Anna underwent her First Change. With the full moon shining and Garou dancing in a frenzied whirl, she lost control of her deep-seated anger for her father. She did not permanently harm anyone, but she did embarrass her parent. He promptly disowned her and ordered her to leave the caern. Anna, knowing all too well the consequences of being a Ronin Garou, challenged her father to single combat; it was her only chance to redeem herself. The fight was brief but decisive. Anna knew her parent's capabilities, but he didn't know a few things she had learned beyond his training. Revolted by her actions but proud of her accomplishment, Anna took up her father's klaive and declared herself a Garou and Shadow Lord. The elders promptly recognized her.

Since that day, Anna has dedicated her life to fighting the Wyrm and defending Garou society. She still carries her father's klaive and wears it proudly. She regrets taking his life and the lives of other Garou, but knows that such deaths are for the greater good.

Carleson Ruah

Breed: Homid
Auspice: Ragabash
Nature/Demeanor: Competitor/Director
Physical: Strength 3 (5/7/6/4), Dexterity 3 (3/4/5/5), Stamina 3 (5/6/6/5)
Social: Charisma 4, Manipulation 4 (3/1/1/1), Appearance 2 (1/0/2/2)
Mental: Perception 3, Intelligence 4, Wits 5
Talents: Alertness 3, Brawl 2, Dodge 2, Empathy 3, Intimidation 3, Primal-Urge 3, Streetwise 3, Subterfuge 4
Skills: Drive 1, Etiquette 3, Firearms 2, Melee 4, Leadership 1, Stealth 3
Knowledges: Computer 1, Enigmas 2, Investigation 3, Law 1, Occult 1, Rituals 1, Politics 2
Backgrounds: Allies 4, Contacts 4, Resources 3
Gifts: (1) Fatal Flaw, Persuasion, Open Seal; (2) Blissful Ignorance, Luna's Armor, Taking the Forgotten
Rank: 2
Rage 4, Gnosis 4, Willpower 7
Rites: (Mystic) Talisman Dedication
Fetishes: Helios Bauble (Level: 5, Gnosis: 6. This small ball [fits in the pocket] can be hurled at someone. If it hits [Athletics + Dexterity], it bursts into a blazing ball of fire. Roll the Ball's Gnosis vs. the target's Gnosis [or Humanity]. The number of successes is the amount of flame damage taken *plus* the number of rounds that the fire continues to burn [one Health Level lost per round].)

Image: Ruah is a charcoal-gray wolf with a white underbelly and white flecks on the crest of his forehead. In Homid form he is a short, stout, pug-nosed Caucasian man with receding black hair and a devilish, black mustache and beard. He wears suits in the exact same hue as his Garou fur. He is in his late 30s.

Roleplaying Notes: You smile a devilish smile, tend to press your forefingers together and always listen, listen, listen. You are vigilant for flaws, hesitations, momentary blunders and betrayals of inner weakness. These you pounce upon when you tear apart your subject, whomever that might be. Snort gruffly when you're done with your "meal."

History: Carleson Ruah is a clever Garou who works with the New York City business community and underworld to fight the Wyrm from within.

He has established extensive business contacts and has tricked many of his mortal enemies into backing him. He has even been successful in infiltrating Empire Oil, a local Pentex front, and can keep the Shadow Lords one step ahead on raids and lightning strikes led by Sylvan-Ivanovich-Sylvan, New York's Shadow Lord leader.

Ruah has also met and formed alliances with Sabbat vampires in New York City. He has not told other Garou of the scope of his alliances, preferring to hold that as a trump card in case he feels the need to challenge the current

Carleson Ruah

leadership. He has also helped Giovanni vampires exterminate some of their Sabbat and Camarilla foes so that the vampires may cling to their eroding control of New York City's crime rackets.

Ruah's mortal and vampire ties make him as much a liability as an asset in the War of the Apocalypse. While he can manipulate his associates to achieve tribal and personal power, he will be called upon to defend those mortals and Wyrm creatures when they come under Garou attack. If he does not defend his allies, any survivors will certainly hunt him down as a traitor. Furthermore, if other Garou learn the extent and immorality of Ruah's relationships, they will undoubtedly eye him along with his associates as pawns of the Wyrm.

Edgewalker

Breed: Homid
Auspice: Theurge
Nature/Demeanor: Conniver/Survivor
Physical: Strength 1 (3/5/4/2), Dexterity 5 (5/6/7/7), Stamina 2 (4/5/5/4)
Social: Charisma 2, Manipulation 3 (2/0/0/0), Appearance 2 (1/0/2/2)
Mental: Perception 4, Intelligence 2, Wits 4
Talents: Alertness 3, Brawl 1, Dodge 3, Streetwise 3, Subterfuge 3
Skills: Drive 2, Firearms 2, Melee 1, Repair 1, Stealth 3

Knowledges: Computer 3, Rituals 1, Science 1
Backgrounds: Contacts 3, Resources 2
Gifts: (1) Fatal Flaw, Mother's Touch, Persuasion, Smell of Man ; (2) Jam Technology, Luna's Armor, Sight from Beyond
Rank: 2
Rage 5, Gnosis 6, Willpower 5
Rites: (Mystic) Rite of Talisman Dedication
Fetishes: None

Image: There is something gloomy about Edgewalker, even on the best of days. He rarely smiles, and when he does it is a weak attempt at best. Depression and pessimism seem to be his lot in life. His Homid form is a red-bearded, stocky man with blue eyes, prone to dark, drab patterns of dress.

Roleplaying Notes: Expect bad things. Be a nay-sayer. You know the glass is neither half-empty nor half-full; it's leaking. The Apocalypse is coming soon on a global scale, and you expect it sooner on a personal one. Even so, you press ever onward, looking for that special angle, surviving.

History: Edgewalker was named for his tendency to psychologically walk the edge of the abyss, ever in danger of falling into despair and self-destruction. For years, he has lived at that edge and not given in to nihilism, but some Ragabash actually make bets on when he will crack.

Still, he has gained a small measure of respect in the Shadow Lord community for his sensitivity to omens, both

Edgewalker

in his dreams and in the world around him. He is hypervigilant and terrified of change and thus immediately notices the smallest detail gone awry or strange and has become adept at reading meanings in such changes. He is very rarely a bearer of glad tidings, however.

Ivan Korda

Breed: Homid
Auspice: Philodox
Nature/Demeanor: Autist/Confidant
Physical: Strength 3 (5/7/6/4), Dexterity 2 (2/3/4/4), Stamina 2 (4/5/5/4)
Social: Charisma 2, Manipulation 3 (2/0/0/0), Appearance 3 (2/0/3/3)
Mental: Perception 3, Intelligence 4, Wits 3
Talents: Alertness 2, Brawl 2, Dodge 2, Intimidation 2, Streetwise 2, Subterfuge 2
Skills: Disguise 1, Drive 2, Escapology 2, Etiquette 3, Firearms 2, Melee 2, Leadership 2, Stealth 2
Knowledges: Computer 2, Investigation 4, Linguistics 2, Politics 3
Backgrounds: Contacts 2, Resources 3
Gifts: (1) Persuasion, Scent of the True Form, Fatal Flaw
Rank: 1
Rage 3, Gnosis 5, Willpower 5
Rites: None
Fetishes: None

Image: Ivan is in his mid-30s, with long black hair and a long mustache. He is of average height and build. He carries himself with an air of quiet confidence and usually dresses conservatively. In Lupus form, Ivan is a dark-brown wolf with black markings.

Roleplaying Notes: You are everyone's friend — or so you would have them believe. You are very cordial and willingly accept behaviors and personality quirks that others find irritating. Your friendliness has a dark, ugly side, though. You use your relationships to find out as much as you can about others while revealing very little, if anything, about yourself (or at least anything that is true or would be considered "useful" by others).

You use the information you learn to blackmail others into doing whatever you want. This has proven especially useful during moots, wherein you have been able to manipulate votes. And if your pawns should dare vote against you? Well, you have no qualms about bringing truths to light for all to see.

History: Ivan was born in Leningrad, Russia, to a working-class family. In school, Ivan was quiet but friendly and quickly gained a reputation for telling the truth — usually truths no one wanted told. This behavior attracted the attention of a KGB agent who had been appointed to the school. Shortly before graduation, Ivan was approached by the agent, who sought to recruit the boy. Ivan immediately

Ivan Korda

Talents: Athletics 2, Brawl 2, Dodge 3, Empathy 3, Expression 3, Intimidation 1, Subterfuge 2.

Skills: Drive 1, Etiquette 2, Firearms 1, Hypnotism 2, Leadership 1, Performance 3

Knowledges: Computer 1, Enigmas 2, Linguistics (English, Russian, German) 3, Occult 2, Rituals 2, Wyrm Lore 3

Backgrounds: Contacts 1, Kinfolk 2, Past Life 2, Resources 3

Gifts: (1) Aura of Confidence, Call of the Wyld, Fatal Flaw; (2) Disfigurement, Staredown; (3) Paralyzing Stare, Song of the Siren

Rank: 3

Rage 6, Gnosis 5, Willpower 5

Rites: (Death) Gathering for the Departed; (Mystic) Rite of Talisman Dedication, Rite of Summoning; (Punishment) Voice of the Jackal

Fetishes: Baneskin

Flaw: Dark Secret

Image: Nadia is attractive in the manner of Old World nobility; her features are startlingly similar to those of her family. Her skin is fair and her eyes are large and luminous. This latter trait carries over into her lupus and Crinos forms as well. Her hair is as black as the stormcrows that sometimes accompany her and just as shiny. Nadia carries herself with regal bearing and tends to wear dark-colored clothing to accent her hair and offset her eyes.

accepted. With the dissolution of the Soviet Union and the dismantling of the KGB, Ivan had to find work within another Russian intelligence agency and continues to serve his country.

For whatever reasons, Ivan's First Change just occurred during the past year. In fact, Garou who were aware of him assumed him to be Kinfolk, although Ivan wasn't aware of his heritage. Naturally, he was quite surprised when he woke one morning to find his bed in shreds. He considered checking into an asylum for evaluation, but knew that to do so would have ended his career as an intelligence agent. A short time after his First Change, he was apprehended on his way home from work and put through his Rite of Passage. He has since returned to work and uses his new abilities to serve not only his country, but his tribe and himself.

Nadia Wyrmfoe

Breed: Homid

Auspice: Galliard

Nature/Demeanor: Fanatic/Competitor

Physical: Strength 3 (5/7/3/4), Dexterity 3 (3/4/5/5), Stamina 4 (6/7/7/6)

Social: Charisma 4, Manipulation 3 (2/0/0/0), Appearance 3 (2/0/3/3)

Mental: Perception 2, Intelligence 2, Wits 3

Nadia Wyrmfoe

Roleplaying Notes: Some accuse you of being condescending, but that's simply not true; you really *are* better than almost everyone else you run into. Time is always of the essence with you, and you have little to waste on trivialities. You are by no means lazy, but others just have to realize that certain tasks are beneath you, though you have no difficulty understanding what must be done in any situation. You wish to be instrumental in your tribe's inevitable ascension to the throne that the Silver Fangs currently hold, and you will slay any number of Wyrm creatures that try to inhibit your personal and tribal progress.

History: Nadia was born into a noble Romanian house at the nadir of its power, though her indomitable will and grating arrogance would lead one to believe she was the daughter of Louis XIV. In addition, her family's ancient connection to the Shadow Lord line did little to abate her self-importance. Nadia had studied the many faces of the Wyrm even before her First Change, swearing to destroy it and help lead her blood-relations into the power that they should rightfully wield.

Her Rite of Passage entailed stealing a scale from a mighty Russian Zmei dragon, and much to the surprise of her elders, she came back utterly unscathed, scale in hand. Fellow Shadow Lords saw this as an omen of a great power over malignant servants of the Wyrm and asked Nadia to join a sept intent on holding a caern against an influx of Banes. Nadia accepted, never knowing that this responsibility would change her life forever.

During the final clash with the Banes, the spirit Nuag-hyr possessed Nadia's body, using it to destroy his Garou enemies. When Nadia awoke, the bodies of her fallen comrades lay broken around her, and the hollow laugh of Nuag-hyr echoed within her mind. She returned to her elders, claiming that she was the only survivor of the battle, and her lie has haunted her ever since, though no one but she and Nuag-hyr knows the truth. She has, as a result, made a vow to combat the Wyrm in any guise and to destroy Banes wherever she encounters them.

Roar of Storms

Breed: Lupus
Auspice: Galliard
Nature/Demeanor: Director/Traditionalist
Physical: Strength 3 (5/7/6/4), Dexterity 4 (4/5/6/6), Stamina 3 (5/6/6/5)
Social: Charisma 2, Manipulation 4 (3/1/1/1), Appearance 2 (1/0/2/2)
Mental: Perception 2, Intelligence 2, Wits 3
Talents: Alertness 2, Athletics 3, Brawl 2, Expression 2, Intimidation 3, Primal-Urge 1, Subterfuge 3
Skills: Animal Ken 1, Etiquette 2, Performance 3, Stealth 3, Survival 2
Knowledges: Investigation 3, Medicine 2, Politics 3

Roar of Storms

Backgrounds: Kinfolk 2, Pure Breed 1, Totem 2
Gifts: (1) Fatal Flaw, Mindspeak, Sense Prey; (2) Clap of Thunder, Distractions; (3) Paralyzing Stare
Rank: 3
Rage 5, Gnosis 6, Willpower 5
Rites: None
Fetishes: Bane Arrow

Image: In Lupus form, Roar of Storms is a long, gray-black wolf with smoldering eyes and large paws. His Homid form is a dignified-looking gentleman in his early 40s. When he wears clothes, he prefers them to be loose-fitting and comfortable.

Roleplaying Notes: You're very good at getting what you want. Manipulating others comes naturally; many young Garou tend to follow your lead. Even elders lend you their ears at moots and on other occasions.

History: Born a Lupus and raised as a wolf, Roar of Storms has adapted to both Garou and human societies. After his Rite of Passage, his eyes opened to the "big picture."

Roar prefers to play second fiddle. He selects a strong alpha, supports him, and acts as advisor, all the while quietly guiding his pack to pursue his own agendas. He prefers to live with other Garou as opposed to wolves or humans. Yet Roar of Storms can secure a favorable position for himself in any environment.

Silent Striders

Grek Twice-Tongue

Breed: Metis
Auspice: Philodox
Nature/Demeanor: Visionary/Judge
Physical: Strength 3 (5/7/6/4), Dexterity 4 (4/5/6/6), Stamina 3 (5/6/6/5)
Social: Charisma 4, Manipulation 4 (3/1/1/1), Appearance 1 (0/0/1/1)
Mental: Perception 5, Intelligence 5, Wits 4
Talents: Alertness 3, Brawl 3, Dodge 4
Skills: Empathy 4, Expression 5, Primal-Urge 3, Performance 5, Stealth 3, Survival 3
Knowledges: Enigmas 5, Rituals 4
Backgrounds: Contacts 2, Kinfolk 3
Gifts: (1) Mother's Touch, Sense Wyrm, Speed of Thought, Spirit Speech; (2) Curse of Hatred; (3) Adaptation
Rank: 3
Rage 4, Gnosis 6, Willpower 8
Rites: (Accord) Rite of Cleansing, Rite of Contrition; (Caern) Moot Rite, Rite of the Opened Bridge, Rite of the Opened Caern; (Mystic) Rite of Summoning, Rite of Talisman Dedication, Rite of the Totem; (Punishment) Voice of the Jackal
Fetishes: Didgeridoo of the Past (Level 2, Gnosis 6. This didgeridoo is made from ghost gum and heavily patterned in ochres and carvings. When this instrument is played, all who hear it have visions of the stories that are being danced or sung to them.)

Image: In his Homid form, Grek appears as an albino Aboriginal man of middle age. He is bald and usually wears a shapeless hat and dark glasses to protect him from the sun. His clothes are invariably dusty and threadbare. In Lupus form, Grek is a hairless, albino dingo. When performing before Garou he takes Crinos form, naked and adorned with bodypaint and feathers.

Roleplaying Notes: You are enigmatic and slightly cantankerous. You think of yourself as a teacher and behave like one. You are judgmental and do not suffer fools gladly. You are also a performer of great caliber and are aware of your power to sway others through words and music.

History: Grek Twice-Tongue was born in Australia, the only child of a Silent Strider mother and a Stargazer father. Grek's mother ran with a pack called the Gampila Aboriginal Dance Company; Australia's Silent Striders traveled under the guise of circus performers. Grek's father traveled with the pack for only one week — long enough to conceive the albino boy.

Deemed to be a Silent Strider, Grek grew up as a circus child. Always a performer, he was thrust onto the stage at a young age. His life was controlled by his mother, Warratah Utemara, until her untimely death on Grek's 18th birthday. Grek is universally respected for his prodigious storytelling powers. Because of his metis status, he is avoided by Garou who are not Silent Striders.

Grek Twice-Tongue

Grek Twice-Tongue was chosen 12 years ago as the Silent Strider representative to Australia's Jindabyne Council of Garou — not by vote, as is traditional, but by the spirits of the Dreamtime. When the Striders were gathered for the Great Circus, the meeting of all their Australian packs, voices crying Grek's name were heard in the wilderness, and every Theurge present dreamed of Twice-Tongue's destiny. It has been foretold that Grek will be responsible for freeing the tribes of their guilt over the destruction of Australia's ancient Bunyip tribe.

No one knows how or when Grek will free his kind of the sins of their past, but it is likely to occur in the War of the

Apocalypse. In such tragic times, individuals tend to be elevated to heroic proportions, not necessarily out of innate courage but sometimes out of a final, desperate determination to see evil destroyed, regardless of personal sacrifice. Perhaps in some unforeseeable way, Grek shall assume upon himself the murderous sins of his kind and free their souls through some divine victory over the Wyrm.

Natasha "Moon Chaser" Ferdman

Breed: Homid
Auspice: Ragabash
Nature/Demeanor: Rebel/Gallant
Physical: Strength 2 (4/6/5/3), Dexterity 5 (5/6/7/7), Stamina 4 (6/7/7/6)
Social: Charisma 4, Manipulation 4 (3/1/1/1), Appearance 4 (3/0/4/4)
Mental: Perception 5, Intelligence 2, Wits 4
Talents: Alertness 3, Athletics 3, Brawl 2, Dodge 5, Primal-Urge 3, Streetwise 3, Subterfuge 4
Skills: Animal Ken 2, Firearms 2, Leadership 2, Stealth 3
Knowledges: Computer 1, Enigmas 4
Backgrounds: Resources 3, Contacts 3, Kinfolk 2, Pure Breed 4
Gifts: (1) Blur of the Milky Eye, Persuasion, Speed of Thought; (2) Blissful Ignorance, Jam Technology, Summon Talisman; (3) The Great Leap, Silence
Rank: 3
Rage 6, Gnosis 8, Willpower 8
Rites: None
Fetish: Mirrorshades (Level 1, Gnosis 7. This is a pair of American mirrorshade sunglasses that, when activated, produces a mirrored surface on the inside of the glasses that allows the wearer to step sideways with ease. The shades reduce all Gauntlet difficulties by 2, and the user does not need to stare into a reflective surface.)

Image: In Lupus form, Natasha is a sleek, quick wolf with jet-black fur and deep, soulful eyes. In Homid form, she is a riveting, beautiful woman standing 5'6" tall. She has short-cut black hair.

Roleplaying Notes: You used to be a happy and carefree wanderer. That has changed. Now you are paranoid and always looking over your shoulder. Being hunted does that to you.

History: Natasha Ferdman came to the Soviet Union a few years ago with the intention of staying only a short time. However, during her visit, the ancient vampire Baba Yaga came out of the slumber of torpor and set in motion a devious plan to corrupt and ultimately control all of Russia. In league with the Wyrm, Baba Yaga distanced the Russian material world from the spirit world, corrupted Garou caerns and infected the populace with Wyrm taint.

As an outsider and privy to the secrets learned and kept by Russia's Silent Striders, Moon Chaser recognized the corruption of the land. She also recognized that Baba

Natasha "Moon Chaser" Ferdman

Yaga's agents were everywhere and that her awareness made her a target for elimination.

Today, Natasha wants nothing more than to leave Russia. However, the severing of the material and spirit worlds and the blindness of Russia's Garou to their own plight keeps her there. She strives to make Russian Garou see past their petty differences to recognize the destruction of their homeland.

Her work must be discreet, though. Blatant efforts to communicate with and unite Russia's Garou will certainly attract the attention of Baba Yaga's minions and that would mean her destruction. Even more importantly, Moon Chaser must be careful of whom she approaches, for even Russian Garou may be under the Hag's sway.

In the War of the Apocalypse, Moon Chaser grows increasingly willing to be daring in her confrontations with the Wyrm, especially as the War escalates. She hopes that bold actions will wake Russia's Garou from their slumber and force Baba Yaga to show her hand in a way that Garou and mortal alike will recognize. Natasha is steeling herself to make a personal sacrifice to save Russia.

Nephthys Mu'at

Breed: Homid
Auspice: Galliard
Nature/Demeanor: Caregiver/Judge

Nephthys Mu'at

Rank: 4

Rage 3, Gnosis 7, Willpower 7

Rites: (Caern) Rite of the Opened Bridge, Rite of the Opened Caern; (Mystic) Rite of Binding, Rite of Spirit Awakening, Ritual of the Questing Stone, Talisman Dedication; (Punishment) The Rending of the Veil

Fetishes: Spirit Tracer, Phoebe's Veil

Image: In Lupus form, Nephthys is long, lean and trim, with sleek, blue-black fur. She has a long, angular jaw and a unique rainbow of peacock reds and violets at the base of her ears. In Homid form she is a slender, graceful Egyptian woman. She has very dark skin and short, black hair. She is in her 40s.

Roleplaying Notes: You are quiet, stately and patient. You think a long time before speaking and often say nothing at all. When you do speak, it is often in questions: "Why do you ask?"

History: Nephthys is the unofficial leader of the Silent Striders in the Northeast U.S. and Canada. She is wise and strong and organizes independent, itinerant Striders to make sure they regularly meet to pool vital information. She has lately become disturbed by reports of parents selling or disposing of their children with Wyrm-tainted kidnappers. She has learned that the Seventh Generation is dealing in the child market, but does not yet perceive the full scope of the plan. She is on the Seventh Generation's trail and is looking for any available information on the people who act as "Snatchers."

In the War of the Apocalypse, Nephthys makes the destruction of abusers her primary pursuit. She applies secrets and information learned as a Silent Strider to her hunt for those who would harm the innocent and defenseless. Her crusade is not limited to helpless mortals and children; on more than one occasion she has come to the aid of Bone Gnawers and other Garou being assaulted by more numerous opponents. Though she does not yet know it, Nephthys' self-appointed mission will ultimately lead to conflict with Pink Tom, the leader of the skinhead gang called the Bastards of Fenris. That fight may ultimately draw in Tom's Garou father, Arn Guth Stormbright, leader of New York's Get of Fenris, and self-exiled mother, Bladetooth.

Passer

Breed: Metis

Auspice: Theurge

Nature/Demeanor: Penitent/Survivor

Physical: Strength 1 (3/5/4/2), Dexterity 3 (3/4/5/5), Stamina 4 (6/7/7/6)

Social: Charisma 1, Manipulation 4 (3/1/1/1), Appearance 1 (0/0/1/1)

Mental: Perception 3, Intelligence 3, Wits 4

Passer

Talents: Dodge 2, Expression 1, Primal-Urge 2

Skills: Animal Ken 2, Etiquette 1, Stealth 3, Survival 3

Knowledges: Enigmas 4, Linguistics 2, Occult 3, Politics 1, Rituals 3

Backgrounds: Pure Breed 2, Rites 3

Gifts: (1) Create Element, Speed of Thought, Spirit Speech

Rank: 1

Rage 2, Gnosis 3, Willpower 3

Rites: (Accord) Rite of Contrition, (Death) Gathering for the Departed, (Mystic) Rite of Talisman Dedication

Fetishes: None

Image: Passer is indeed a horrid sight, due to his pitiful metis deformity. Regardless of which form he takes, Passer has the face of a man. Unsettling in Crinos form and disgusting in Lupus, this affliction is emphasized by his otherwise scrawny body. Wiry brown fur covers him, and his limbs are fragile and spindly.

Roleplaying Notes: If anyone lives a more wrongful existence than you, you don't want to meet them. You do what you have to do to redeem your blighted self, but you know it will never be good enough. Still, the Garou need all able bodies in the impending Apocalypse, and yours will have to do.

History: Passer grew up never knowing his parents, though his all-Silent Strider sept in the Libyan deserts treated him as a somewhat less pathetic wretch than he was. Trained early on in the role of a messenger, Passer served his packmates humbly and with grim determination, using his abilities as best he could. He has always possessed a keen insight into the doings of the spirits, an ability that has helped him save his hide delivering messages more than once.

Sees-through-Stars

Breed: Homid

Auspice: Philodox

Nature/Demeanor: Visionary/Lone Wolf

Physical: Strength 3 (5/7/6/4), Dexterity 3 (3/4/5/5), Stamina 4 (6/7/7/6)

Social: Charisma 4, Manipulation 2 (1/0/0/0), Appearance 2 (1/0/2/2)

Mental: Perception 4, Intelligence 3, Wits 3

Talents: Alertness 3, Athletics 3, Brawl 3, Empathy 3, Expression 3, Subterfuge 1

Skills: Etiquette 3, Melee 2, Leadership 1, Stealth 2, Survival 2

Knowledges: Enigmas 2, Linguistics 1, Medicine 2, Occult 3, Politics 1, Rituals 2

Backgrounds: Pure Breed 5

Gifts: (1) Persuasion, Resist Pain, Scent of the True Form, Sense Wyrm, Speed of Thought, Truth of Gaia; (2) Messenger's Fortitude, Strength of Purpose; (3) Adaptation, Wisdom of the Ancient Ways; (4) Attunement

Rank: 4

Rage 5, Gnosis 7, Willpower 8

Rites: (Caern) Moot Rite, Rite of the Opened Caern; (Mystic) Rite of Becoming, Rite of Binding, Rite of Summoning, Rite of Talisman Dedication

Fetishes: Monkey Puzzle

Image: In Homid form, he is a tall, gaunt Egyptian of magnetic mien, somewhere in his 50s. His Crinos form is a lanky but muscular gray werewolf. In both forms, there is a sense of greatness and wisdom about him, and his eyes seem to see the secrets in the hearts of others.

Roleplaying Notes: Peaceful and wise, you have traveled long and far and have seen more than most. Truth is the calm eye at the heart of a storm of chaos. It is your gift to look into that eye. Other Garou see violence as the path toward truth, but you realize it is but a tool and that often there are better tools to use in approaching difficult matters. You expect respect and usually receive it. Greet those who do not offer you that respect with calm disdain; if they push it too far, firmly put them in their place then walk away.

Sees-through-Stars

History: No Garou will refuse passage through their territories to Sees-through-Stars. In fact, he is often reckoned a member of all septs, and his presence at a caern is such an honor that the caern's controllers will often ask the Philodox to act in one of their positions for moots. He always does, with wisdom and good humor. Afterwards, he inevitably shares stories of his travels and of the wonders he has seen, making each a subtle parable pointing to new visions, new paths toward harmony.

Sees-through-Stars is among the purest of the purebred, and the greatness of his previous incarnations radiates from him in an aura felt by all who are near him. He is thought to be "kissed by Gaia" and reckoned to be far more powerful than he actually is. It is known that years ago, he took a journey far and deep into the Umbra and returned imbued with a vision of gentleness and wisdom that strikes deep into the hearts of all but the most rage-filled Garou. He is a prophet of Gaia herself, and if he has his way, the Garou will ultimately join together in a balanced and cooperative nation that will easily repel the Wyrm and its minions.

Tanzût

Breed: Lupus

Auspice: Philodox

Physical: Strength 2 (4/6/5/3), Dexterity 4 (4/5/6/6), Stamina 3 (5/6/6/5)

Social: Charisma 2, Manipulation 3 (2/0/0/0), Appearance 2 (1/0/2/2)

Mental: Perception 3, Intelligence 4, Wits 3

Talents: Alertness 4, Athletics 3, Brawl 3, Dodge 3, Empathy 2, Primal-Urge 2

Skills: Animal Ken 2, Drive 1, Kailindo 3, Melee 4, Stealth 3, Survival 2

Knowledges: Enigmas 3, Investigation 2, Rituals 1

Backgrounds: Contacts 3, Past Life 5

Gifts: (1) Heightened Senses, Resist Pain, Scent of the True Form, Speed of Thought; (2) Scent of Sight, Summon Talisman

Rank: 2

Rage 4, Gnosis 5, Willpower 6

Merits/Flaws: Driving Goal (destroy all Setites)

Rites: Rite of Talisman Dedication

Fetishes: Stalk the Heart (Level 4, Gnosis 7. This is an Egyptian wand that will lead the user to the location of a vampire's heart — whether it is in the vampire's body or placed elsewhere, such as a Setite's heart. A successful activation roll must be made. Tanzût has dedicated this item to herself and can summon it with her Gift.)

Image: In Lupus form, Tanzût is an Ethiopian wolf, lean and sleek with reddish-fur. In Homid form, she appears as a woman of Coptic descent with dark hair and complexion. She has Egyptian hieroglyphs tattooed all over her body; they appear in all her forms. She wears worn-out, loose-fitting clothing.

Tanzût

Roleplaying Notes: You are a very quiet person, for there is very little that needs saying. When you do speak, it is plain and straight with no attempt at subtlety. You are on a mission of vengeance and have little time for anything else.

History: Tanzût came to South America in search of her enemies: the Followers of Set. After a battle in Medein nearly killed her, she fled to the jungles of the Amazon and discovered the war. She quickly joined up for the fight, rising quickly in the ranks.

The war is only a temporary distraction for her. She realizes the need to aid Gaia, but her seething hate for the Followers of Set may drive her to leave soon. Hunting down the vampires who drove her tribe from their homeland ages ago is her driving goal.

The secret behind Tanzût's hate is arcane. She is possessed by an ancestor who died under the fangs of a Setite. The past lives of a Strider's ancestors are normally closed to their experience, but Tanzût is different from the rest of her tribe. She bears this wondrous ability as a curse. Why she alone among her tribe has this ability to call upon her ancestors is a mystery, but the dead have seized the opportunity and use her as a tool for vengeance. They are currently leading her on a quest for an ancient sword, one they claim will give her an edge over the serpentine undead.

Walks-with-Might

Breed: Lupus

Auspice: Ahroun

Nature/Demeanor: Predator/Alpha

Physical: Strength 5 (7/9/8/6), Dexterity 5 (5/6/7/7), Stamina 5 (7/8/8/7)

Social: Charisma 2, Manipulation 2 (1/0/0/0), Appearance 2 (1/0/2/2)

Mental: Perception 4, Intelligence 2, Wits 4

Talents: Alertness 3, Athletics 2, Brawl (Leaping Bite) 4, Dodge (Sidestep) 4, Intimidation 3, Primal-Urge (Hunting) 4

Skills: Animal Ken 3, Leadership 3, Melee (Klaives) 4, Stealth (Hiding in Shadows) 4, Survival 3

Knowledges: Enigmas 2, Medicine 2, Occult 3, Rituals (Death) 4

Backgrounds: Kinfolk 2, Pure Breed 2, Totem 1

Gifts: (1) Heightened Senses, Razor Claws, Sense Wyrm; (2) Messenger's Fortitude, Spirit of the Fray, True Fear; (3) Adaptation, Silver Claws; (4) Stoking Fury's Furnace, Touch of Death; (5) Kiss of Helios

Rank: 5

Rage 8, Gnosis 7, Willpower 9

Rites: (Death) Gathering for the Departed, Rite of the Winter Wolf

Fetishes: Klaive, Nightshade

Walks-with-Might

Image: Huge, well-muscled, and perpetually calm, Walks-with-Might carries himself with an incredibly regal air. He moves with a near-feline grace and a purpose that command attention whenever he is present. He has remarkably fine features for a wolf; these features are a direct result of his breeding and Egyptian origin and carry a look of predatory intelligence in whichever form he takes. His coat is always a shiny, dusky tan.

Roleplaying Notes: You are the consummate killer; cold, calculating, ruthless and utterly without mercy. You have fully embraced your Ahroun auspice, though you do not revel in it as do some lesser, bloodthirsty Ahrouns. You have killed hundreds if not thousands of opponents, and you no longer have any shred of remorse for any foe you face in mortal combat. After all, only one of you will leave the combat, and you're not ready to die yet. Sometimes, especially of late, you allow yourself to savor the terror of your prey before you extinguish their life like a candle in a brutal wind.

History: Walks-with-Might was born into a wartime sept in northern Egypt that was dedicated to combating the incessant scheming of the vampires known as the Followers of Set. Vile and unholy minions of the Wyrm, these vampires trafficked in drugs, slaves, weapons, vice, and other decadent aspects of the monkeys that populated the cities. As a youth, Walks-with-Might led numerous effective attacks against these vampires, though they seemed to get stronger after every conflict. His sept finally realized that the Followers of Set were merely making more vampires to replace the ones killed by fellow Garou.

At this point, Walks-with-Might began to understand the Sisyphian nature of his sept's position; no matter how many Setites were killed, there would always be more, and all he and his packmates could ever hope to do was retard the vampires' efforts; they would never be able to stop them. This point was driven home when the Followers of Set managed to capture the leader of the sept, turning him into an utterly corrupt combination of vampire and Garou, an Abomination, in a grand gesture of mockery.

Steeling his heart, Walks-with-Might cornered and slew the former leader of his once-mighty sept as every ounce of his being revolted against the desperate and tragic loss of one of Gaia's greatest avengers. Cold and barren after being forced to destroy one of Gaia's chosen, Walks-with-Might has since reinforced within himself his true role in the imminent Apocalypse, though the screams of his slain enemies follow him into his sleep every night.

Silver Fangs

Amanda Withers-in-Sun

Breed: Metis
Auspice: Theurge
Nature/Demeanor: Caregiver/Confidant
Physical: Strength 2 (4/6/5/3), Dexterity 3 (3/4/5/5), Stamina 1 (3/4/4/3)
Social: Charisma 4, Manipulation 3 (2/0/0/0), Appearance 2 (1/0/2/2)
Mental: Perception 4, Intelligence 4, Wits 4
Talents: Alertness 1, Dodge 2, Empathy 2, Instruction 2
Skills: Animal Ken 2, Archery 2, Meditation 3, Melee 1, Stealth 1, Survival 2
Knowledges: Enigmas (Existential) 4, Investigation 1, Linguistics (Garou Sign Language) 1, Occult 3, Rituals (Mystic) 5
Backgrounds: Past Life 1, Pure Breed 3, Resources 3, Rites 1
Gifts: (1) Mother's Touch, Sense Wyrm, Spirit Speech; (2) Awe, Command Spirit, Luna's Armor; (3) Exorcism, Eyes of the Cat, Wrath of Gaia

Amanda Withers-in-Sun

Rank: 3
Rage 3, Gnosis 7, Willpower 4
Rites: (Caern) Moot Rite, Rite of the Opened Caern; (Mystic) Baptism of Fire, Rite of Binding, Rite of Spirit Awakening, Rite of Summoning
Fetishes: Phoebe's Veil

Image: In her Homid form, Amanda is plain-looking. She is of average height, though a little pudgy, and wears her long, gray-flecked brown hair pulled back, which reveals her widow's peak. In Lupus form, she is a short-haired gray wolf with brown dappling. Her Crinos form is thinly furred and vaguely lethargic-looking, owing to her heavier but unathletic proportions.

Roleplaying Notes: Keep out of bright light, as your condition makes you uncomfortable, but don't skulk. You are amiable and have no compunctions about sharing your knowledge with others. In fact, you are so open that other people come to you when they need to speak their mind. You are a true friend, however, and will not use these confidences to your own advantage.

History: Amanda is the illegitimate offspring of two renowned homid Silver Fangs who, due to the Litany, could not publicly acknowledge their relationship. Amanda was born under a sliver of a moon, close to the new moon of the Trickster. Some intolerant elders point to this as an omen of her birth, saying that she is just as close to being an affront to Gaia. Her metis disfigurement is a bizarre and mystic allergy to light, although she is not an albino. Nonetheless, Amanda is a strong and caring individual, well-versed in the customs of her culture. As her allergy somewhat hinders her martial abilities, she tends to guard her pack's caern when they are abroad and otherwise fulfill the healer's role.

Amanda often finds herself acting as a go-between for other packmates or tribe members. Her calm and understanding nature often help cooler heads prevail, and a few of the Gifts she has learned serve to further her efforts in this regard. Among her pack, she is rightfully considered an expert when questions concerning spirits or the Umbra are concerned, though she commonly finds respect given begrudgingly due to her metis birth.

Greyfist

Breed: Homid
Auspice: Philodox
Nature/Demeanor: Caregiver/Judge
Physical: Strength 4 (6/8/7/5), Dexterity 3 (3/4/5/5), Stamina 3 (5/6/6/5)

Social: Charisma 3, Manipulation 2 (1/0/0/0), Appearance 3 (2/0/3/3)

Mental: Perception 4, Intelligence 4, Wits 3

Talents: Alertness 3, Brawl 2, Dodge 2, Empathy 2, Intimidation 2, Primal-Urge 2

Skills: Drive 2, Etiquette 3, Leadership 3, Melee 2

Knowledges: Law 3, Politics 3, Rituals 3

Backgrounds: Allies 2, Contacts 2, Pure Breed 3, Resources 3, Rites 3

Gifts: (1) Lambent Flame, Persuasion, Truth of Gaia; (2) Awe, Staredown, Strength of Purpose; (3) Disquiet, Silver Claws, Wisdom of the Ancient Ways

Rank: 3

Rage 5, Gnosis 7, Willpower 7

Rites: (Accord) Rite of Cleansing; (Caern) Moot Rite; (Minor) Breath of Gaia, Greet the Moon; (Mystic) Rite of Talisman Dedication; (Punishment) Rite of Ostracism, Stone of Scorn; (Renown) Rite of Accomplishment

Fetishes: Klaive

Image: Greyfist is a tall, powerfully built man with blond hair and gray eyes. He carries himself with a regal air and dresses well but practically. His Lupus form is a large, handsome, silver wolf.

Roleplaying Notes: You are proud of your service to the Silver Fang tribe and especially to the Silver Fang king. Your pride borders on arrogance though, and from time to time you have been known to look upon others, even those in your own tribe, as inferior. Sometimes you feel you must "father" others through their shortcomings. Generally, you tend to be a practical individual and realize that nearly everyone (with the obvious exception of the Wyrm-tainted) plays a role in Gaia's plan.

History: Greyfist was identified at birth as Garou and spent his youth aware of his proud heritage, eagerly awaiting his First Change. When it finally occurred, he was immediately withdrawn from his private school, sent on his Rite of Passage and educated in the ways of the Silver Fangs.

Greyfist is descended from a long line of seneschals to the Silver Fang king, and both he and his family expect him to assume the role. To that end, Greyfist studied both human law and Garou Litany to be a better advisor to and judge for the king. When he was called to service in the Silver Fang court of the United States, Greyfist closed his law practice and left his native England for rural Vermont.

Greyfist is a well-respected lawyer in his adopted community and a well-respected advisor and friend to King Morningkill. He has no aspirations to be king himself, even though he is of noble blood. He feels there are others better suited to lead the Garou Nation and is content to be advisor and judge. In the War of the Apocalypse, that role lends power, but also the personal freedom that the throne would deny.

Grimfang

Breed: Lupus

Auspice: Theurge

Nature/Demeanor: Traditionalist/Confidant

Physical: Strength 4 (6/8/7/5), Dexterity 4 (4/5/6/6), Stamina 4 (6/7/7/6)

Social: Charisma 3, Manipulation 5 (4/2/2/2), Appearance 2 (1/0/2/2)

Mental: Perception 5, Intelligence 5, Wits 5

Talents: Alertness 5, Athletics 2, Brawl 3, Dodge 4, Empathy 5, Intimidation 5, Primal-Urge 5, Subterfuge 1, Stealth 3

Skills: Animal Ken 4, Leadership 3, Stealth 3, Survival 4

Knowledges: Enigmas 4, Linguistics 2, Medicine 3, Occult 5, Politics 1, Rituals 5

Backgrounds: Past Life 5, Pure Breed 3

Gifts: (1) Heightened Senses, Mother's Touch, Sense Wyrm, Spirit Speech; (2) Command Spirit, Luna's Armor, Name the Spirit, Sense the Unnatural, Sight from Beyond; (3) Catfeet, Detect Spirit, Exorcism, Pulse of the Invisible; (4) Beast Life, Mindblock, Spirit Drain; (5) Elemental Gift, Malleable Spirit, Paws of the Newborn Cub; (6) Rebirthing (This gift is a special one bestowed upon Grimfang by Gaia herself. Upon his death, he will be reborn in the form of a cub somewhere within 2,000 miles of his demise. This is not a Past Life, but an actual reincarnation. At maturity, the cub will come into Grimfang's true powers.)

Greyfist

Grimfang

Rank: 6

Rage 7, Gnosis 10, Willpower 10

Rites: (Caern) Moot Rite, Rite of Caern Building, Rite of the Opened Bridge, Rite of the Shrouded Glen, The Badger's Burrow; (Death) Rite of the Winter Wolf; (Mystic) Rite of Becoming, Rite of Binding, Rite of Spirit Awakening, Rite of Summoning, Rite of the Fetish, Rite of the Totem; (Punishment) Gaia's Vengeful Teeth; (Renown) Rite of Passage

Fetishes: Soulstone (Level 5, Gnosis 8. The soulstone allows Grimfang to look into the soul of any other Garou. By using the stone, Grimfang can tell when someone is not speaking the truth, what her plans are, what her dreams are, and the source of her deepest fears. The fetish doesn't work on Silver Fangs.)

Image: Grimfang is a small, silver wolf with a sprinkling of black fur and only half of his left ear. In Homid form, he is a bright-eyed, smiling old mountain man. He occasionally walks with a cane.

Roleplaying Notes: Be happy, friendly, helpful and eager to teach. When someone manages to rouse your ire, mutter about "upstart young pups," change to wolf form and vanish into the woods. If someone truly angers you, only then will you frown, and Gaia rest the souls of those you frown upon. Let all of the young pups, and they are all young pups, have no doubt that the caern comes first. You enjoy talking people's ears off about nothing.

History: Grimfang is as old as many of the trees in the forest, and he remembers planting several of them. He was born to one of the many wolf packs that inhabit his caern's region under the protection of the Garou and has known little of life other than that of a shapechanger.

Throughout his long life, Grimfang has traveled the length and breadth of Russia, Europe and even the Orient to combat the Wyrm and its manifestations. He is old now and has held the position as Warder of the Caern since the previous Warder's death 30 years ago. He is considered to be one of the wisest Theurges in Russia and recently has begun receiving messages and visits from Garou questioning him about the draining of caerns.

This possibility troubles him greatly, and in his concern he has greatly increased the security of the caern. He also seeks any news of the truth behind what is happening to the other caerns. In fact, he will occasionally disappear and travel to nearby caerns to warn them and assist in shoring up their defenses. Wherever he goes, this sagest of Theurges is always welcome.

Lord Albrecht

Breed: Homid

Auspice: Ahroun

Nature/Demeanor: Survivor/Rebel

Physical: Strength 4 (6/8/7/5), Dexterity 3 (3/4/5/5), Stamina 4 (6/7/7/6)

Social: Charisma 3, Manipulation 2 (1/0/0/0), Appearance 3 (2/0/3/3)

Mental: Perception 3, Intelligence 2, Wits 4

Talents: Alertness 2, Athletics 3, Brawl 5, Dodge 3, Expression 2, Intimidation 3, Primal-Urge 4, Streetwise 2

Skills: Drive 2, Etiquette 1, Firearms 2, Leadership 3, Melee 5, Repair 1, Stealth 3, Survival 2

Knowledges: Enigmas 2, Investigation 2, Law 1, Medicine 1, Occult 2, Politics 3, Rituals 2

Backgrounds: Allies 1, Fetish 5, Kinfolk 1, Past Life 1, Pure Breed 4, Resources 1

Gifts: (1) Lambent Flame, Resist Pain, Sense Wyrm, Smell of Man, The Falling Touch; (2) Awe, Luna's Armor, Spirit of the Fray, True Fear; (3) Silver Claws, Wrath of Gaia; (4) Stoking Fury's Furnace

Rank: 4

Rage 8, Gnosis 4, Willpower 8

Rites: (Caern) Moot Rite, Rite of the Opened Caern; (Death) Gathering for the Departed; (Mystic) Rite of Talisman Dedication; (Renown) Rite of Wounding

Fetishes: Grand Klaive

Image: Albrecht is a rough-looking man in his late 20s. He wears his long silver-white hair in a ponytail and is usually unshaven. He is typically in the company of a cigarette or drink. In Crinos form he is massive and white.

Lord Albrecht

Albrecht is capable of achieving tremendous things, but has some lessons to learn before he gets there. If he can learn to value others as much as he does his own hide, he will prove to be a worthy heir to the Silver Fang throne.

(Albrecht's **Rage** statistics represent him as he was before he rescued Evan Heals-the-Past and formed a truce with Mari. Accordingly, he is presented here at that stage of the journey. By the time the Silver Crown opens, he is likely Rank 5, with all the increased abilities that implies.)

Roshen One-Arm

Breed: Lupus
Auspice: Ragabash
Physical: Strength 3 (5/7/6/4), Dexterity 3 (3/4/5/5), Stamina 4 (6/7/7/6)
Social: Charisma 3, Manipulation 3 (2/0/0/0), Appearance 2 (1/0/2/2)
Mental: Perception 2, Intelligence 2, Wits 3
Talents: Alertness 2, Athletics 2, Brawl 3, Dodge 3, Primal-Urge 3
Skills: Leadership 3, Melee 4, Performance 2
Knowledges: Linguistics 1, Medicine 2, Politics 1, Rituals 1
Backgrounds: Allies 2, Pure Breed 3
Gifts: (1) Heightened Senses, Lambent Flame, Scent of Running Water

He occasionally wears ornate battle armor if he's expecting a fight.

Roleplaying Notes: So you're surly and bitter. Who wouldn't be? You've given up on thinking of yourself as a prince a long time ago. However, you're still a Silver Fang, and you don't take well to insults against yourself or your tribe. You still value honor, even if it doesn't seem to get you anywhere. Walk by yourself, be civil to the Gnawers (they're decent folks, anyway), and if anybody messes with you, rip their guts out.

History: Jonas Albrecht is a prince in exile. The grandson of King Jacob Morningkill of the North Country Protectorate, he was once the favored son of the Silver Fang court. But madness was slowly devouring his grandfather, and the old Garou began lashing out at anyone handy. The final blow came when Albrecht singlehandedly defeated a Wyrm-beast that was preying on the protectorate. When he presented the carcass to the king, Morningkill demanded that Albrecht kneel in supplication. Albrecht refused to cheapen his glory by showing submission and was banished.

He began wandering New York City, where he was accepted by the local Bone Gnawers. His pride and regal bearing gradually slipped away, and he turned to the bottle to help ease the pain. During one of his forays, he ran across the territory of Mari Cabrah of the Black Furies. The two fought, and Albrecht barely beat her, giving her a nasty battle scar. She's been angry at him ever since.

Roshen One-Arm

Rank: 1

Rage 4, Gnosis 5, Willpower 5

Merits/Flaws: One Arm, Metamorph

Rites: (Mystic) Talisman Dedication

Fetishes: Severed Arm (Gnosis 7. This is Roshen's old arm, turned into a fetish. It is a Crinos-form arm that Roshen uses as a club. It delivers Strength + 2 aggravated damage when it hits).

Image: Roshen is a scraggly guy of about 20 years. He is 5'2" and weighs 120 pounds. He has a nutty smile and likes to walk waving his severed arm. His wolf form is lean and dirty gray.

Roleplaying Notes: Pretend you're crazy. You get a lot of attention that way and your enemies fear you. You know it's just a put-on, as does your pack, who plays along with you.

History: Roshen One-Arm lost his arm in battle some years ago. The arm, severed while he was in Crinos form, was preserved and made into a fetish. Now, Roshen uses it as a club in battle, wielding the tattooed limb without mercy against his enemies.

He came to the Amazon from California, where he was a member in a Napa Valley sept of Silver Fangs. In the Amazon he tries to make a name for himself, attempting to rise in Rank despite his obvious handicap. Many of his allies find him unsettling and bizarre, but it often proves equally shocking to his enemies when they catch a glimpse of the crazed Silver Fang whirling his arm over his head.

Sings-for-the-Beast

Breed: Metis

Auspice: Galliard

Nature/Demeanor: Martyr/Autist

Physical: Strength 3 (5/7/6/4), Dexterity 3 (3/4/5/5), Stamina 3 (5/6/6/6)

Social: Charisma 4, Manipulation 3 (2/0/0/0), Appearance 4 (3/0/4/4)

Mental: Perception 3, Intelligence 2, Wits 3

Talents: Alertness 3, Brawl 5, Dodge 5, Empathy 2, Instruction 3, Primal-Urge 3, Subterfuge 3

Skills: Animal Ken 2, Etiquette 2, Performance 5, Investigation 2

Knowledges: Linguistics 2, Rituals 1

Backgrounds: Pure Breed 4, Past Life 1

Gifts: (1) Call of the Wyld, Create Element, Lambent Flame; (2) Awe, Dreamspeak

Rank: 2

Rage 4, Gnosis 5, Willpower 6

Metis Disfigurement: Bestial Reflection

Rites: None

Fetishes: Harmony Flute, Sanctuary Chimes, Spirit Whistle

Image: In Homid form, Sings-for-the-Beast is cultured, refined and downright beautiful, but she looks a little older

Sings-for-the-Beast

each day — she has the Flaw: Wolf Years. In Lupus, she is a true white wolf, going gray fast.

Roleplaying Notes: You are a follower. True, you prefer that people not know you are metis, and you are embarrassed at how fast you are aging, but both of these are products of the purity of your breeding. Since time seems so short for you, you try to be where everything is happening or where people are gathering. You want to teach, but before anyone will listen, you have to become famous. You need glory, so you try to be where it can be found. You are living as fast as you can.

History: Sings-for-the-Beast was born and raised in Russia, the product of a Silver Fang mating with one of the Lost, a Garou who had lost her Kin Fetch and had not undergone the Change. Sings' mother underwent her First Change shortly after becoming pregnant and went through her Rite of Passage while heavy with child. After Sings was born, her father prepared her way in Garou society.

Sings-for-the-Beast's greatest dream in life, even from youth, was to become a legend — that one day her story would grace the Cliff of Heroes, a monument to Silver Fang greatness maintained by the Ural Mountains' Sept of the Crescent Moon. As fate would have it, though, Sings' weakness as a Silver Fang manifested as accelerated aging. Determined to make a name for herself before it was too late, she fled Russia to travel West, believing that the

Wyrm's greatest corruption festered there, and there she would face it.

Ironically, after Sings left the Soviet Union, the ancient vampire Baba Yaga rose from the slumber of torpor and cast a shadow over the land. Now Russia is virtually impenetrable to outside Garou, and those still within cannot leave. Free of Baba Yaga's curse, Sings realizes that only by returning to her homeland can she become a true legend. Yet, the time that she spends away from Russia and the time she dedicates to returning are squandered, for with each passing day she grows increasingly older and is no closer to becoming a hero. Perhaps what she does not realize is that she must accept what she is and has, and if she is to become a legend, she must act where she is. Until she comes to that conclusion, she is only a passing threat to the Wyrm.

Sofya Softkiller

Breed: Homid
Auspice: Ahroun
Nature/Demeanor: Bravo/Alpha
Physical: Strength 3 (5/7/6/4), Dexterity 3 (3/4/5/5), Stamina 4 (6/7/7/6)
Social: Charisma 3, Manipulation 3 (2/0/0/0), Appearance 4 (3/0/3/3)
Mental: Perception 3, Intelligence 2, Wits 3
Talents: Alertness 2, Athletics 2, Brawl 3, Dodge 3, Intimidation 3

Sofya Softkiller

Skills: Etiquette 4, Leadership 2, Melee 3
Knowledges: Linguistics 1, Politics 3, Rituals 1
Backgrounds: Pure Breed 4, Resources 1
Gifts: (1) Inspiration, Lambent Flame, Persuasion, Razor Claws; (2) Awe
Rank: 2
Rage 5, Gnosis 2, Willpower 4
Rites: (Mystic) Rite of Talisman Dedication
Fetishes: None

Image: Cold and beautiful, Sofya Softkiller clearly springs from the purest of Silver Fang bloodlines. Her ferocity in battle and her breeding are much respected, but she herself is an arrogant bully and thus hated by many who come into regular contact with her. Even when she shows respect to her elders there is always a touch of mockery in her smile, as if she knows that she is actually their superior.

Roleplaying Notes: The blood of heroes and kings runs in your veins. You are destined for legend. Make sure everyone knows it. Stare down those who are beneath you, make sure they know who they are dealing with. Seek renown at every opportunity; you would be in the Silver Record already if those lowborn Galliards knew what the hell they were doing.

History: Raised among poor Silver Fang Kinfolk in a small mountain village near the Sept of the Crescent Moon, Sofya always knew she was destined for greatness. Her parents encouraged her in this, praying that she would be Garou and bring their family once more into the realm of the true Silver Fang nobility. As a result, she did indeed develop the bearing of many high-born: she became haughty and demanding and spoiled rotten. The coming of her First Change only made her even more insufferable.

During her Rite of Passage, Sofya and her packmates fought a band of horrid fomori, and Sofya cut a swath through them so easily and with such fearlessness that she was given the name "Softkiller." Upon completion of the rite, her family presented her with the sword of her great-grandsire, a Garou hero. She treats this ornate weapon like her own firstborn.

Since that time, Sofya has distinguished herself in many battles. She is, indeed, a master of casual violence, and that worries her sept leaders. Those so close to savagery are often the ones easily seduced by the bloodlust of the Wyrm….

That Sofya is blessed with innate greatness no one denies, but it is rare to hear anyone saying anything positive about her. She struts and prances, glaring coldly down at others, and has made few friends; even her packmates have reservations, though they appreciate her combat finesse. In time, it is hoped, she will mature beyond her haughty self-centeredness and realize that the purpose for her natural prowess isn't for her own aggrandizement, but to make a positive difference in the world and in the lives of those around her.

Stargazers

Antonine Teardrop

Breed: Homid

Auspice: Philodox

Nature/Demeanor: Visionary/Fanatic

Physical: Strength 3 (5/7/6/4), Dexterity 4 (4/5/6/6), Stamina 3 (5/6/6/5)

Social: Charisma 4, Manipulation 4 (3/1/1/1), Appearance 3 (2/0/3/3)

Mental: Perception 4, Intelligence 5, Wits 5

Talents: Alertness 4, Brawl 5, Dodge 4, Empathy 3, Primal-Urge 3

Skills: Animal Ken 2, Etiquette 2, Melee 4, Leadership 2, Stealth 3, Survival 3

Knowledges: Enigmas 5, Investigation 4, Medicine 3, Occult 4, Rituals 4

Backgrounds: Past Life 3, Pure Breed 3

Gifts: (1) Persuasion, Resist Pain, Scent of the True Form, Truth of Gaia; (2) Inner Strength, Surface Attunement; (3) Merciful Blow; (4) Preturnatural Awareness, Scent of Beyond

Rank: 4

Rage 4, Gnosis 7, Willpower 9

Rites: (Accord) Rite of Cleansing, Rite of Contrition; (Caern) Rite of the Opened Bridge, Rite of the Shrouded Glen, The Badger's Burrow; (Death) Gathering for the Departed; (Mystic) Rite of Spirit Awakening, Rite of the Fetish, Rite of the Totem, Ritual of the Questing Stone, Talsiman Dedication; (Renown) Rite of Passage

Fetishes: Klaive with a Paradox spirit bound into it (provides the Gift: Distractions).

Image: Antonine has medium-length golden fur with a white-gold underbelly. In Homid form he looks like a tanned, middle-aged outdoorsman, with leathery skin and blond-flecked brown hair. He is in his late 40s.

Roleplaying Notes: You remain supremely calm no matter what happens. Smile at odd times, as if you recognize something humorous that nobody else understands or perceives.

History: Antonine Teardrop is among the few Stargazers in the New York area. There are only two Gazers who actually reside in the state. One is located in New York City. Antonine makes his home in the Catskill Mountains, where he has an observatory that's fitted with telescopes and scientific arcana. He is available for consultation and receives Garou and Kinfolk on a regular basis.

Antonine is a wise Stargazer who has recently read some frightening portents. He has seen the Wyrm as a great hydra uncoiling a horrible new head: one studded with the faces of screaming children. He does not know the meaning of the omen, but knows the nature of the beast.

He has insisted at several revels that the new beast cannot be destroyed by tooth and claw, but will require all Garou to purify themselves and re-dedicate themselves to Gaia's true way. He calls for all Garou to become adept at healing their inner wounds, the wounds of homids and the wounds of mortal society. He calls for a great revel in which the Garou tribes will present their grievances to each another, acknowledge the grievances of others, ask forgiveness, forgive offenses committed, and accept the forgiveness of other tribes. Anything less, he predicts, will doom the tribes to tear at each other's throats while the enemy gloats.

Antonine's calls for tribal healing have made even the Children of Gaia uncomfortable, and Antonine has received very few visitors since he announced his plan.

The tribes of New York would be wise to listen to Antonine, for he has seen the future of the War of the Apocalypse. Whether he realizes it or not, his role in the war is to unite the tribes. Unless he can find some common ground on which to appeal to them or can find a Garou who

Antonine Teardrop

is well respected and willing to hear him out, Antonine's vision of Wyrm invasion will come to pass. Antonine realizes that, in wartime, heroes and leaders may emerge from the lowliest of the ranks and is glad to have the support of any Garou willing to believe in him, hoping that one might rise to become the champion of his cause.

Gesar

Breed: Homid

Auspice: Ragabash

Nature/Demeanor: Jester/Jester

Physical: Strength 2 (4/6/5/3), Dexterity 5 (5/6/7/7), Stamina 2 (4/5/5/4)

Social: Charisma 3, Manipulation 4 (3/1/1/1), Appearance 4 (3/0/4/4)

Mental: Perception 3, Intelligence 3, Wits 5

Talents: Alertness 4, Athletics 4, Dodge 3, Expression 3, Streetwise 4, Subterfuge 4

Skills: Drive 2, Firearms 3, Kailindo 2, Performance 4, Stealth 4

Knowledges: Computer 2, Enigmas (Word Games) 4, Linguistics (Chinese, English) 2, Occult 2, Philosophy 1, Rituals 5, Tactics 1

Backgrounds: Contacts (Hong Kong) 3, Resource 4, Totem (East Wind) 5

Gifts: (1) Balance, Open Seal, Persuasion, Scent of Running Water; (2) Jam Technology, Surface Attunement, Taking the Forgotten; (3) Clarity, Open Moon Bridge

Rank: 3

Rage 3, Gnosis 10, Willpower 5

Rites: (Caern) Rite of the Opened Bridge, Rite of the Opened Caern; (Mystic) Rite of Talisman Dedication; (Punishment) Satire Rite

Image: A slender, attractive youth of 20 years, Gesar has traded in the silk suits of his Hong Kong days for more practical leather and canvas. Gesar has a wicked sense of humor and a charming smile; he is also an incorrigible ladies' man. In Lupus, he's mottled gray and laughs like a hyena.

Roleplaying Notes: Life was a lot more fun back in Hong Kong where you ran with the Urban Primitives and hit all the hot spots. And, of course, there were all the girls.

Then one day it was over. Dad came back from "finding himself" in Tibet and "requested" that you return with him. Next thing you knew, you were stuck in a musty old temple in the middle of nowhere — some place in Tibet called the "Sept of the Snow Leopard" — with a bunch of rejects from *The Ten Commandments*.

Dad turned out to be a bigwig there and started teaching you cool stuff about Moon Bridges and so on, until — Bam! Dad was killed by Red Hats and you were the only one left at the caern who had the keys to the Bridge.

Gesar

That old geezer Lungtok says you're the worst gatekeeper he's ever seen, and he wants you out, which is fine by you. Still, you aren't completely without honor, so you'll stay until you train someone else; you'll even obey the rules — to a point. Yeah, the place isn't all bad. The Cheng sisters are a lot of fun. And that Tara: Hot!

History: Gesar was raised by his mother while his estranged Garou father, a respected Theurge, involved himself in the affairs of Tibet's Caern of the Snow Leopard. In his youth, Gesar became a thrill-seeking thief. Most of his Hong Kong packmates were Glass Walkers, and he learned a few of their tricks.

The Leopards know Gesar's history and do not trust him completely, so have embarked upon a campaign to "straighten him out."

Morihei High-Mountain

Breed: Homid

Auspice: Galliard

Nature/Demeanor: Penitent/Survivor

Physical: Strength 3 (5/7/6/4), Dexterity 3 (3/4/5/5), Stamina 4 (6/7/7/6)

Social: Charisma 3, Manipulation 1 (0/0/0/0), Appearance 3 (2/0/2/2)

Mental: Perception 5, Intelligence 4, Wits 4

Talents: Alertness 3, Athletics 2, Dodge 3, Empathy 2, Expression 2

Skills: Drive 1, Etiquette 1, Firearms 1, Kailindo 4, Melee 1, Performance 2, Repair 1, Stealth 2, Survival 3

Knowledges: Enigmas 2, Linguistics 2, Medicine 5, Occult 1, Rituals 2, Science 1

Backgrounds: Mentor 4, Pure Breed 1

Gifts: (1) Balance, Beast Speech, Persuasion, Sense Wyrm; (2) Distractions, Inner Strength, Staredown, Surface Attunement; (3) Clarity, Merciful Blow, Reshape Object, Song of Rage; (4) Bridge Walker, Cocoon

Rank: 4

Rage 6, Gnosis 9, Willpower 8

Rites: (Accord) Rite of Cleansing, Rite of Contrition; (Caern) Rite of the Opened Caern; (Mystic) Rite of Becoming, Rite of the Questing Stone, Rite of Talisman Dedication; (Renown) Rite of Accomplishment

Fetishes: Coin of Wealth, Tears of Gaia

Image: Morihei's Homid form is a dashing and fit man in his late 40s, wearing adventure clothing like a contemporary Indiana Jones. In Crinos, he is a large gray werewolf of strangely gentle aspect. In both forms, he is solemn and quiet; there is sadness in his eyes.

Roleplaying Notes: Go ever forward, trying not to look back. Memory is pain. Somewhere ahead of you are absolution, enlightenment and joy. Keep looking for that place in the world and in yourself that will bring them to you.

History: Already the source of several tales in the Silver Record, Morihei High-Mountain travels the earth and the Umbra like a one-man commando squad, hunting the Wyrm's minions to their darkest hiding places and destroying them, bringing corrupted locales back to Gaia's blessing. He is a driven man, relentless in his mission, and this has made him incredibly knowledgeable and highly skilled.

Yet he came late to this life and to his existence as a Garou. He was a lost pup, an internationally recognized thoracic surgeon, with a wife and a baby daughter. Then the First Change came, and he slaughtered them both in a fit of dark rage that had been building for years. Madness and self-loathing filled him, and had he not been recognized then by the Garou of the Sept of the Green, he would certainly have taken his own life. Mother Larissa helped him to understand his true nature and his place in the grand scheme. In time, he left Central Park and embarked on a rigorous journey through the Himalayas, ultimately dragging himself exhausted and injured to the door of the Shigalu Monastery in Tibet, home of the Sept of the Snow Leopard.

Some say he actually died at that door and was returned to life by the Stargazers within, but this is just legend. However it happened, he was accepted into the Sept by his tribe and undertook the Path of the Adventurer, rigorously throwing himself into the spiritual practices of the monastery and into the study of Kailindo. If his *raison d'etre* was to

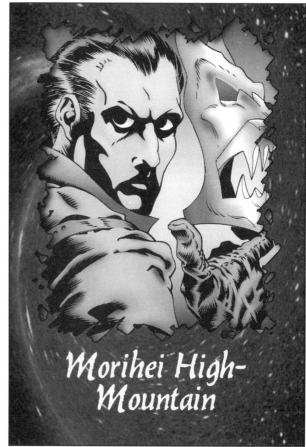

Morihei High-Mountain

serve Gaia, then that he would do. His spirit was so great that Lungtok, the Sept Leader, took him as a personal student. Their relationship as teacher and student continues even now, even as Morihei High-Mountain roams the worlds running from his pain and to the fate of a true hero.

Rainpuddle

Breed: Lupus

Auspice: Theurge

Nature/Demeanor: Visionary/Caregiver

Physical: Strength 1 (3/5/4/2), Dexterity 3 (3/4/5/5), Stamina 2 (4/5/5/4)

Social: Charisma 3, Manipulation 1 (0/0/0/0), Appearance 4 (3/0/4/4)

Mental: Perception 4, Intelligence 3, Wits 3

Talents: Alertness 3, Athletics 2, Brawl 1, Dodge 3, Empathy 4

Skills: Animal Ken 2, Performance 2, Stealth 1, Survival 2

Knowledges: Enigmas 4, Occult 3, Rituals 3

Backgrounds: Kinfolk 2, Pure Breed 3

Gifts: (1) Heightened Senses, Mother's Touch, Sense Wyrm, Spirit Speech

Rank: 1

Rage 2, Gnosis 6, Willpower 5

Rainpuddle

Rites: (Accord) Rite of Cleansing; (Mystic) Rite of Becoming, Rite of Binding, Rite of Spirit Awakening.

Fetishes: Spirit Drum

Image: Rainpuddle is a wolf of snow and ice, with pure white fur and eerie blue-white eyes. In Homid form, she is a pale beauty, wild and graceful. There is something ethereal and magical about her. She is quiet and gentle, a calming presence radiating wisdom.

Roleplaying Notes: You see through surfaces, so much so that often you're unaware of them; where others may remember a dark-furred alpha wolf, you remember a wolf of bright heart. Where others remember a rugged, harsh ridge tough to travel, you remember a mountain spirit of wondrous memory. All things have a spirit and you wish communion with them, a fact made easier by your innate ability to interact fully with both worlds at all times. You speak simple truths and are often surprised when others find you cryptic.

History: Though all Garou are creatures of both the Umbra and the physical world, Rainpuddle exists in both at once. The world that she experiences is a world of spirits with physical presence, and it is the spiritual side of things that most concerns her.

Birthed in the eternal winter of Siberia, Rainpuddle was always strangely different than her wolf brothers and sisters. Her eyes were shining ice, strange and frightening; had she not been beyond dominance games, no wolf could have

stared her down. Yet hierarchy and conflict had no meaning to her, not in a world that was so filled with wonder. The wolves of her pack gave her the name Rainpuddle after she spent three spring days watching the ripples in a pool of fallen rain. They had no way of knowing that she saw through to another world.

One day, while wandering, Rainpuddle encountered a strange two-legged creature, covered in the skins of other animals. He spoke to her in the language of wolves, and she was excited to find that he knew of the things she saw, things none of the others saw or understood. He explained that she was Garou, like him, and he became a wolf to show what he meant. She grasped this truth instantly and changed into a lovely young girl, naked in the snow. He told her she was a Crescent Moon and that her destiny was to be healer and teacher to both man and wolf, and he wrapped her in furs for warmth and took her to meet others like him in a mountain village far away. Since that time, she has moved between the worlds of man and wolf as easily as she moves between the worlds of spirit and flesh, seeking to bring all worlds together in harmony.

Seeks-the-Truth

Breed: Lupus
Auspice: Philodox
Nature/Demeanor: Deviant/Visionary
Physical: Strength 2 (4/6/5/3), Dexterity 3 (3/4/5/5), Stamina 4 (6/7/7/6)

Seeks-the-Truth

Social: Charisma 4, Manipulation 1 (0/0/0/0), Appearance 1 (0/0/1/1)

Mental: Perception 4, Intelligence 3, Wits 3

Talents: Alertness 1, Brawl 2, Dodge 2, Primal-Urge 1

Skills: Etiquette 3, Stealth 4, Survival 2

Knowledges: Enigmas 4, Linguistics 2, Medicine 1, Occult 3, Rituals 3

Backgrounds: Fetish 3, Rites 3

Gifts: (1) Balance, Heightened Senses, Scent of the True Form, Truth of Gaia; (2) Call to Duty, Sense the Unnatural, Strength of Purpose; (3) Catfeet

Rank: 3

Rage 4, Gnosis 7, Willpower 7

Rites: (Mystic) Baptism of Fire, Rite of Binding, Rite of Summoning, Rite of Talisman Dedication, Rite of the Fetish, Rite of the Questing Stone

Fetishes: Key to the Umbra, Phoebe's Veil

Image: Wiry and tawny complexioned in Homid form, Seeks-the-Truth is an Asiatic adult of indeterminate age. He is walleyed, which fosters the illusion that he never looks directly at anyone or anything, but he misses nothing. His emotions are muted; for him, raising an eyebrow constitutes an extreme expression. He does not warm easily to others, but anyone who excites his mind can call him a loyal friend.

Roleplaying Notes: Lies, usually revealed to you through the Gift: Truth of Gaia, offend you gravely. Your response is invariably, "It is unso." Because you learned English after mastering Chinese, your syllables are clipped and angular.

History: Seeks-the-Truth earned his name through ardent quests into the Umbra. He was born in a Chinese zoo, from which members of the Tibetan Snow Leopard caern liberated him at age two. His aptitude for the mystical arts manifested early, and his fellow Stargazers had high hopes for him. Alas, Seeks-the-Truth's discomfort around other Garou was also apparent. Even among the mostly ascetic Snow Leopards he was considered remote. His first ventures into the Umbra revealed a world wherein he felt much more at home. He gradually acquainted himself with the spirit world and its denizens in the vicinity of the caern.

Seeks developed a passion for Zen riddles during those moony Umbral days, as he conversed with Chimerlings and Jagglings. The spirits began to call him "He Who Seeks the Truth with Both Halves of His Head." They referred to his relentless pursuit of Truth by whatever paths, whether credible or crazed. There was his short-lived vegetarianism, for example, which ended with his frenzied consumption of a local yak.

The first fetish Seeks-the-Truth crafted for himself was a Key to the Umbra. He fashioned it from the antique key to a strongbox said to contain vials of powerful toxins. After he won the box in a puzzle contest with a Sherpa peddler, he inserted the key into the lock. "What use have you for these poisons?" the Sherpa asked.

"None," said Seeks-the-Truth as he broke off the key in the lock. "Neither, now, has any other." He gave the box to the Snow Leopards, but kept the remnant of the key. Before he departed the caern on an American pilgrimage, he made an earring from the remnant and bound to it a willing spirit to ease his way through the Gauntlet. Now he travels throughout North and South America, comparing philosophies, delving into secrets and hoping to find some elusive, Triat-unifying truth.

Thunder Tiger

Breed: Lupus

Auspice: Ahroun

Nature/Demeanor: Martyr/Bravo

Physical: Strength 4 (6/8/7/5), Dexterity 4 (4/5/6/6), Stamina 3 (5/6/6/5)

Social: Charisma 3, Manipulation 1 (0/0/0/0), Appearance 2 (1/0/2/2)

Mental: Perception 3, Intelligence 2, Wits 5

Talents: Alertness (Ambushes) 4, Athletics 2, Brawl 3, Dodge (Bodyguard) 4, Empathy 3, Expression 1, Intimidation 1, Primal-Urge (Tracking Prey) 4

Skills: Animal Ken 3, Etiquette 1, Firearms 1, Kailindo (Leaping Kick) 4, Leadership 2, Melee 1, Stealth 3, Survival (Jungle) 4

Knowledges: Enigmas 1, Medicine 3, Occult 1

Thunder Tiger

Backgrounds: Familiar Spirit 4 (East Wind; gives +2 Dodge), Pack Totem 2, Past Lives 1

Gifts: (1) Balance, Heightened Senses, Leap of the Kangaroo, Razor Claws; (2) Inner Strength, Sense the Unnatural, Shriek (Bastet Gift); (3) Silver Claws, Whispering Wind

Rank: 3

Rage 7, Gnosis 6, Willpower 8

Rites: None

Fetishes: Tiger-Scar (Level 2, Gnosis 5. A gift from the Bastet Panthesilea, this is a mark of great pride and respect. Thunder Tiger is at -2 to any Social roll difficulty with the Bastet.)

Image: In Lupus form, Thunder Tiger is a gray wolf with yellow eyes. He has a large scarlike marking on his left flank that's in the shape of a leaping tiger. In Homid form, the tiger-scar transforms into a tiger tattoo that marks him as a member of the East Wind school of Kailindo. Thunder Tiger dresses in the battered fatigues worn by the Ghost Raptors.

Roleplaying Notes: You usually grunt replies to all questions. When you do speak intelligibly, you use the fewest words necessary. You constantly watch those around you, even when not on duty.

You are gay. Your lover is the Garou Steps Lightly.

History: The Garou to be known as Thunder Tiger was born in the Pacific Northwest and went through his First Change while alone in the wilderness. His cries of anguish attracted a Theurge Stargazer named Windsinger. Windsinger took the young pup to a mountain hideaway and befriended him. The cub was taught how to wear the Homid shape, and Windsinger began to prepare the young Garou for a destiny that the Stargazer had foreseen in a vision.

Thunder Tiger received his name from his Kailindo tutor. Tiger's natural instincts and fluid motions made him a perfect study for the discipline. He was also noted for channeling his rage and, in his instructor's words, "could concentrate in the now-time of eternal vigilance."

When Windsinger's pack, the Ghost Raptors, decided to join the war in the Amazon, Thunder Tiger requested to join them and was accepted. He rose in rank during the pack's tour of duty and soon became one of the chief bodyguards of White Father, the pack leader.

When the pack first met the Amazon's Bastet, Thunder Tiger quickly bested their champion. His vanquished foe taught him one of her ancient Gift-secrets: the werejaguar's Shriek.

Thunder Tiger is perhaps too devoted in his role as bodyguard to White Father. He does anything to protect the pack leader from harm, even challenging anyone in defense of White Father's honor. Such fanaticism gets Thunder Tiger into trouble, but such loyalty has brought him far in the pack's hierarchy. None among the Ghost Raptors challenges Thunder Tiger, although he rarely asserts his own dominance.

Uktena

Anna "Eyes-of-the-Sun" Pelfrey

Breed: Homid

Auspice: Galliard

Nature/Demeanor: Maker/Traditionalist

Physical: Strength 3 (5/7/6/4), Dexterity 3 (3/4/5/5), Stamina 3 (5/6/6/5)

Social: Charisma 3, Manipulation 3 (2/0/0/0), Appearance 3 (2/0/3/3)

Mental: Perception 4, Intelligence 4, Wits 4

Talents: Alertness 2, Brawl 2, Dodge 2, Empathy 3, Expression 3, Primal-Urge 3, Streetwise 3, Subterfuge 3

Skills: Drive 2, Firearms 3, Performance 2, Repair 2

Knowledges: Area Knowledge (Chicago) 4, Computer 3, Enigmas 3, Spirit Lore 2, Law 5, Linguistics 4, Occult 3, Rituals 3

Backgrounds: Allies 4, Contacts 4, Influence 2, Kinfolk 4, Past Life 4, Pure Breed 2, Resources 2, Retainers 4

Gifts: (1) Beast Speech, Call of the Wyld, Mindspeak, Persuasion, Sense Magic, Shroud; (2) Dreamspeak, Spirit of the Bird; (3) Call Flame Spirit

Rank: 3

Rage 7, Gnosis 7, Willpower 7

Rites: (Punishment) Voice of the Jackal; (Renown) Rite of Accomplishment, Rite of Passage, Rite of Wounding

Fetishes: Boots of the Stag, which grant Speed of Thought and Leap of the Kangaroo Gifts; Sanctuary Chimes

Image: In Homid form, Anna carries herself with a strict business bearing: her hair is pulled back neatly, she affects a need for reading glasses and she wears dresses made after the fashion of men's business suits, to better fit into the human-male-dominated field that she deals in. In Lupus form, she is thin, her ribs apparent under her fine brown fur. Her eyes shine brightly, not pale like the light of the moon.

Roleplaying Notes: You spent most of your life as a human and still have strong ties to humanity. While other Garou condemn mortals for their corrupt ways, you defend your mundane kind. However, the discovery of your animal side has completed your once-aching spirit, and you are quick to defend Garou from human depradations.

History: Anna Pelfrey discovered her Garou heritage only recently, after years of living as a human, but with a sense of lacking. Indeed, she remained out of the fold so long that she acquired a law degree and raised herself to the position of Chicago assistant district attorney. It was through her career that she learned the truth of herself, when prosecuting members of the city's Sept of Jupiter. Investi-gation of strange goings-on led her to the Temple of the Fanum, a local institution known for its academia and esoteric library.

In truth, the Fanum was the caern of the Sept of Jupiter and an institution operated by Chicago's Uktena. Immersed in the very spirit of her buried nature, Anna's true self came forth — literally.

With the teaching and guidance of members of Jupiter, Anna came to accept and embrace her heritage. Though raised a human, she began a new life among the Garou. Anna still practices law, but now largely in defense of Garou subjected to humanity's laws.

Anna is loved and respected by her true kind; no one is more trusted by sept members. However, given her dealings with the mortal world, often on human terms, Garou leaders outside Fanum mistrust her motives. As a warrior against Apocalypse, Anna "Eyes-of-the-Sun" Pelfrey has the potential for great power among Chicago's Garou.

Anna "Eyes-of-the-Sun" Pelfrey

Guides-to-Truth

Breed: Lupus

Auspice: Theurge

Nature/Demeanor: Lone Wolf/Confidant

Physical: Strength 3 (5/7/6/4), Dexterity 3 (3/4/5/5), Stamina 4 (6/7/7/6)

Social: Charisma 3, Manipulation 4 (3/1/1/1), Appearance 3 (2/0/3/3)

Mental: Perception 5, Intelligence 3, Wits 3

Talents: Alertness 5, Brawl 3, Dodge 3, Empathy 3, Primal-Urge 4

Skills: Leadership 4, Stealth 4, Survival 5

Knowledges: Enigmas 3, Occult 4, Rituals 4

Backgrounds: Fetish 4, Kinfolk 2, Pure Breed 4, Rites 4

Gifts: (1) Heightened Senses, Sense Magic, Sense Wyrm, Shroud, Spirit Speech; (2) Command Spirit, Scent of Sight, Sense the Unnatural, Sight from Beyond; (3) Exorcism, Name Spirit, Pulse of the Invisible; (4) Call Elemental, Grasp the Beyond; (5) Elemental Gift, The Malleable Spirit

Rank: 5

Rage 8, Gnosis 10, Willpower 8

Rites: (Caern) The Badger's Burrow, Rite of the Opened Bridge, Rite of the Opened Caern; (Minor) Hunting Prayer, Prayer for the Prey; (Mystic) Baptism of Fire, Rite of Becoming, Rite of Binding, Rite of Spirit

Awakening, Rite of Summoning; (Seasonal) The Great Hunt, Rite of Keres, Rite of Reawakening

Fetishes: Incarna Sigil

Image: In Homid form, Guides-to-Truth is an average-sized Native American man, with reddish-black hair and large black eyes. His Lupus form is a black wolf with strong red hues and dark eyes.

Roleplaying Notes: You are in almost constant contact with the spirits of the Umbra and find it much easier than most to cross into the spirit realm. While others are often disoriented in the Umbra, you're at home. In fact, the spirit realm has grown closer to you than the material world. You enjoy listening to the lessons from and rantings of spirits and use what they tell you to help others realize truths about themselves and the world, whether physical or spiritual. You often mutter under your breath; you're talking to your spirit friends, not yourself.

History: Guides-to-Truth was born in the Badlands of North Dakota, near a Sioux reservation. When food became scarce, his pack traveled close to Bismarck to find scraps to eat. Guides studied the humans in their city and was confused and disgusted by what he witnessed.

His First Change occurred while on one such expedition. His pack was foraging near the city, and Guides stopped to drink from a pool. As he gazed into the water, he saw the moon reflected on the water's surface. Pausing to admire the moon, he sensed his surroundings change. Startled, he found the world that he was accustomed to had changed. Odd creatures stared at him; his pack had vanished.

Guides bristled with fear as the odd creatures advanced toward him. As they did, he instinctively grew larger, stronger. A few of the creatures paused; some even backed away. Guides-to-Truth found himself in a form similar to that of the men he had seen, only taller and prouder. He lashed out at the creatures that dared to remain where they stood, and a brief battle began. He was able to destroy many of the things; the rest fled. As Guides-to-Truth began changing back to natural shape, he felt his surroundings change again. He had returned to the world he knew; his pack stared at him, full of questions that he couldn't answer.

Days later, three men from the nearby Sioux reservation were spotted tracking the pack as it hunted. Two nights after that, three strange wolves seemed to follow the pack. Guides waited for the wolves and sensed their difference from his packmates. The wolves explained that they, like him, were Garou and were there to teach him of his heritage. Guides was reluctant at first, but the three finally convinced him to join them. He was put through his Rite of Passage, taught the ways of the Garou and quickly learned the ways of the Umbra.

The spirit realm and its inhabitants have become a source of fascination for Guides-to-Truth. Few Garou have traveled the Umbra as extensively as Guides-to-Truth. He spends a great deal of time communicating with and learning from spirits. The spirit-knowledge that he has acquired and shared

Guides-to-Truth

with other Garou is not always pleasant or sought after, but always profound.

Jacky Gecko

Breed: Homid

Auspice: Galliard

Nature/Demeanor: Confidant/Maker

Physical: Strength 3 (5/7/6/4), Dexterity 3 (4/5/6/6), Stamina 2 (4/3/5/4)

Social: Charisma 2, Manipulation 3 (2/0/0/0), Appearance 3 (2/0/3/3)

Mental: Perception 2, Intelligence 4, Wits 5

Talents: Alertness 3, Brawl 3, Empathy 3, Primal-Urge 4

Skills: Animal Ken 3, Boomerang 3, Drive 3, Pilot Aircraft 3, Repair 3, Stealth 3, Survival 4

Knowledges: Enigmas 1, Law 3, Linguistics 1, Medicine 4, Occult 1, Rituals 2

Backgrounds: Allies 4, Mentor 3, Resources 1

Gifts: (1) Call of the Wyld, Mother's Touch, Sense Magic, Smell of Man

Rank: 1

Rage 4, Gnosis 2, Willpower 6

Rites: (Mystic) Rite of the Fetish, Rite of the Questing Stone

Fetishes: Yongar's Wings (Level 4, Gnosis 7. This is a throwing boomerang with a spirit servant of Yongar, the kangaroo totem, bound into it. Any kangaroos brought down in a hunt with this weapon are considered to be gifts from Yongar. The boomerang does Str +2 aggravated damage and always returns to its user.)

Image: Jacky is a tall, thin Aboriginal in early manhood. He is always clothed in faded blue jeans and some kind of ripped or intentionally torn T-shirt. In Lupus form he is a sandy-colored dingo with faint, dark-brown markings along his spine. He can stand patient and unmoving for hours on end. Few know that he can actually sleep on his feet.

Roleplaying Notes: You are quiet in social circles, especially among strangers and non-Aboriginals. Though others may assume you aloof or close-chested, you are actually uncertain of your manners. When forced to talk, you resort to clichés, such as calling others "mate" and engaging in empty banter.

History: Born of what he has been told was a Kinfolk mother in the Northern Territory, Jacky has spent his life exposed to the suffering of his Aboriginal people. Determined to improve the lot of his native Australians, Jacky determined from an early age to become a doctor.

Jacky learned of his true nature at an early age and underwent his First Change under the tutelage of Tjinderi

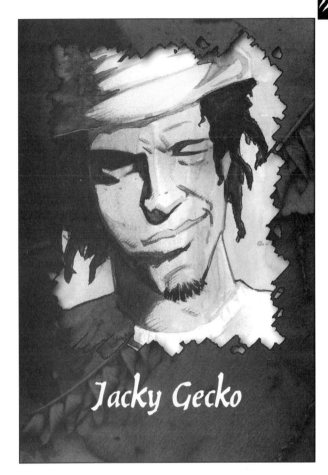

Jacky Gecko

Knowing-Smile, leader of his newfound sept. Little did he know that she was already molding him to become her successor, to pursue her dream of Uktena superiority over other tribes, regardless of Jacky's devotion to his mortal roots. With the support of Tjinderi Knowing-Smile, Jacky was able to complete his education and began work with the Australian Flying Doctors, treating Aboriginals for miles around.

After setting aside enough money to buy his own plane, Jacky found that more than his mortal kind needed his aid. On several ocassions he came to the aid of injured and lost Garou, to the point of learning rites to help find them. Thus did Jacky's altruistic bent broaden — all the while under the suspicious eye of his sept-leader mentor.

Jacky's most recent supplicant, Innana of the Children of Gaia, taught him the Gift: Mother's Touch as thanks for his help. For Tjinderi Knowing-Smile, such extratribal relations are evidence of Jacky's fall from a true path of tribal purity and superiority. It cannot be long before the value differences of mentor and student divide them, especially in the War of the Apocalypse. Surely Jacky will believe that all Garou must fight side by side against the common foe, rather than seek power for themselves or their individual tribes.

Jubatí

Breed: Homid

Auspice: Ragabash

Physical: Strength 2 (4/6/5/3), Dexterity 2 (2/3/4/4), Stamina 3 (5/6/6/5)

Social: Charisma 3, Manipulation 3 (2/0/0/0), Appearance 2 (1/0/2/2)

Mental: Perception 3, Intelligence 4, Wits 4

Talents: Alertness 2, Athletics 3, Brawl 2, Dodge 2, Empathy 3, Primal-Urge 4

Skills: Animal Ken 4, Stealth 3, Survival 5

Knowledges: Enigmas 3, Occult 2, Rituals 2

Backgrounds: Allies 5 (Balam and Mokolé), Mentor 4 (native elder)

Gifts: Blur of the Milky Eye, Shroud, Smell of Man; (2) Alter Scent, Spirit of the Fish

Rank: 2

Rage 3, Gnosis 4, Willpower 5

Merits/Flaws: Phobia (Mild): Heavy Machinery

Rites: (Accord) Rite of Cleansing; (Mystical) Rite of Binding, Rite of Spirit Awakening, Rite of Summoning, Rite of the Questing Stone, Rite of Talisman Dedication

Fetishes: Tsansti's Blowgun (Level 4, Gnosis 7. This 10-foot-long blowgun once belonged to a local Uktena hero. It has some magical abilities associated with it: a

range of 40 yards and a damage pool of 5 dice, used for penetrating armor only. Jubatí has 15 darts and enough curare for them.)

Image: In Homid form, Jubatí is a Native Indian of the Yanomami tribe. He is 4'7" and weighs 100 pounds. His body is painted with many of the war and beauty marks of his tribe. In Lupus, he is a sleek wolf with reddish fur.

Roleplaying Notes: You used to smile a lot, for you were happy. Now the world is dying and you are very sad. Your friends worry about you, warning you to "not let Harano take you." You cannot stop worrying. Let Harano come.

History: Jubatí lived in the first village that Pentex took over when they entered the jungle. He had fled when the machines first came; they scared him like nothing he had ever seen. When he returned and discovered the machines living in his village, he went to visit Atahualpa, his Bastet friend who lived in her realm near the village, and was horrified to discover what she had become. He barely escaped her trap and fled to the Caern of Rain Spirits, where the rest of his Yanomani tribe lived.

Since the outsider Garou have come, he has felt a little better. They worry him with their strange and destructive ways, but they are here to help, aren't they? More than anything, though, he cannot help but dwell on the loss of his home and his Bastet friend. If he is given the chance to save her, he would take it.

Lamurun

Breed: Lupus

Auspice: Philodox

Nature/Demeanor: Visionary/Curmudgeon

Physical: Strength 4 (6/8/7/5), Dexterity 4 (4/5/6/6), Stamina 5 (7/8/8/7)

Social: Charisma 4, Manipulation 2 (1/0/0/0), Appearance 2 (1/0/2/2)

Mental: Perception 4, Intelligence 3, Wits 4

Talents: Alertness 3, Athletics 2, Brawl 3, Dodge 4, Intimidation 3, Primal-Urge 4

Skills: Animal Ken 3, Firearms 2, Leadership 5, Melee 2, Stealth 4, Survival 4

Knowledges: Area Knowledge (Outback) 4, Enigmas 2, Rituals 3

Backgrounds: Contacts 3, Past Life 2, Pure Breed 1

Gifts: (1) Heightened Senses, Leap of the Kangaroo, Sense Magic, Shroud; (2) Sense the Unnatural; (3) Call Flame Spirit, Weak Arm; (4) Gnaw, Roll Over; (5) Song of the Great Beast

Rank: 5

Rage 7, Gnosis 8, Willpower 10

Rites: (Caern) Moot Rite, Rite of the Opened Caern; (Death) Gathering for the Departed; (Mystic) Rite of the Fetish, Rite of the Totem; (Renown) Rite of Passage, Rite of Wounding

Lamurun

rivalries of the Uktena and too little time discovering the meanings of old patterns and mysteries.

Lamurun is especially supportive of bringing to bear any powers or persons that could help the Uktena learn the mysteries of the Bunyip. He spends much time dreaming in his sept, trying to discover the forgotten lore of the lost tribe. When he does leave the sept, it is only because he hopes to find greater understanding in the battles against the Wyrm.

Naomi

Breed: Homid
Auspice: Theurge
Nature/Demeanor: Visionary/Lone Wolf
Physical: Strength 3 (5/7/6/4), Dexterity 4 (4/5/6/6), Stamina 3 (5/6/6/5)
Social: Charisma 2, Manipulation 2 (1/0/0/0), Appearance 4 (3/0/4/4)
Mental: Perception 4, Intelligence 4, Wits 3
Talents: Alertness 4, Athletics 3, Brawl 2, Empathy 4, Primal-Urge 2
Skills: Animal Ken 3, Stealth 2, Survival 4
Knowledges: Enigmas 4, Medicine 3, Occult 3, Rituals 2
Backgrounds: Past Life 3, Pure Breed 4, Totem 1

Fetishes: Fang Dagger, Spirit Whistle, various talens

Image: Lamurun is a large-boned, shaggy, brindled wolf with a gray face and muzzle. Although obviously old, his fur is still full and shines with health. In Homid form, he is a medium-built Aborigine with startling green eyes and gray hair; his body is just beginning to show the infirmities of old age. His face has been aged into great craggy paths by the burning rays of the Australian sun.

Roleplaying Notes: Shake your head and smile ironically at the foolishness that so often goes on around you. You spend much of your time in dreaming and are adept at interpreting symbols. Watch the body language of others and treat all with dignity until they prove themselves unworthy (as most soon do). You seldom speak, but when you do, it is because the words are so weighty you can no longer hold them back.

History: Lamurun grew up in far north Australia with a group of dingoes. Being different both physically and mentally, he had a difficult time before he discovered his true heritage. However, once he was initiated into his sept, Lamurun began to turn his unique understanding of patterns and symbols to the world around him, even venturing into human establishments. A great traveler, Lamurun has spent countless years exploring the continent. Since becoming his sept's Warder, Lamurun has been forced to spend too much time, for his taste, mediating the internal

Naomi

Gifts: (1) Mother's Touch, Persuasion, Sense Magic, Spirit Speech; (2) Command Spirit, Sight from Beyond, Staredown; (3) Call Flame Spirit, Exorcism

Rank: 3

Rage 6, Gnosis 8, Willpower 6

Rites: (Accord) Cleansing; (Mystic) Binding, Spirit Awakening, Summoning

Fetishes: Spirit Tracer, Moonglow

Image: Naomi is a beautiful, raven-haired Native American. Her eyes are pale brown and peer out from behind the wispy strands of hair that frame her face. She is tall, standing almost six feet, with a model's build.

Roleplaying Notes: You are shy and contemplative, yet resolved. You know what your goal is and accept sacrifices in its pursuit. You have developed a strong mistrust of humankind and prefer the company of spirits and other Umbral travelers to all else.

History: Adopted daughter of Looks-beyond-Trees, Naomi seemed destined to follow in her father's footsteps and lead her sept. She spent most of her adolescence and early adulthood preparing to take his place. When the time came, Looks-beyond-Trees underwent the Rite of the Winter Wolf.

In the days that followed, another Uktena came forward to claim leadership of the sept. Naomi, prepared to defend her rightful role, accepted his challenge. The fight was cut short, however, as Naomi found herself whisked into the Umbra. Before she was fully aware of what had happened, she was facing an Incarna of the mighty Uktena. It spoke to her of a greater goal, a larger responsibility than leading her sept. Now Naomi travels the Umbra, aiding other packs of Garou in accordance with the mighty Uktena's wishes.

Naomi serves the Uktena totem with honor. However, the pain of her lost station weighs heavily on her. She has vowed to stay out of Garou politics until she restores her honor in the eyes of her old sept members.

Running Creek

Breed: Homid

Auspice: Ahroun

Nature/Demeanor: Reluctant Garou/Director

Physical: Strength 3 (5/7/6/4), Dexterity 3 (3/4/5/5), Stamina 4 (6/7/7/6)

Social: Charisma 2, Manipulation 2 (1/0/0/0), Appearance 3 (2/0/3/3)

Mental: Perception 3, Intelligence 3, Wits 2

Talents: Alertness 3, Athletics 4, Brawl 2, Dodge 2, Empathy 1, Streetwise 1

Skills: Animal Ken 2, Drive 2, Firearms 2, Melee 4, Stealth 2

Knowledges: Investigation 1, Linguistics 1, Medicine 2, Rituals 1

Backgrounds: Allies 1, Fetish 2, Mentor 2, Rites 1

Running Creek

Gifts: (1) The Falling Touch, Mother's Touch, Shroud, Smell of Man; (2) Spirit of the Bird, Spirit of the Fish

Rank: 2

Rage 3, Gnosis 1, Willpower 6

Rites: (Mystic) Rite of Talisman Dedication

Fetishes: None

Image: In Lupus form Running Creek is a sleek, chocolate-brown wolf. When Homid, which she often is, she favors oddly archaic tunics in combination with Spandex tights. Only hints of Running Creek's native Brazilian accent survive her extensive schooling abroad.

Roleplaying Notes: You've learned from your fellow Uktena how privilege for the few creates want for the many. You're always ready to mount a soapbox and denounce the evils of capitalism, so speechify. Deep down, however, you are still a hurt child yanked away from all you knew and loved. Your new politics help you ignore that ache, but they don't cure it.

History: The girl who would become known as Running Creek was the perfect daughter of perfect parents, and she lived a perfect life. Then she was kidnapped and changed.

When no one came to claim the ransom, her parents thought they'd followed the instructions incorrectly. The kidnappers, however, were in no condition to claim anything. A week passed. Her parents spent a tiny fraction of their fortune to hire an army of detectives, who located only the shredded remains of three Cali Cartel graduates. No trace of the girl was found — because no one was looking for a wolf.

Running Creek wandered in Lupus form for weeks, subsisting on rodents and the like. One morning she awakened on a sand dune and heard the roar of the sea. She remembered everything. She was naked, stripped of her fine clothes, her privilege and her perfect life. She was a monster. She was alone. There the Garou found her.

They dubbed her Running Creek because she could move across the ground like a rush of water. She accepted the name to mark her new life. Before her first transformation she was training assiduously for the Olympiad. Now

she applied herself equally to the challenge of becoming an Uktena spy. Her duty was to make certain the tribe's myriad secrets remained secret.

She once — and only once — used her new abilities to observe her parents. Unseen, she watched her mother sit for hours on end before a shrine commemorating a lost and only child. Her father, she concluded, now occupied the guest house and communicated with his wife only through servants. Running Creek promised herself never to spy on her kin again.

Currently, Running Creek submerges herself in her work. Alert to the arcane and numb to her past, she travels among the Garou and polices the unknowable.

Wendigo

Rites: (Caern) Rite of the Opened Caern; (Mystic) Rite of the Fetish, Rite of the Totem
Fetishes: Fang Dagger

Image: In Homid form, Blood-on-the-Wind is a tall, dark-haired man with pale features. In Lupus form, he is stark white with gray stripes running from his ears to his tail.

Roleplaying Notes: You are calm and collected, always ready and always cautious. The enemy comes in many forms and surrounds you on all sides. Stupidity rules the foolish who would rather fight than think, and you will not be part of it. Other Garou must be taught their errors. Nature will prevail, and when it does, so will Gaia.

History: Blood-on-the-Wind became the leader of the Sept of the Siberian Wilds several years ago when he challenged and beat the former leader. He has brought a new vigor to Russia's Wendigo, but it is a vigor entrenched in maintaining the tribe's isolation from the rest of the world.

Isolated as he is, Blood-on-the-Wind has felt little of the dire influence that the newly risen vampire Baba Yaga has had on Russia. That is certainly beneficial for his people, for it makes them a force that could confront the Hag when ready. However, that same isolation may doom Blood-on-the-Wind and his tribe, for Baba Yaga is more likely to discover Blood's existence before he discovers hers. Then again, if the Hag were allowed to reign and the Wendigo went even further afield in their isolation, Blood-on-the-Wind might find the safety that he seeks for his kind. Mortals and rival Garou would pose no further threat, and all attention could be brought to bear on watching for one enemy: the Wyrm. As far as Blood-on-the-Wind is concerned, the wise bide their time.

Blood-on-the-Wind

Blood-on-the-Wind

Breed: Lupus
Auspice: Galliard
Nature/Demeanor: Survivor/Director
Physical: Strength 4 (6/8/7/5), Dexterity 4 (4/5/6/6), Stamina 5 (7/8/8/8)
Social: Charisma 2, Manipulation 3 (2/0/0/0), Appearance 3 (2/0/2/2)
Mental: Perception 5, Intelligence 3, Wits 4
Talents: Alertness 3, Athletics 4, Brawl 5, Dodge 3, Intimidation 4, Primal-Urge 4, Subterfuge 4
Skills: Animal Ken 2, Melee 4, Survival 3
Knowledges: Rituals 4
Backgrounds: Familiar Spirit 4, Past Life 4
Gifts: (1) Call of the Wyld, Camouflage, Leap of the Kangaroo, Sense Prey; (2) Curse of Aeolus, Dreamspeak, Eye of Eagle, Sense the Unnatural; (3) Catfeet, Chill of Early Frost; (4) Attunement, Bridge Walker; (5) Song of the Great Beast
Rank: 5
Rage 7, Gnosis 8, Willpower 7

Charging Bull

Breed: Homid
Auspice: Ragabash
Nature/Demeanor: Caregiver/Gallant
Physical: Strength 3 (5/7/6/4), Dexterity 4 (4/5/6/6), Stamina 3 (5/6/6/5)
Social: Charisma 3, Manipulation 2 (1/0/0/0), Appearance 2 (1/0/1/1)
Mental: Perception 3, Intelligence 3, Wits 4
Talents: Alertness 3, Athletics 2, Brawl 3, Dodge 4, Primal-Urge 3
Skills: Animal Ken 3, Etiquette 1, Melee 4, Performance 1, Stealth 5, Survival 2
Knowledges: Enigmas 2, Linguistics 2, Medicine 2, Rituals 3, Science 1
Backgrounds: Kinfolk 4, Resources 1

Charging Bull

Gifts: (1) Blur of the Milky Eye, Camouflage, Persuasion, Scent of Running Water; (2) Blissful Ignorance, Cutting Wind, Jam Technology, Sense of the Prey, Staredown, Taking the Forgotten; (3) Chill of Early Frost, Gremlins, Sky Running; (4) Luna's Blessing, Spirit Ward, Whelp Body

Rank: 4

Rage 6, Gnosis 6, Willpower 7

Rites: (Mystic) Rite of Binding, Rite of the Questing Stone, Rite of Talisman Dedication, Rite of Spirit Awakening, Rite of Summoning, Rite of the Fetish

Fetishes: Fang Dagger, Phoebe's Veil

Image: In his Homid form, Charging Bull is a sun-baked Lakota-Sioux in his early 50s. He is usually clad in worn old work clothes, though for ceremonial purposes and in action he will don traditional war garments. In his Crinos form, he is a weathered yet handsome figure of a werewolf, strong and elegant, radiating a warrior's pride.

Roleplaying Notes: You are a wily old trickster, alert for opportunities to pester those around you, though always in a playful, good-natured way. You do this with a great degree of style, however; the in-your-face pranks of a young Ragabash are far behind you. Often, all it takes is a sly statement to help someone look foolish and protect their ego from harmful expansion. Beyond the fun of life, you care deeply for your people and All Your Relations in Wakan Tanka's (Gaia's) world and have made a name for yourself as a dedicated warrior in their cause.

History: Raised in a small Kinfolk community in South Dakota, Charging Bull was the youngest of 12 children and the only one of the bunch born Garou. He established a reputation well before his First Change of being an utter brat, always into things, teasing his playmates and stealing items from his elders. In his eyes, this was all keeping with the tradition of counting coup, a tradition he fell in love with. In his eyes, it worked quite well to justify his Ragabash ways.

It was during a Black Spiral Dancer attack on his village that Charging Bull gained his name. The elder warriors were away for a Grand Concolation, and the Dancers had a group of Kinfolk cornered in a cave; the Kinfolk were barely holding the corrupt werewolves back with a small store of silver bullets and a couple of rifles. Then a rumble like thunder filled the night, and the ground quaked, a huge herd of buffalo stampeded into the Black Spiral Dancers. The Dancers had nowhere to go and disappeared beneath the herd's hooves. On the back of one of the bulls rode young Charging Bull, whooping and yipping crazily in Crinos form. In the wake of the stampede, the Kinfolk simply walked among the crushed Dancers and shot each in the head with a round of silver. Charging Bull was a hero.

In the years since, he has become known for his playful wisdom and warmth, and he has continued the practice of counting coup. His reputation is so strong among the Wendigo that he often gets credit for things lost, such as one sock from the laundry or a mislaid $10 bill, and the soft caress of a stray breeze is likened to his touch.

Evan Heals-the-Past

Breed: Homid

Auspice: Philodox

Nature/Demeanor: Visionary/Judge

Physical: Strength 2 (4/6/5/3), Dexterity 3 (3/4/5/5), Stamina 3 (5/6/6/7)

Social: Charisma 3, Manipulation 3 (2/0/0/0), Appearance 3 (2/0/3/3)

Mental: Perception 3, Intelligence 3, Wits 4

Talents: Alertness 2, Brawl 2, Dodge 2, Empathy 3, Expression 3, Primal-Urge 3

Skills: Etiquette 1, Leadership 3, Stealth 2, Survival 1

Knowledges: Computer 1, Enigmas 2, Medicine 3, Occult 2, Politics 1, Rituals 2

Backgrounds: Past Life 4, Pure Breed 2

Gifts: (1) Call the Breeze, Persuasion, Truth of Gaia; (2) Cutting Wind, Strength of Purpose

Rank: 2

Rage 4, Gnosis 6, Willpower 7

Rites: (Accord) Rite of Cleansing, Rite of Contrition; (Mystic) Rite of the Questing Stone

The Dancers killed Evan's parents and tried to kidnap him. Two things stopped them — the intervention of the disgraced Silver Fang Lord Albrecht and Evan's first conscious Change. Albrecht spirited him away afterward, enlisting the help of Mari Cabrah, and the three ran a merry chase across several continents. Evan's education was quick and dirty, but productive.

At the climax of their quest, Evan entered the Umbra, where he watched the long-ago massacre of a Wendigo clan at the hands of invading Garou. He then learned from Great Wendigo that it was his task to heal these wounds and bring the Garou together. It was an incredible responsibility for one cub, but Evan accepted. With the help of his packmates, Evan hopes to unite Gaia's defenders so that the War of the Apocalypse can be won.

Eyes-of-Frost

Breed: Homid
Auspice: Theurge
Nature/Demeanor: Lone Wolf/Maker
Physical: Strength 2 (4/6/5/3), Dexterity 3 (3/4/5/5), Stamina 2 (4/5/5/4)
Social: Charisma 4, Manipulation 2 (1/0/0/0), Appearance 2 (1/0/2/2)
Mental: Perception 4, Intelligence 3, Wits 3
Talents: Alertness 2, Dodge 2, Empathy 1, Expression 1
Skills: Drive 2, Firearms 1, Leadership 3, Melee 2, Survival 1
Knowledges: Enigmas 3, Investigation 2, Linguistics 2, Medicine 3, Occult 3
Backgrounds: Kinfolk 2, Mentor 1, Past Life 5
Gifts: (1) Camouflage, Persuasion, Spirit Speech
Rank: 1
Rage 2, Gnosis 3, Willpower 4
Rites: None
Fetishes: None

Image: Old before his years, Eyes-of-Frost carries himself with dignity and pride. In Homid form he stands only 5'8" tall and has a slim, agile build. His most noticeable feature is his eyes, which are cold steel-blue.

Roleplaying Notes: You have seen much in your few years among the Garou, and your experiences have left you distant from and distrustful of your brethren. Having only recently completed your Rite of Passage, you are still too new to be fully accepted into Garou society; you are an afterthought for your pack. You prefer to be alone rather than suffer the abuses of your condescending, ignorant packmates.

History: Eyes-of-Frost is still very new to Garou society. He passed his Rite of Passage with great bravery and honor, much to the satisfaction of his elders. Although recently thrust into a new world, Eyes-of-Frost has quickly taken to being Garou. It's almost as if he's done it all before — and he has.

Evan Heals-the-Past

Fetishes: Storm Spear (Level 5, Gnosis 6. This spear was given to Evan by Wendigo himself. By spending two Gnosis points and activating the fetish, Evan can call down a lightning bolt to strike his enemies. He must roll Dexterity + Occult to hit; the lightning inflicts 10 dice of normal damage.)

Image: Evan is a slender, unimpressive 14-year-old kid. Although Wendigo, he doesn't look even remotely Native American. He tends to dress practically rather than keeping up with fashion. His Crinos form is almost noble, and his eyes glitter with quiet insight in all his forms.

Roleplaying Notes: Nothing disgusts you more than Garou fighting among themselves. That sort of thing gets all the wrong people killed, opening a hole for the Wyrm. You're very loyal to your packmates, and don't complain when the going gets a little rough. People tend to underestimate you when they see you next to Albrecht and Mari — that's fine by you. If they aren't threatened by you, maybe they'll listen when you talk some sense into them.

History: Evan grew up a normal kid in most respects. His father was a heavy disciplinarian, however, and grew increasingly hostile as Evan became a teenager. When Evan started having strange dreams and waking up in the town park, his father took his behavior as proof that Evan had joined a gang. After a particularly vivid night, Evan came home and was confronted by his father. In midharangue, Black Spirals came calling.

Eyes-of-Frost

Mental: Perception 2, Intelligence 2, Wits 2
Talents: Alertness 3, Athletics 3, Brawl 3, Expression 1, Intimidation 3, Streetwise 2
Skills: Drive 1, Leadership 2, Melee 1, Repair 1, Stealth 2, Survival 2
Knowledges: Computer 1, Linguistics 1, Medicine 3
Backgrounds: Allies 1, Kinfolk 2, Pure Breed 2
Gifts: (1) Camouflage, Inspiration, Smell of Man; (2) Sense Silver
Rank: 2
Rage 4, Gnosis 2, Willpower 4
Rites: None
Fetishes: None

Image: Allison is a tall, pretty woman of American Indian and Italian descent. Her hair falls like a thick mane around her face and is a rich amber hue. She has the build of an athlete and the look and moves of a predatory animal.

Roleplaying Notes: You always look your prey in the eyes and rarely lose a staredown. You try to remain calm, cold and calculating, although your Rage often gets the better of you in the heat of battle. You and your twin brother, Thomas, are very active against the Wyrm. You would die to protect him.

Eyes-of-Frost is the reincarnation of a great Wendigo Theurge from the time of the Impergium. Eyes-of-Frost can unwittingly contact his ancestor from time to time, gaining great power. When connected to his ancestor he can banish powerful totems. However, the effort leaves him weakened, without Gnosis and unable to use his Gifts until recovered.

Eyes-of-Frost doesn't truly realize his connection to the ancient spirit. His remarkable talents have not gone unnoticed by his elders, though, who watch him from afar. In time, the War will forge Eyes-of-Frost into the very image of his ancestor. When that time comes, Eyes-of-Frost will assume his rightful role as leader of his people.

The Kachina Twins

Allison Kachina

Breed: Homid
Auspice: Ahroun
Nature/Demeanor: Predator/Survivor
Physical: Strength 3 (5/7/6/4), Dexterity 4 (4/5/6/6), Stamina 3 (5/6/6/5)
Social: Charisma 2, Manipulation 3 (2/0/0/0), Appearance 3 (2/0/3/3)

Allison Kachina

Thomas Kachina

Breed: Homid

Auspice: Ahroun

Nature/Demeanor: Gallant/Reveler

Physical: Strength 4 (6/8/7/5), Dexterity 2 (2/3/4/4), Stamina 4 (6/7/7/6)

Social: Charisma 3, Manipulation 2 (1/0/0/0), Appearance 3 (2/0/3/3)

Mental: Perception 2, Intelligence 2, Wits 2

Talents: Alertness 1, Athletics 3, Brawl 3, Empathy 2, Expression 2, Intimidation 2, Streetwise 1

Skills: Drive 1, Firearms 1, Leadership 2, Melee 2, Performance 1, Repair 1, Stealth 2, Survival 1

Knowledges: Investigation 2, Occult 2, Politics 1

Backgrounds: Allies 1, Kinfolk 2, Pure Breed 2

Gifts: (1) Call the Breeze, Inspiration, Razor Claws; (2) Curse of Aeolus

Rank: 2

Rage 5, Gnosis 2, Willpower 4

Rites: None

Fetishes: None

Image: A large man with dark piercing eyes, Thomas looks unkempt nearly all the time. He wears a tribal vest and deerskin pants. He has many tattoos and tribal brands on his body.

Thomas Kachina

Roleplaying Notes: You are carefree, happy and adventurous. You live life to the fullest and never look back. You often work with your sister, Allison, but don't always approve of her methods. In spite of this, you're very protective of her and would sacrifice your life for hers.

History: The Kachina twins were born in the middle of a desert thunderstorm under a full moon, and their lives have been just as dramatic ever since. On the night of their births, their parents were murdered by a Pentex First Team, and their tribe laid to waste. Allison and Thomas were spirited away by a Gaffling of the great Wendigo. They were left in the care of an unsuspecting couple who owned a farm in Montana.

The humans raised the twins as their own, but always knew something was special about the children, who had a temperament that bordered on the bestial. One day the truth was revealed. After three weeks of being bullied by a young Duncan MacGregor, Allison snapped in her gym class. Allison grabbed the bully by the throat and shifted to Glabro form, hoisting him off of the ground. A moment later she was in Crinos form and beating poor Duncan with his own arm — which she had torn off. The class was hysterical. Only Thomas kept his composure. He felt the rage rise within him and felt his body grow and change. He beat Allison away from Duncan, and the twins ran off into the countryside.

It didn't take long for members of the White Eagle sept to find the two cubs.

Allison and Thomas underwent their Rites of Passage nearly three years ago and have been inseparable ever since. Each has an intuitive knowledge of when the other is in danger. This bond, combined with their formidable fighting skills, makes the twins a powerful force in the War of the Apocalypse.

Wahya-Ohni

Breed: Lupus

Auspice: Ahroun

Nature/Demeanor: Lone Wolf/Alpha

Physical: Strength 3 (5/7/6/4), Dexterity 3 (3/4/5/5), Stamina 5 (5/8/8/7)

Social: Charisma 3, Manipulation 1 (0/0/0/0), Appearance 2 (1/0/2/2)

Mental: Perception 2, Intelligence 2, Wits 4

Talents: Alertness 3, Athletics 1, Brawl 4, Dodge 1, Primal-Urge 3, Streetwise 3

Skills: Animal Ken 2, Leadership 2, Stealth 2, Survival 3

Knowledges: Enigmas 2, Linguistics 1, Occult 2

Backgrounds: Allies 2, Fetish 4

Gifts: (1) Camouflage, Heightened Senses, Razor Claws; (2) Spirit of the Fray, True Fear; (3) Combat Healing

Rank: 3

Rage 6, Gnosis 5, Willpower 4

Rites: None

Fetishes: War Paint of Wahya-Ohni (Level 4, Gnosis 5. The Garou regenerates at twice the normal speed, healing aggravated damage at the rate of one Health Level for every 12 hours' rest. The difficulty of healing in combat is reduced by one.)

Image: Wahya-Ohni's Lupus form is a large, gray-brown wolf with haunting yellow eyes. In Crinos form, his fur lightens in color and turns red. When he does switch to Homid form (which is rare), he stands approximately 5'10" tall and weighs around 210 pounds — all muscle. He is Native American and forgoes clothing or (if convention requires) dresses in simple tribal clothes.

Roleplaying Notes: You are seen by many as a leader, although you want to stand and fight alone. You are quite capable of leading other Garou, but seek to avoid the responsibility that comes with the role. You say little, believing that actions speak louder than words.

History: As a young cub, new to Garou society, Wahya-Ohni was called Dreams-Far. Immediately following his Rite of Passage, he embarked on a long Umbral Quest. He was away from his tribe and pack for nearly eight years. In that time he learned many secrets and gained many spirit allies.

In one of his more prominent adventures he freed a group of Lunes from captivity in Malfeas. While escaping, Dreams-Far fought a deadly battle against two Black Spiral Dancers who sought to block his escape. Although victorious, Dreams-Far was mortally wounded. Grateful for his sacrifice, two Lunes pledged themselves to him. One bound itself to Dreams' very fur, doubling his healing time as long as he remained in the Umbra. The other fashioned itself into richly colored paints, to be used as war dressing.

Tales of Dreams' adventures in Malfeas eventually reached his sept. While Dreams-Far lay in hiding, recovering from his wounds, his sept gave him up for dead. They renamed him Wahya-Ohni, or Lost Wolf, in tribute to his actions and passing.

When Dreams-Far/Wahya-Ohni finally returned, there was a Grand Moot called to honor his return. He told many of his tales and spoke with pride and reverence about the sacrifices the Lunes had made. He announced that he would keep his new name and return to the Umbra. He promised to come back and aid his sept in times of dire need, but that his first responsibility was to Luna and her honorable Lunes.

Wahya-Ohni

Bastet

Black Claw

Tribe: Balam
Breed: Feline
Physical: Strength 5 (6/8/7/6), Dexterity 4 (5/7/7/7), Stamina 4 (6/7/7/6)
Social: Charisma 3, Manipulation 2 (1/0/0/0), Appearance 2 (1/0/2/2)
Mental: Perception 4, Intelligence 5, Wits 4
Talents: Alertness 5, Athletics 4, Brawl 5, Dodge 5, Intimidation 5, Primal-Urge 3
Skills: Animal Ken 3, Stealth 4, Survival 3
Knowledges: Area Knowledge 4, Enigmas 2, Rituals 3
Backgrounds: Allies 4, Den-Realm 3 (27 square miles, Gauntlet 8), Kinfolk (Yanomami Natives) 2, Pride (Jaguars) 5
Gifts: (1) Heightened Senses, Razor Claws, Sense Wyrm; (2) Eyes of the Cat, Eerie Eyes, Shriek; (3) Call the Pride, Trackless Waste; (4) Attunement, Walking between Worlds; (5) Song of the Great Beast (Black Claw can summon a *Hoplophoneus* — a saber-tooth tiger. This creature is huge and vicious; stats are left to the Storyteller.)
Rank: 5

Rage 8, Gnosis 3, Willpower 7

Rites: (Accord) Rite of Fealty; (Caern) Badger's Burrow, Taghairm Rite
Fetishes: Skin of the Toad (Level 4, Gnosis 5. This is the shed skin of a giant poisonous toad. Black Claw pulls it from his pouch, wraps it about his hand over a grass glove, and then rakes his foe with his other claw. After he opens a wound, he touches this glove to it, thus introducing the poison into his foe's body. The victim must make a Stamina roll against a difficulty of 8 or lose three Health Levels per touch).

Image: Black Claw is very large and muscular in all forms from human to jaguar. His Homid form appears to be a Yanomami, and he also wears the garb of this tribe.

Roleplaying Notes: You are exceptionally stern. Unlike your fellows, you don't like to play with the others often. With your anger, you'd tear them to pieces. No, you must reserve your rage for the invaders, both Pentex and Garou. You refuse to speak to any werewolves except a native Garou or an acknowledged pack leader.

History: Black Claw has always been respected. He stood up against the humans long ago, when the rest of the Balam thought there was little to fear from the apes. Now the War for the Amazon is worse than ever, and he has grown bitter from the losses in battle. The Balam's over-confidence is affecting their strategy — if they don't learn quickly, they might never win. Those Balam who have sworn obediance to him through the Rite of Fealty must follow his orders explicitly or they will be thrown from his realm.

He is enraged at Golgol Fangs-First's arrogance and imperialism. He loathes the idea that any Garou, no matter how strong, has the audacity to assume that they are the only ones capable of winning this war. If it were not for Golgol, in fact, the Garou might have allied with Black Claw long ago. Now they suffer Black Claw's raids, for he will not rest until all outsiders are forced from the jungle.

Those Garou who know of Black Claw's existence dislike his single-mindedness, but many seek to enlist his aid. If peace can be struck between the Garou and the native Balam, Gaia has a fighting chance. If Black Claw can gather in the Mokolé as well, the alliance will be unprecedented. Alas, the ancient hatreds between the Changing Breed make such an alliance nothing more than a Children of Gaia pipe dream... for now....

Black Claw

Frenar

Breed: Feline

Tribe: Balam

Nature/Demeanor: Show-Off/Cub

Physical: Strength 3 (4/6/5/4), Dexterity 4 (5/7/7/7), Stamina 3 (5/6/6/5)

Social: Charisma 2, Manipulation 1 (0/0/0/0), Appearance 3 (2/0/3/3)

Mental: Perception 3, Intelligence 3, Wits 2

Talents: Alertness 3, Athletics 2, Brawl 3, Dodge 2, Primal-Urge 3

Skills: Stealth 3, Survival 4, Swimming 2

Knowledges: Enigmas 3, Occult 2

Backgrounds: Kinfolk 2, Mentor 3

Gifts: (1) Beastmind, Lick Wounds, Razor Claws

Rank: 1

Rage 4, Gnosis 6, Willpower 5

Rites: None

Fetishes: None

Image: In his feline form, Frenar is a sleek jaguar. His human form is that of a long-haired native South American, but one without tribal markings. He has a taste for unusual clothing.

Roleplaying Notes: You are young, impressionable and eager to please. In your vanity and insecurity, you feel that you have something to prove. You often rush into battle before the rest of your companions, so that you can affirm your role in Gaia's plan.

History: Frenar was born in the jungles of the Amazon River Valley and, as is the case with many Bastet, was raised by Kinfolk before being taught the ways of his race. During his youth, he became fascinated with humans and studied villagers who lived along the river, as well as the occasional stranger who traveled upriver from unknown lands. Indeed, Frenar still sits and watches the ebb and flow of humanity, but since the War of the Apocalypse has come to his home, his observation is now dedicated to gathering information rather than satisfying curiosity.

Frenar's vanity and fascination with humans has led to the development of habits that amuse other Bastet. When in Crinos, Glabro and Homid forms, Frenar enjoys wearing a large black jacket that he found, and he smokes. He believes these manners heighten his allure and allow him to pass among humans unnoticed.

Frenar is frustrated by the Garou who have come uninvited to the Amazon to fight a war that he believes is not theirs. From time to time he has stood beside Garou packs not only to fight the Wyrm but also to keep an eye on the invaders. He looks forward to an end to the War, anticipating the departure of the Garou. In the meantime, he uses the War to gain a name for himself and prove that he is a warrior worthy of Gaia.

Frenar

Markhat

Breed: Feline

Tribe: Balam

Nature/Demeanor: Survivor/Predator

Physical: Strength 4 (5/7/6/5), Dexterity 5 (6/8/8/8), Stamina 5 (7/8/8/7)

Social: Charisma 3, Manipulation 3 (2/0/0/0), Appearance 4 (3/0/4/4)

Mental: Perception 5, Intelligence 3, Wits 5

Talents: Alertness 4, Athletics 5, Brawl 4, Dodge 4, Intimidation 4, Primal-Urge 5

Skills: Animal Ken 4, Firearms 2, Melee 4, Leadership 3, Stealth 5, Survival 5

Knowledges: Enigmas 3, Medicine 2, Rituals 1

Backgrounds: Den-Realm 3, Kinfolk 2

Gifts: (1) Blur of the Milky Eye, Cat Feet, Lick Wounds, Razor Claws, Sense Wyrm; (2) Eerie Eyes, Eyes of the Cat, Sense of the Prey, Shriek; (3) Cat Fear, Purr; (4) Attunement, Spirit Claws, Walking between Worlds

Rank: 4

Rage 8, Gnosis 7, Willpower 9

Rites: (Bastet) Rite of Claiming

Fetishes: Klaive

Markhat

Image: In his Feline form, Markhat is a preternaturally large, frightening jaguar. In Crinos, he is a towering werecat, all wiry muscle with many battle scars. He usually adorns himself with feathers and skins.

Roleplaying Notes: You are fierce and strong and do not take orders well. Your love of the forests that are your home is exceeded only by your bitter anger toward those who would defile them. Snarl menacingly to those who stand in the way of your protection of these forests, even if they be your allies. Revel in carnality, even in the sensory flow of battle. Life is sweet.

History: Markhat's world has always been the rich rainforest of the Amazon basin, and it is a world he has never left. Though he has heard many tales of the lands and cities beyond that world, he has never felt even mild curiosity about them, much less any desire to see them. He feels that those who dwell in those other places are no longer in touch with the sacredness of the wilds, as he himself is, and he counts the Garou as pretenders to a natural hegemony they actually lost long ago.

Though he is extremely iconoclastic even for a Bastet, Markhat has always been smart enough to see when coop-

eration is necessary and thus has been counted as an ally to the Uktena and Black Furies of the Amazon for years. For the most part, however, his activity has been that of lone operative, a stealthy killer in the jungle, striking from the shadows and leaving his enemies torn to shreds behind him. Unfortunately, he counts the Get of Fenris, Shadow Lords, and the Silver Fangs as enemies and has secretly slain many warriors of these tribes, thus weakening the anti-Wyrm forces protecting his homelands, even as he himself struggles against the true defilers. Publicly, he is never to be seen when members of these tribes are present.

Svajda

Breed: Homid
Tribe: Balam
Nature/Demeanor: Autist/Show-Off
Physical: Strength 3 (4/6/5/4), Dexterity 3 (4/6/6/6), Stamina 2 (4/5/5/4)
Social: Charisma 4, Manipulation 4 (3/1/1/1), Appearance 5 (4/0/5/5)
Mental: Perception 2, Intelligence 2, Wits 3
Talents: Alertness 3, Brawl 3, Dodge 1, Intimidation 2, Subterfuge 3
Skills: Animal Ken 3, Drive 2, Escapology 2, Firearms 2, Melee 3, Leadership 1, Stealth 3
Knowledges: Computer 1, Law 1, Linguistics (English) 1, Occult 2, Politics 1
Backgrounds: Fetish 3, Pure Breed 2
Gifts: (1) Lick Wounds, Razor Claws; (2) Eerie Eyes, Night Terror; (3) Purr
Rank: 3
Rage 5, Gnosis 4, Willpower 4
Rites: (Mystic) Rite of Talisman Dedication
Fetishes: Bastet Klaive

Image: Svajda is one of the most beautiful women that most people have ever seen. In any of her forms, her body is curvaceous and lithe, and she carries herself with such grace that those looking at her often have to do a double-take. Her coat in her feline and Crinos forms is a shiny honey brown, as is her hair in her Homid form.

Roleplaying Notes: Make them understand the importance of Gaia. Beat it into their heads if you have to; take off their heads if they won't listen. On a personal level, never let anyone know you, because no matter who they are, they will let you down. It is better to stay in a bad situation than to acknowledge your weakness to someone else.

History: A native of the Amazon jungle, Svajda has long been jealously xenophobic of visitors to her natural home. The encroachment of the evil corporation Pentex

Svajda

has been a constant thorn in her side, and the Garou that followed them have only made matters worse. Now she and the other Balam are faced with a war waged on two separate fronts, fought on their native soil by invaders and foreigners. She has teamed up with Garou in the past, but such alliances are temporary at best and only serve to weaken their common enemy. She knows the effect that her beauty has on people and will not hesitate to use it to her advantage, either against the werewolves or the corporate poisoners.

A creature of savage fury, Svajda is actually thankful to some degree that these invaders make such convenient scapegoats while giving her an opportunity to vent her Rage, though she will be glad when they are gone. She has recently begun communication with a third entity in the conflict, a group of werewolves known as the Ghost Raptors. Though they are members of the Garou and she still feels the wounds of the War of Rage, they seem to operate independently of the other Garou and sometimes even to cross-purposes. She respects them for their fierce individuality and their devotion to the cause, though her racial prejudice prohibits her from ever considering working with them as allies for any length of time.

Corax

Petrov Tzarovitch

Breed: Homid

Nature/Demeanor: Visionary/Jester

Physical: Strength 3 (4/2), Dexterity 4 (5/5), Stamina 3 (4/3)

Social: Charisma 3, Manipulation 3 (1/0), Appearance 3 (0/3)

Mental: Perception 4 (7/8), Intelligence 3, Wits 5

Talents: Alertness 2, Dodge 3, Brawl 2, Expression 2, Primal-Urge 3, Subterfuge 3

Skills: Drive 1, Meditation 1, Performance 3, Piloting 1, Stealth 3

Knowledges: Art 2, Enigmas 3, Investigation 2, Occult 4, Rituals 3

Backgrounds: Kinfolk 1, Rites 3

Gifts: (1) Voice of the Mimic, Enemy Ways; (2) Omens and Signs; (3) Dark Truths, Hear the Corpse Whisper

Rank: 4

Rage 5, Gnosis 6, Willpower 4

Rites: Rite of Talisman Dedication, Rite of the Sun's Bright Ray

Fetishes: None

Petrov Tzarovitch

Image: Tzarovitch is a slim, young man in his late teens to early 20s with dark eyes that always have a glimmer of mischief in them. He dresses in black, not because he is a grim, foreboding person, but because he is colorblind and knows that by wearing black and similar basic solid colors, he won't end up looking foolish.

Roleplaying Notes: You are a highly spiritual freethinker and enjoy looking at the lighter side of life; you enjoy helping others to see the lighter sides of things — even the lighter sides of themselves (whether they want to or not). You have heard the place known as the Dark Umbra, or Shadowlands, and you have an interest in going there to search for your mother, but what you have heard does not encourage you to go rushing off to find her, either. You *do* have a logical, practical side, after all. You are also a bit vain and hate to admit to being color-blind, so you dress in grays, blacks and blues, keeping your wardrobe simple so that you don't end up wearing red plaids with orange stripes. You are somewhat materialistic as well and can't resist the flash and glitter that modern society has to offer.

History: Tzarovitch is the son of Russian-Jewish immigrants. His family emigrated to the United States in the 1970s when his mother contracted leukemia and the family sought better medical attention than was available in the Soviet Union. His father, an artist, found his work very well received in the States, so the family decided to stay. Tzarovitch's mother died a few years later, while Petrov was still a young boy, leaving his father alone. His father began doing commercial art to provide for his young son and him, and he encouraged Tzarovitch to be a freethinker and to look past the surface value of things.

Tzarovitch's First Change came as quite a surprise to him. The young boy sat in his backyard, watching birds fly over his head, wishing he could do the same, when he felt his body began to change. Panicked, the young boy began to run toward his house, but suddenly found himself flying above his house instead. After recovering from the initial shock, the young boy began to enjoy living his daydreams and took advantage of the situation to perpetrate a few practical jokes on his father and the neighborhood children. Realizing that he would not be believed, he decided to keep his secret to himself. A few days later, another Corax arrived and taught Tzarovitch what he was exactly and all that it implied.

Tzarovitch still lives with his father, who has now retired, and he continues his studies to be a pilot; his first love remains the joy of flight. He frequents his mother's grave to "talk with" her and is the only "person" he's ever told of his dual life.

Tzarovitch has taken an active role in the War of the Apocalypse and in spite of some rather spectacular misadventures, has risen in rank rapidly. He is committed to removing the Wyrm's influence from the Tellurian, and he has the potential to be one of Gaia's greatest warriors.

Mokolé

Breath of Fire

Breed: Suchid

Aspect: The Rising Sun, "Strike"

Nature/Demeanor: Traditionalist/Survivor

Physical: Strength 5 (4/7), Dexterity 2 (1/1), Stamina 5 (9/8)

Social: Charisma 2 , Manipulation 2 (0/0), Appearance 2 (0/2)

Mental: Perception 3, Intelligence 4, Wits 3

Talents: Alertness 3, Athletics 4, Brawl 5, Dodge 2, Intimidation 5, Primal-Urge 3

Skills: Animal Ken 4, Stealth 5, Survival 5

Knowledges: Enigmas 4, Occult 4, Rituals 4

Backgrounds: Kinfolk 4, Mnesis 4

Gifts: (1) Bellow, Razor Claws, Resist Pain, Talk; (2) Armor of the Tortoise, Become Log, Clap of Thunder; (3) Clear Mind, Dragon's Breath, Eyes of the Cobra; (4) Hot Ichor, Infest, Rule; (5) Sleep of the Dragon, Song of the Great Beast, Walking between Worlds

Rank: 5

Rage 7, Gnosis 7, Willpower 8

Rites: The Badger's Burrow, Feed the Wallow, Save Hatchling

Archid Characteristics: Armor (+3 Soak), Long Teeth, Terrible Claws

Fetishes: None

   Image: In his Suchid form, Breath of Fire is a very large crocodile. In Archid form, he resembles the land dragons of legend. No Garou has ever seen his Homid form.

   Roleplaying Notes: You've had enough. For years you enjoyed the tranquility of the jungle, but the arrival of Wyrm-tainted creatures and Garou has disturbed your peace. You are a vicious combatant and know that, as soon as the Wyrm is driven from your home, the Garou will leave as well, so you fight the Wyrm in all its forms.

   History: For many years Breath of Fire enjoyed life on the Amazon River. He had long since passed his dreaming, shaping his Archid form, when *they* came — when Wyrm creatures arrived in droves and began destroying his home. Breath of Fire fought back viciously. A short while later he began dreaming of wolves. He dreamed of them running through his jungle, and he prayed that it wasn't so. Then he saw them and realized that a war had come to his home. The Garou, when they weren't fighting each other, fought Wyrm creatures, but some of the things they did "in the service of Gaia" repulsed Breath of Fire. He knew that his time of peace had gone and that now was the time to fight — for home and Gaia.

Breath of Fire

   At first the Garou were frightened by the fearsome werealligator, but gradually realized that he was a formidable ally. They now welcome the Mokolé when he makes appearances, which are becoming more frequent with every passing day.

Juki, "Sun Halo"

Breed: Homid

Aspect: Noonday Sun, "Shadowless"

Nature/Demeanor: Cub/Competitor

Physical: Strength 4 (8/6), Dexterity 2 (1/1), Stamina 4 (8/7)

Social: Charisma 2, Manipulation 2 (0/0), Appearance 2 (0/2)

Mental: Perception 3, Intelligence 3, Wits 4

Talents: Athletics 1, Brawl 3, Dodge 1, Expression 3, Primal-Urge 2

Skills: Animal Ken 2, Melee 2, Survival 1

Knowledges: Enigmas (Visual) 4, Herbalism 2, Medicine 3, Occult 2, Rituals 2

Backgrounds: Mnesis 1, Rites 2

Gifts: (1) Bellow, Talk

Rank: 1

Rage 2, Gnosis 3, Willpower 2

Rites: (Mokole) Feed the Wallow, Save Hatchling

Fetishes: None

Archid Characteristics: Bipedal Walking, Poison Sacs, Throat Sac and Wattles (+1 Expression)

Image: In his Homid form, Juki is a thick-skinned and tanned young man. In his Suchid form, he is a slim and deep-green alligator. In Archid, Juki is a seven-foot bipedal dinosaur with frills and a throat sac that accentuate his voice.

Roleplaying Notes: Until the dread Wyrm brought its plague to the wallow, life was a pleasant dream. With it, the Wyrm brought death, poison, destruction and the Garou. You are tired now, an uncommon trait for one as young as you, but fighting constantly makes you weary. You do whatever is necessary to bring these tumultuous conflicts to an end because you wish to get back to your dreaming.

History: Juki's early years were spent as a young tribesman until he manifested the aspects of his Mokolé nature. His proud parents brought him to the wallow of the indigenous werealligators, telling them of their son's pride in becoming one of them. It was also a sad day for them, as they left their only child behind, and Juki has never forgotten the bittersweet look of longing on his mother's face.

Juki, "Sun Halo"

He quickly adapted to his newfound family, becoming a talespinner and dreamteller. Juki relishes the days when he was able to dream to his heart's content. But then the Wyrm came, with its smoldering bulldozers, gun-carrying monsters, and poisonous chemicals. As if it were not enough to have his home invaded by the giant corporations of the city, the ancient foes of the Mokolé followed the Wyrm — the Garou.

Now Juki sings songs of the war being fought in the ancestral lands of the Mokolé by two foreign groups. He is very interested in the Garou, however, and his curiosity has led him into encounters with them. These encounters give him hope, as none of them have ended in the violence that he remembers with his racial memory, and he longs to make true friends among these strange shapeshifters who call themselves werewolves.

Roars-Like-Thunder

Breed: Homid

Aspect: The Rising Sun, "Strike"

Nature/Demeanor: Confidant/Judge

Physical: Strength 3 (7/5), Dexterity 3 (2/2), Stamina 4 (8/7)

Social: Charisma 5, Manipulation 2 (0/0), Appearance 5 (3/5)

Mental: Perception 4, Intelligence 5, Wits 4

Talents: Alertness 5, Athletics 5, Brawl 3, Dodge 4, Empathy 3, Expression 2, Primal-Urge 3

Skills: Animal Ken 3, Leadership 3, Melee 3, Performance 3, Stealth 3, Survival 4

Knowledges: Enigmas 4, Medicine 2, Occult 3, Rituals 1

Backgrounds: Mnesis 3, Rites 2

Gifts: (1) Bellow, Talk, Razor Claws; (2) Clap of Thunder, Tame Sunbeam; (3) Dragon's Breath, Clear Mind

Rank: 3

Rage 4, Gnosis 7, Willpower 6

Rites: (Mokole) Feed the Wallow, Save Hatchling

Archid Characteristics: Armor (+2 Soak), Feathers, Huge Size, Long Neck, Terrible Claws, Wings

Fetishes: Bane Arrows (6)

Image: In Homid form, Roars-Like-Thunder is a tall, beautiful woman: lanky and fast, with a dancer's grace. She is usually clad in traditional Black Fury garb, as she is an accepted member of the tribe. In Archid form, she becomes a saurian bird, huge and fearsome, with a serpentine neck and a beak large enough to snap a man in two.

Roleplaying Notes: Remain calm in the face of chaos. Fight fiercely and loudly when you must, but always seek alternate ways of resolving problems. You benefit from a greater historical perspective than your short-lived allies, and you know this makes you wiser than they are, though you act more as a gentle advisor than as a superior or leader.

History: Over 100 years old, Roars-Like-Thunder has long been an ally to the Black Furies of the Amazon Basin

Roars-Like-Thunder

Knowledges: Enigmas 2, Medicine 2, Occult 1
Backgrounds: Mentor 3, Mnesis 2
Gifts: (1) Bellow, Cooking, Resist Pain; (2) Armor of the Tortoise
Rank: 2
Rage 5, Gnosis 2, Willpower 3
Fetishes: None
Archid Characteristics: Bipedal Walking, Spikes on Tail

Image: In Suchid form, Rytti is an "unassuming" crocodile. His Archid, or "Crinos," form is a stocky, bipedal lizard with a barbed tail and horns on the back of his head. He rarely assumes Homid form, but when he does he looks like a well-muscled native.

Roleplaying Notes: Mmmmm, the sun feels good. The water feels good. You live to lounge around, eat and mate. You only spring into action if you or your family is threatened.

History: Rytti spent most of his life swimming, basking, eating and mating. He lived near a small pond deep in the Amazon jungle. All of that changed when Pentex developers arrived. Rytti's family was forced from its home and had to flee to survive. Rytti wanted to fight, but wanted to see his family to safety even more. Now that his loved ones are secure, Rytti is back and looking for anything that smells like Pentex. He's met many strange allies who also hate Pentex. With the help of these strange man-dogs, Rytti hopes to drive the evil from his home.

and has undergone initiation into the tribe. Naturally, as the War for the rainforests began and the Amazons were drawn in, she joined the battle and has served as a vicious foe of the Wyrm.

Roars-Like-Thunder is much more social toward people and Garou than others of her species, and her racial memory of times past allows her to look at matters with a tempered perspective; among the Black Furies, she is considered a Philodox because of her wisdom and insight. This does not mean she is averse to conflict, only that she is good at resolving problems by whatever means necessary. If battle is the only way, she joins in with ferocity. Many is the foe whose final sight has been the roaring descent of this winged behemoth.

Rytti, "Horned Thunder"

Breed: Suchid
Aspect: The Rising Sun, Strike
Nature/Demeanor: Caregiver/Maker
Physical: Strength 4 (8/6), Dexterity 3 (2/2), Stamina 4 (8/7)
Social: Charisma 3, Manipulation 2 (0/0), Appearance 2 (0/2)
Mental: Perception 4, Intelligence 2, Wits 3
Talents: Alertness 4, Brawl 4, Intimidation 3, Primal-Urge 3
Skills: Leadership 2, Stealth 4, Survival 4

Rytti, "Horned Thunder"

Nuwisha

Laughs-at-Death

Breed: Homid

Auspice: Ragabash

Nature/Demeanor: Caregiver/Conniver

Physical: Strength 2 (3/4/4/2), Dexterity 3 (4/6/6/6), Stamina 4 (6/7/7/7)

Social: Charisma 3, Manipulation 4 (3/2/1/1), Appearance 3 (3/0/3/3)

Mental: Perception 5, Intelligence 3, Wits 4

Talents: Alertness 2, Athletics 3, Brawl 2, Dodge 3, Empathy 2, Expression 1, Intimidation 1, Primal-Urge 1, Streetwise 1, Subterfuge 2

Skills: Animal Ken 2, Melee 1, Performance 2, Repair 1, Stealth 2, Survival 4

Knowledges: Enigmas 1, Medicine 1, Occult 1, Rituals 2, Science 1

Backgrounds: Contacts 3, Kinfolk 3

Gifts: (1) Blur of the Milky Eye, Rabbit Run, Smell of Man, Spirit Speech; (2) Odious Aroma; (3) Sheep's Clothing, Umbral Howl

Rank: 3

Rage 3, Gnosis 5, Willpower 5

Rites: (Accord) Rite of Cleansing; (Mystic) Rite of Spirit Awakening, Rite of Talisman Dedication; (Nuwisha) Rite of Dansing

Fetishes: None

Image: In her Homid form, Laughs-at-Death is an earthily attractive Native American woman in her early 30s, usually wearing either comfortable, semi-traditional garb or outdoor clothing like T-shirts, hiking shorts, and river sandals. In her Manabozho form, she is a wiry bundle of energy, athletic in a spidery way, reminding one of the coyote in those wonderful old cartoons.

Roleplaying Notes: Smile. Smile a lot. Laugh often. Pick on others, but always playfully, never with malice. Smile some more. Tell jokes that make yourself look foolish but that teach lessons of humility and humor. Sing. Smile. Above all, make sure that people learn the lessons of their own folly in the classroom of experience. Telling people something doesn't teach it to them. Trip them so they fall into their lessons. Oh, and smile some more.

History: Born on a Navajo reservation in Arizona, Alicia Lopez was always into something. Neighbors knew she had Coyote in her, but didn't realize just how much. In truth, her mother had an affair with a local rascal without knowing he was Nuwisha, and little Alicia was the result. Her real father, who she knew as a good-natured friend of the family, took her for a ride in his pickup shortly after her 13th birthday and left her in the desert. As she made her way back, strange things happened to her. A tortoise spoke, telling her the story of how Coyote placed the stars. She tripped and fell on her face every mile or two, and it was always exactly the same rock tripping her up, as if it were somehow following her. When she tried carrying it, it simply disappeared at some point and she tripped over it again. Finally, her father appeared again, sitting under a cottonwood tree, and he told her the truth about herself and taught her how to change.

Since that time, she has become a true Nuwisha, having been initiated into the Umbral Dansers and joining the battle against the Wyrm in the spirit world. Like most Nuwisha, she lives mainly in the Umbra, though during the summers she works as an instructor at a wilderness skills school in the Escalante region of southern Utah. There she teaches humans the traditional ways of living on the Earth, according to Gaia's wishes, in the hope that they'll return to their homes with a new understanding of what is truly valuable in life.

Minions of the Wyrm

Ananasi

Amelia

Breed: Homid

Allegiance: Hatar

Nature/Demeanor: Bravo/Confidant

Physical: Strength 2 (5/6), Dexterity 4 (7/6), Stamina 3 (5/5)

Social: Charisma 3 , Manipulation 3 (0/0), Appearance 4 (0/0)

Mental: Perception 3, Intelligence 2, Wits 3

Talents: Alertness 1, Brawl 3, Dodge 2, Empathy 4, Subterfuge 3

Skills: Etiquette 3, Melee 1, Stealth 5

Knowledges: Enigmas 1, Investigation 2, Medicine 3, Occult 3

Backgrounds: Contacts 2, Resources 4

Gifts: (1) Control Simple Machines, Eyes of the Cat, Fatal Flaw; (2) Insect Eyes; (3) Wall Crawling

Rank: 3

Gnosis 6, Willpower 5, Blood Pool: variable (usually between 6 and 10)

Amelia

Rites: None

Fetishes: None

Image: In her Homid form Amelia is an alabaster beauty, with flawless ivory skin and full red lips. She favors short dresses and skirts that reveal her long, shapely legs. Her Pithus form is a huge, towering spider with a humanoid torso. Her skin and fur colors range from pale green-yellow to lobster red.

Roleplaying Notes: You delight in and savor the pain of others, be it the emotional pain you cause with your feminine wiles or the physical pain that you inflict. You almost seem contemplative when talking to others. It puts people at ease. In reality, you're usually bored and trying to decide whether to eat them.

History: Little is known about this reclusive art collector from New York City. Amelia, as she's known by her associates, has refined tastes and a smooth social manner. She entered the social scene about three years ago and has been selectively building a collection of masterpieces ever since.

In truth, Amelia loves art; it is timeless, profound and beautiful. The flesh is frail and flawed; only art surpasses the limitations of the mortal world. It reminds her of herself, although her vanity is not quite as strong as her passion for the aesthetic.

She owns a building in the Village. When she's not collecting art, she's investing in real estate and doing freelance consultation for the Bryant Land Developers Group, a subsidiary of the Pentex Corporation. She's been known to do on-site eviction on recently acquired properties. She's particularly inclined to do so when Kinfolk or Garou need to be ousted from their precious tribal lands.

Bastet

Atahualpa, "Blood of the Incas"

Tribe: Balam

Breed: Feline

Physical: Strength 3 (4/6/5/4), Dexterity 5 (6/8/8/8), Stamina 4 (6/7/7/6)

Social: Charisma 2, Manipulation 4 (3/1/1/1), Appearance 3 (2/0/3/2)

Mental: Perception 4, Intelligence 2, Wits 3

Talents: Alertness 4, Athletics 4, Brawl 4, Dodge 5, Intimidation 4, Primal-Urge 5, Subterfuge 2

Skills: Animal Ken 2, Etiquette 1, Stealth 5, Survival 4

Knowledges: Area Knowledge 3, Enigmas 2, Linguistics (English, Native Yanomami) 2, Medicine 2, Occult 2, Rituals 1

Backgrounds: Den-Realm 2 (9 square miles, Gauntlet 6), Pride (Corrupt Jaguars) 3

Gifts: (1) Catfeet, Heightened Senses, Razor Claws; (2) Eyes of the Cat, Sense of the Prey; (3) Call the Pride

Fomori Powers: Lashing Tail, Roar of the Wyrm

Rank: 3

Rage 9, Gnosis 4, Willpower 6

Rites: (Mystic) Rite of Talisman Dedication

Fetishes: Dragon's Ichor (3 applications), Soul Ruby (gives the following: Science 2, Black Spiral Sign Language 2, Computer 1)

Image: Atahualpa appears to be a very sick jaguar. Her fur is falling out in patches, and she has an incessant cough. These are all effects from the Bane that inhabits her body. In Homid form, she appears as a local native with very purebred features and is 25 years old. She is really from an almost extinct Incan bloodline.

Roleplaying Notes: Pace about often. You are a jaguar in a cage. Your own home has become your hell. That's what you got for staying to defend it. You now fight the Bane within you to control your actions. Snarl and growl to the unjust skies.

History: Atahualpa's Den-Realm is in the Umbra, right where Pentex decided to build its Amazon headquarters. She tried with all her might, but could not stop them. Her realm is now a home to Banes, which have possessed Atahualpa and her pride. She is desperate for escape, but most days she cannot remember her real identity and her place in Gaia's plan. The Bane is winning possession of her.

She knows only one way out now: to attack as many Garou as she can. Atahualpa hopes they are fierce enough to kill her and give her peace. The cursed Bane will not allow this. It has a strong self-preservation instinct and has caused her to run wounded from two battles. She is mustering all of her will for the next fight to ensure that she dies on that field.

Atahualpa, "Blood of the Incas"

Rokea

Morgan

Tribe: Spynha

Nature/Demeanor: Predator/Bravo

Physical: Strength 4 (8/8), Dexterity 4 (5/4), Stamina 4 (8/7)

Social: Charisma 2 (0/0), Manipulation 2 (0/0), Appearance 2 (0/0)

Mental: Perception 3, Intelligence 1, Wits 4

Talents: Athletics 1, Brawl 5, Dodge 1, Intimidation 4 (8/8), Primal-Urge 2, Streetwise 3

Skills: Firearms 3, Melee 3, Stealth 3, Survival 2

Knowledges: Linguistics 3, Medicine 2

Backgrounds: Contacts 2

Gifts: (1) Heightened Senses, Razor Teeth (treat as Razor Claws); (2) Scent of Sight, Spirit of the Fray, True Fear; (3) Cat Feet

Rank: 3

Rage 8, Gnosis 3, Willpower 7

Rites: None

Fetishes: None

Image: Towering and huge, Morgan in his Homid form is enough to give the faint-hearted a panic attack. He looks like what he is: a creature of unrestrained cruelty and violence. In his Crinos form, he is a sleek, humanoid hammerhead shark standing over 10 feet tall.

Roleplaying Notes: Vicious. Cruel. Hungry. You do things only in that they satisfy these impulses. Subtlety is not your strong suit. You have no sense of humor at all. Violence is the only form of entertainment.

History: Early on, Morgan became interested in the surface world after witnessing a bloody battle between a band of drug runners and the U.S. Coast Guard off the coast of California. After gorging himself on the carcasses of the dead, he trailed the victorious pirates to a small coastal village in Baja. He followed them ashore with the dim thought of joining them and further enjoying their bloody exploits. Unable to communicate this desire, Morgan was met with fear and violence in the form of automatic gunfire. Though he healed nearly immediately, the pain enraged him, and in his bloodlust he slaughtered those he had thought to join.

Fortunately for Morgan, the conflict was observed by a stranger in the village, a former mercenary turned Pentex

Morgan

soldier named T.F. MacNeil. MacNeil called in reinforcements and managed to stun and capture the hulking wereshark. Initially enraged at his entrapment, Morgan gradually learned enough English from his captors to realize they were offering him exactly what he wanted: a life of blood and violence.

Given the name "Morgan" by MacNeil (after the soldier's favorite rum), he began this new life working directly for Pentex as a security expert (read: professional thug) for Endron International, Pentex's primary oil concern, quickly becoming known for his ferocity and the tendency to eat those he killed. In time, however, he grew weary of constant corporate supervision and struck out on his own, freelancing his immense capacity for violence to anyone willing to pay. Even so, he still feels a weak loyalty to MacNeil and to Pentex for freeing him from the limitations of his previous existence.

Black Spiral Dancers

Fangs-through-Eye

Breed: Metis
Auspice: Ahroun
Nature/Demeanor: Visionary/Bravo
Physical: Strength 4 (6/8/7/5), Dexterity 3 (3/4/5/5), Stamina 3 (5/6/6/5)
Social: Charisma 4, Manipulation 3 (2/0/0/0), Appearance 1 (0/0/1/1)
Mental: Perception 2, Intelligence 2, Wits 2
Talents: Alertness 1, Athletics 1, Brawl 3, Dodge 2, Intimidation 3, Primal-Urge 3
Skills: Leadership 1, Melee 2, Stealth 3, Survival 3
Knowledges: Politics 2, Occult 3
Backgrounds: Allies 3, Mentor 2
Gifts: (1) Bane Protector, Sense Wyrm, Shroud; (2) Ears of the Bat, Horns of the Impaler
Rank: 2
Rage 4, Gnosis 2, Willpower 7
Rites: None
Fetishes: None

Fangs-through-Eye

Image: Fangs is a rather awkward-looking young man in his late teens with greasy, jet-black hair and large teeth. In Crinos form he is large, jet-black, and has large fangs. In Lupus, he is a mangy black wolf with a sickly green tint to his fur.

Roleplaying Notes: Fomori suck. Black Spiral Dancers rock. Everyone else can come or go, preferably go — far, far away. You are proud to serve the Wyrm, and you want everyone to know it. You are ruthless, both in combat and in daily living. Everyone around you is either an asset or a liability. If they're assets, no problem. If they're liabilities, spill their blood and send flowers to their families. That or send some body part that you don't want to eat, and eat the flowers.

History: Fangs-through-Eye earned his name before his Rite of Passage, when a littermate teased him about his large teeth. Fangs responded by thrusting his teeth into her eyes to spare her looking at them any longer. Two weeks later, Fangs killed and ate the same littermate after an argument over dinner.

Fangs' ruthlessness and arrogance quickly made him a favorite of his parents and Hive. He looks down upon most other Wyrm creatures as pathetic and incapable of serving the Wyrm as can the Black Spirals. Fangs holds particular contempt for fomori, whom he considers useless half-breeds. If a Wyrm ally is in combat, Fangs will refuse to defend the creature, allowing it to stand or fall on its own merit. If it falls, there's proof of the creature's inferiority.

Fangs gleefully danced the Black Spiral. He looks forward to undergoing the Rite of Transmogrification, when he will be able to gaze upon the Wyrm's face and know the rapture of Truth. In the War of the Apocalypse, Gaia's warriors will learn of Fangs-through-Eye and will know fear.

Fangthane Bloodjaw

Breed: Homid
Auspice: Ahroun
Nature/Demeanor: Autist/Reveler
Physical: Strength 4 (6/8/7/5), Dexterity 3 (3/4/5/5), Stamina 3 (5/6/6/5)
Social: Charisma 2, Manipulation 3 (2/0/0/0), Appearance 1 (0/0/1/1)
Mental: Perception 3, Intelligence 3, Wits 2
Talents: Alertness 1, Athletics 2, Brawl 3, Intimidation 3, Primal-Urge 2, Streetwise 2
Skills: Drive 2, Melee 2, Repair 2, Stealth 3
Knowledges: Computers 3, Law 2

Fangthane Bloodjaw

Sometimes a kindly family member takes pity on the lost doggy and takes him home. Fangthane has been known to maintain the charade for as long as a week before lashing out. He begins by killing pets, and then moves from the oldest to the youngest family member, killing them all in the space of one night. He often lingers in the homes of his victims for a few days, playing with his food.

Hunts-at-Night

Breed: Lupus
Auspice: Ragabash
Nature/Demeanor: Predator/Lone Wolf
Physical: Strength 3 (5/7/6/4), Dexterity 3 (3/4/5/5), Stamina 3 (5/6/6/5)
Social: Charisma 1, Manipulation 4 (3/1/1/1), Appearance 1 (0/0/1/1)
Mental: Perception 4, Intelligence 3, Wits 4
Talents: Alertness 3, Athletics 2, Brawl 4, Dodge 2, Intimidation 1, Primal-Urge 3, Subterfuge 2
Skills: Animal Ken 3, Stealth 5, Survival 4
Knowledges: Enigmas 2, Occult 2, Rituals 2
Backgrounds: Kinfolk 2, Past Life 3
Gifts: (1) Blur of the Milky Eye, Heightened Senses, Leap of the Kangaroo, Scent of Running Water, Shroud; (2) Blissful Ignorance, Ears of the Bat, Scent of Sight,

Backgrounds: Kinfolk 2, Past Life 1, Resources 2
Gifts: (1) Bane Protector, Inspiration, Smell of Man
Rank: 1
Rage 5, Gnosis 2, Willpower 4
Rites: None
Fetishes: None

Image: In Homid form, Fangthane has short, curly red hair. He is small and stocky. His face is horribly scarred; he usually wears a mask to hide his deformities. The most noticeable quality of his Crinos form is his protruding lower teeth that are each approximately six inches long and usually covered with the blood of a victim. In Lupus form he looks like a large, mangy stray.

Roleplaying Notes: You are very shy and avoid personal contact with others. Although an Ahroun, you are a coward at heart and often flee battle. This has caused you problems with your pack, but you've managed to avoid the consequences of your actions thus far.

History: The proverbial runt of his litter, Fangthane has grown up with well over a dozen psychological problems. He fears almost everything he encounters and haphazardly upholds his convictions. He rarely remains in the same pack very long; he's usually driven out when others lose patience with him.

Fangthane likes to play a private game. It involves approaching an unsuspecting family while in Lupus form.

Hunts-at-Night

Sense of the Prey, Wyrm Hide; (3) Catfeet; (4) Gnaw, Whelp Body

Rank: 4

Rage 6, Gnosis 7, Willpower 6

Rites: (Mystic) Rite of Becoming, Rite of the Questing Stone

Fetishes: None

Image: A ghostly albino wolf who seldom sees the sun, Hunts-at-Night rarely if ever speaks. He watches. He listens. He is there, then he is not. When he returns, it is usually with blood on his muzzle and claws and a meal of fresh meat to regurgitate and share with his Hive-mates.

Roleplaying Notes: You listen to everything said, watch the body language of the speakers and never forget anything. You are ever-focused on what the next hunt will be. Are the others discussing a Get of Fenris warrior who took several lives in a recent, bloody skirmish? Are they discussing a betrayal by a Pentex First Team? Are they laughing about the possibilities for sadistic fun in a new orphanage in the city above? Whatever the case, you listen and you decide. Then you go, unnoticed, without a word, and you kill. The hunt and the kill are all that matter.

History: There is not now and has never been anything in Hunts-at-Night's life but the hunt. He has no use for community; though he shares his kills, it is only instinct that motivates him to do so. He pads silently through the labyrinthine Black Spiral Dancer Hive that is his home, a colorless terror, a ghost, and he for the most part never acknowledges others. He never accepts or seems to need help. He sleeps. He kills. He eats. This seems to be enough.

In spite of his antisocial behavior, Hunts-at-Night has gained much renown as a Black Spiral Dancer assassin. Pups whisper his name and stalk each other, often beating each other brutally in arguments about who gets to "be" Hunts-at-Night. Lower-rank Dancers watch him walk and try to move as he does. And many seek to join him, to touch greatness, to be his packmates. Still, he hunts alone in the darkness of night, and he never fails.

Johnathan Roark

Breed: Homid

Auspice: Ragabash

Nature/Demeanor: Cub/Deviant

Physical: Strength 2 (4/6/5/3), Dexterity 4 (4/5/6/6), Stamina 3 (5/6/6/5)

Social: Charisma 1, Manipulation 4 (3/1/1/1), Appearance 2 (1/0/1/1)

Mental: Perception 2, Intelligence 5, Wits 3

Talents: Alertness 2, Athletics 2, Brawl 2, Dodge 3, Intimidation 1, Streetwise 2, Subterfuge 2

Skills: Drive 1, Firearms 1, Melee 2, Stealth 4, Survival 1

Knowledges: Computer 2, Enigmas 1, Occult 3, Rituals 1

Backgrounds: Allies 1, Contacts 2, Kinfolk 2

Johnathan Roark

Gifts: (1) Bane Protector, Blur of the Milky Eye, Open Seal, Smell of Man; (2) Burrow, Taking the Forgotten

Rank: 2

Rage 4, Gnosis 3, Willpower 3

Rites: (Mystic) Rite of Talisman Dedication

Fetishes: None

Image: In Homid form, Johnathan is a long-haired black man, tattooed and multi-pierced, with one green eye and one strange yellow eye and unusually sharp teeth. His Crinos form is a tall, skinny, shaggy-maned werewolf with crazed eyes and a 15-inch tongue.

Roleplaying Notes: Laugh at the pain of others, especially when you've caused it. Steal things from everybody around you. Play your music too loud and refuse to turn it down. Strut 'cause you're a stud. Try to ignore the fact that no one seems much impressed with you.

History: Johnathan Roark was born in a Black Spiral Dancer Hive beneath Washington, D.C. He grew up with other Black Spiral pups, in darkness, tormented by his depraved and insane elders, and never truly found his place, even after dancing the Black Spiral. If anything, he returned from the Dance with a feeling of true insignificance in the face of all that was the Wyrm. He started going to the surface, looking for thrills, and soon discovered that the only sense of accomplishment he could find was in vicious pranks, petty violence and burglary. Below, in the tunnels that twist beneath the city, Johnathan was just another

Wyrmy thing, but above, he knew that he was a force of evil moving through mortal lives like dark lightning. It was this and this alone that made life worth living.

Johanathan took a room in a flophouse and adapted further to the surface world. He discovered the local music scene and the clubs and in them found easy prey for his sick sensuality. In time, this led him to the joys of murder. Many of his "pickups" are later found mutilated, often with body parts "stolen" by the Ragabash as he descends deeper into his depravity. He has recently taken the words "Spiral Death" as a personal motto and is trying harder than ever to live up to his awful heritage.

Kills-the-Weak

Breed: Metis
Auspice: Ahroun
Nature/Demeanor: Bravo/Bravo
Physical: Strength 5 (7/9/8/6), Dexterity 3 (3/4/5/5), Stamina 4 (6/7/7/6)
Social: Charisma 1, Manipulation 2 (1/0/0/0), Appearance 1 (0/0/1/1)
Mental: Perception 4, Intelligence 1, Wits 4
Talents: Alertness 3, Brawl 3, Dodge 1, Primal-Urge 2
Skills: Drive 1, Firearms 1, Leadership 2, Stealth 2, Survival 3

Kills-the-Weak

Knowledges: Enigmas 1, Medicine 1, Occult (Malignant Entities) 4, Wyrm Lore 3
Backgrounds: Allies 2, Totem 1
Gifts: (1) Create Element, Bane Protector, Shroud; (2) Horns of the Impaler; (3) Patagia
Rank: 3
Rage 5, Gnosis 3, Willpower 7
Rites: None
Fetishes: Wyrm Fang Dagger (Fake)

Image: Kills-the-Weak can only marginally pass for human, as his lower jaw is horrendously and painfully extended and his skin is a particularly disturbing shade of ashen gray. In Crinos form, his fang-bristling jaw is even more pronounced, and his batlike ears flap unceasingly. His fur falls out in patches, as his metis deformity is a constant state of mangelike spalling of his skin. In Lupus, Kills-the-Weak resembles a small pony in the advanced stages of radiation poisoning.

Roleplaying Notes: Find small things; break them. Find small people; hurt them. Find small spirits; smash them. Find werewolves; kill them.

History: Kills-the-Weak spent his nascent years in the hell of the Hive. Both of his parents had long since gone mad in service to the Wyrm and could hardly form complete sentences, let alone raise their "child." Luckily, Kills-the-Weak was born under a full moon and soon began to manifest traits of his warrior nature. When food was scarce, he ate other Black Spiral Dancers or he erupted from his Hive to rampage in a nearby town or on a farm within traveling distance. He grew large, surly and nearly uncontrollable, much to his elder's pleasure. His deep-seated sense of inadequacy has formed him into a bully of sorts; he will only pick a fight when he is more than assured of victory and, as such, only picks fights with those smaller and weaker than himself. Unfortunately, most things fall into this category, and even his hivemates are constantly on the lookout for their own blighted welfare.

Longtooth Soulkiller

Breed: Metis
Auspice: Galliard
Nature/Demeanor: Alpha/Alpha
Physical: Strength 4 (6/8/7/5), Dexterity 4 (4/5/6/6), Stamina 4 (6/7/7/6)
Social: Charisma 4, Manipulation 4 (3/1/1/1), Appearance 2 (1/0/2/2)
Mental: Perception 3, Intelligence 4, Wits 3
Talents: Alertness 4, Athletics 2, Brawl 4, Dodge 2, Intimidation 3, Primal-Urge 2
Skills: Firearms 3, Leadership 2, Melee 4, Stealth 3
Knowledges: Enigmas 2, Occult 3, Politics 2, Rituals 2
Backgrounds: Allies 1, Kinfolk 4

Longtooth Soulkiller

Gifts: (1) Bane Protector, Call of the Wyld, Sense Wyrm; (2) Curse of Hatred, Ears of the Bat, Howl of the Banshee, Wyrm Hide; (3) Eyes of the Cat, Patagia, Song of Rage; (4) Crawling Poison, Shadows by the Fire, Wither Limb

Rank: 4

Rage 8, Gnosis 7, Willpower 8

Rites: (Caern) Moot Rite, Rite of the Opened Caern; (Mystic) Baptism of Fire, Rite of Binding, Rite of Becoming; (Punishment) Rite of Ostracism, Voice of the Jackal; (Renown) Rite of Accomplishment, Rite of Passage, Rite of Wounding

Fetishes: Banesword

Image: A hulking werewolf with ash-gray fur and a gaping maw of teeth, Longtooth Soulkiller carries himself with gusto. He is all-alpha, speaking in a deep and thundering voice, inspiring fear in his enemies and slavering loyalty in his fellow Black Spiral Dancers.

Roleplaying Notes: Lead others to rousing victories against Gaia and her greatest champions. You know no fear and accept no weakness in your fellows. Often, you sing dark martial songs in the midst of combat. Know fully and with certainty that you are the embodiment of Black Spiral Dancer ideals and that in time you will be their king. When Apocalypse comes, it will be on your resume.

History: Longtooth Soulkiller was so large at birth that his mother died delivering him. He was the first pup out,

snarling, eyes open, and the corrupted Garou present at the birth knew they had a champion. Though he was a Galliard, and prone to song at odd times, he could outfight all of the Ahroun cubs who were raised with him. These Ahrouns came to worship Longtooth, recognizing the greatness in him and submitting to it without rancor. By the time he underwent the Rite of the Black Spiral, he was already recognized as a great warrior, and when he finished the Rite with an impromptu song about the scatalogical greatness of the Wyrm itself, he passed into legend.

In the years since, Longtooth has continued to distinguish himself in battle and song and has been given the position of HiveSinger, bringing great renown to himself and his packmates. He is always at the fore of any attack — a towering, fearless presence of violent charisma, a battle song booming from his maw, his Banesword cleaving his enemies and his fellow Black Spiral Dancers rushing to die in his name.

Lotus

Breed: Metis
Auspice: Philodox
Nature/Demeanor: Cub/Show-Off
Physical: Strength 4 (6/8/7/5), Dexterity 3 (3/4/5/5), Stamina 3 (5/6/6/5)
Social: Charisma 2, Manipulation 3 (2/0/0/0), Appearance 1 (0/0/1/1)

Lotus

Mental: Perception 3, Intelligence 1, Wits 4

Talents: Brawl 3, Dodge 3, Intimidation 1, Primal-Urge 3, Streetwise 1, Subterfuge 2

Skills: Melee 2, Stealth 4, Survival 3

Knowledges: Enigmas 1, Occult 4

Backgrounds: Allies 2, Past Life 1, Totem 2

Gifts: (1) Resist Pain, Sense Wyrm, Shroud, Truth of Gaia

Rank: 1

Rage 4, Gnosis 3, Willpower 3

Rites: None

Fetishes: None

Image: Burly and short with long, whipping ears; pig-eyes; a mostly hairless, greenish complexion; and a cavernous mouth, Lotus is just plain ugly. As she waddles through the bowels of the Black Spiral Dancer labyrinths, she calls to mind Gollum from *The Lord of the Rings*, though to hear her singing curses in her little girl's voice is to know that Lotus lacks even Gollum's social graces.

Roleplaying Notes: Do things your way, not because you don't want to do things the way you're told, but because you forget just about everything you're told. Yell. Attract lots of attention. Then, when you irritate someone really badly, run screeching from them, flailing your arms above your head, and dive down the first hidey-hole you find. You are not a fighter, but when cornered you can be a terror.

History: Lotus has never been above ground, has never seen the sun, and has never been around anyone but other Black Spiral Dancers and their equally disturbed allies. She fears Gaia's Garou the way children fear the Boogieman or Pup Pid and isn't actually completely persuaded that they are real. She is 20 years old, but has the emotional makeup of an eight year old. She lives too much in the moment to remember her past or to learn from it and has no thoughts of the future. Usually her activities consist of performing simple tasks and running errands for stronger Black Spiral Dancers, but if adventure ever rears its ugly head, Lotus will likely charge into it without realizing what's happening before it's too late to get away.

In her Hive, Lotus is known as the alpha of a pack of pups called The Bad Kids, none of whom are all that bright. She is always running through the tunnels, singing profanities, throwing things, and dancing grotesque little dances. In spite of her metis status (a plus in Black Spiral society) and her irritating personality (often enough to get you killed), she is generally pitied by the others of her tribe, for she is out of touch with her Rage and unable to experience the gift of frenzy. This is enough to break any Black Spiral Dancer's heart.

Old One-Eye

Breed: Lupus

Auspice: Theurge

Nature/Demeanor: Autist/Maker

Physical: Strength 2 (4/6/5/3), Dexterity 4 (4/5/6/6), Stamina 2 (4/5/5/4)

Social: Charisma 2, Manipulation 3 (2/0/0/0), Appearance 1 (0/0/1/1)

Mental: Perception 4, Intelligence 3, Wits 3

Talents: Brawl 2, Dodge 1, Streetwise 4, Subterfuge 4

Skills: Drive 2, Firearms 2, Melee 2, Repair 5, Stealth 2

Knowledges: Enigmas 3, Linguistics 1, Occult 3, Rituals 2

Backgrounds: Fetish 3, Mentor 2, Rites 2

Gifts: (1) Scent of Sweet Honey, Sense Prey, Spirit Speech; (2) Heat Metal, Odious Aroma, Trash Magnet

Rank: 2

Rage 3, Gnosis 5, Willpower 4

Rites: (Black Spiral) Dance of the Black Spiral; (Mystic) Rite of Spirit Awakening, Rite of Talisman Dedication

Fetishes: None

Image: In his Homid form, Old One-Eye is a lean, grizzled fellow around 40. He is afflicted with perpetual five o'clock shadow, body odor and lice. His Lupus form resembles a pea-green hyena rather than a wolf. A long, serpentine tongue often slides slowly from his mouth, then darts quickly, noisily back. Regardless of his form, a crudely fashioned metal plate covers the space formerly occupied by his right eye.

Roleplaying Notes: You are a packrat. Lovingly fondle any small objects within reach, then pile them around you. You're always hungry due to the Wyrm's Eater-of-Souls

Old One-Eye

influence, so constant noshing on junk food is appropriate. Try to keep that right eye shut.

History: A Ronin Garou sired Old One-Eye on a scraggly wolf in New Orleans' Audubon Zoo. The local Bone Gnawers sprung him just after his second birthday and adopted him. They reared Little Bug-Eyes (as he was then called) on a steady diet of dumpster divings, Mississippi River water and TV reruns. From an early age he accumulated caches of "stuff" hidden all over town.

His troubles began at age 25 when he decided to build a better rat. He became arrogant due to his prodigious mechanical abilities. He created several generations of cyborg rodents with nothing more than some flash and old batteries. None survived the experience. Soon, he worked his way up to bums and hid his failures in the lot near the docks. There, the smell went unnoticed.

As a waste-not, want-not kind of Garou, Little Bug-Eyes began snacking on leftovers from his experiments: a blatant transgression of the Litany. He might have gotten away with a Rite of Contrition as penalty, but when the Glass Walker who had befriended and mentored him discovered the truth, Bug-Eyes panicked. Bug-Eyes murdered his mentor, then, desolate, gave himself up. His acts nearly ignited a tribal war between the Crescent City's Bone Gnawers and Glass Walkers. As punishment, Little Bug-Eyes was subjected to the Hunt, tantamount to a death sentence. Two Black Spiral Dancers intervened in the rite, however, and spirited him away from Gaia's intended justice. The pair convinced Bug-Eyes to tread the Black Spiral, saying he was already halfway down the path. His path has been one of darkness ever since.

Little Bug-Eyes came to be Old One-Eye on his own "laboratory" table. His attempt to replace an eye with a "sensory module" of his own design was as successful as his previous experiments. Old One-Eye's bioengineering efforts in the service of the Wyrm continue.

Rends-the-Innocent

Breed: Homid
Auspice: Galliard
Nature/Demeanor: Deviant/Masochist
Physical: Strength 4 (6/8/7/5), Dexterity 3 (3/4/5/5), Stamina 4 (6/7/7/6)
Social: Charisma 3, Manipulation 3 (2/0/0/0), Appearance 4 (3/0/4/4)
Mental: Perception 3, Intelligence 4, Wits 2
Talents: Alertness 2, Brawl 3, Dodge 2, Intimidation 4
Skills: Drive 3, Firearms 2, Melee 3, Stealth 3, Survival 3
Knowledges: Linguistics 2, Occult 3
Backgrounds: Allies 2, Mentor 3, Fetish 3
Gifts: (1) Bane Protector, Call of the Wyld; (2) Ears of the Bat, Wyrm Hide; (3) Eye of the Cobra, Patagia
Rank: 3
Rage 6, Gnosis 5, Willpower 7

Rends-the-Innocent

Rites: None
Fetishes: Devilwhip

Image: In Homid form, Rends-the-Innocent is a handsome man in his late 20s who frequently wears jungle camouflage. In Lupus, he is a handsome but vicious-looking jet-black wolf with glowing green eyes.

Roleplaying Notes: You always knew you were special, and the fact that you're a Black Spiral Dancer is proof of that fact. Sure, maybe others call you a sociopath, pyschopath and various other cool names, but you know that from the very beginning you were meant to serve the Wyrm.

History: Rends-the-Innocent had a far-from-normal childhood. His father was a writer for Black Dog Game Factory, and his mother was a computer programmer for Sunburst Enterprises. Both parents were aware of who/what they really worked for and what they were doing and were proud of it. For his 10th birthday, Rends, who at the time was named Bob (but he spelled it backward, revealing a hidden message from the Wyrm), received a container of Gooshy Gooze from his parents. Unfortunately, the Gooshy Gooze didn't seem to like Bob; it often slogged through the house as fast as it could go, with Bob in hot pursuit.

Shortly after his 12th birthday, Bob discovered his Garou nature when he changed into Crinos form and ripped apart his best friend for refusing to buy him a booster pack of a popular collectible trading card game. Bob's parents were delighted.

A pack of Black Spiral Dancers arrived shortly thereafter, about the same time as a pack of Get of Fenris that had come in hopes of saving the child from the Wyrm. Rends joined the Black Spirals in combat against Gaia's werewolves. He took great joy in stabbing into Garou stomachs, grabbing a handful of intestine, and running away as fast as his legs could carry him.

After dancing the Black Spiral, he never returned home, choosing to stay and train with the Black Spiral Dancers until such a time as he was ready to travel to the Amazon. He's been there ever since, enjoying the carnage and general havoc he's been allowed to wreak.

Zhyzhak

Breed: Homid

Auspice: Ahroun

Nature/Demeanor: Deviant/Bravo

Physical: Strength 5 (7/9/8/6), Dexterity 3 (3/4/5/5), Stamina 5 (7/8/8/8)

Social: Charisma 3, Manipulation 2 (1/0/0/0), Appearance 4 (3/0/4/4)

Mental: Perception 3, Intelligence 2, Wits 2

Talents: Alertness 2, Athletics 3, Brawl 5, Dodge 4, Intimidation 4

Skills: Firearms 4, Melee 5, Leadership 3, Survival 3

Knowledges: Enigmas 1, Medicine 2, Occult 4, Rituals 3

Backgrounds: Pack Totem 5

Gifts: (1) Razor Claws, Sense Wyrm, Smell of Man; (2) Horns of the Impaler, Sense of the Prey, Snarl of the Predator, Wyrm Hide; (3) Foaming Fury, Heart of Fury, Silver Claws; (4) Clenched Jaw, Crawling Poison; (5) Balefire

Rank: 5

Rage 10, Gnosis 7, Willpower 8

Rites: (Mystic) Rite of Arterial Introduction (a Level Two rite used to initiate new Dancers to Grammaw's bloodstream without getting burned or disoriented), Rite of Summoning; (Punishment) Rending of the Veil

Fetishes: Devilwhip

Image: Zhyzhak is basically a muscle-bound Wagnerian valkyrie who wears dominatrix ensembles. She is far from unattractive, however, and many males are strongly attracted to her dangerous aura as well as her Aryan features and physique. She is dark-haired and has a good Homid complexion for her tribe; in Crinos form, she is 10 feet of black-furred madness. Her Hispo and Lupus forms could almost pass for a Black Fury, if an overlarge one. However, Zhyzhak's irrational fervor dooms any potential deception.

Roleplaying Notes: A klazomaniac, you never speak without shouting. You are the baddest of the bad, and you want to make sure everyone knows it. You are exception-

Zhyzhak

ally impatient, and care little for any pursuit not directly related to smashing skulls and drinking blood. Sometimes you actually feel affection for your victims — how good of them it is to come and offer their bodies for your sport!

History: When Zhyzhak was born, she cracked her mother's pelvis wide open. She has not let up on anyone since. Always a favorite of the Green Dragon, her ungodly strength is a gift of her totem. She rapidly rose to the position of Warder for the Trinity Hive Caern, a hive actually situated in the gut of a colossal Thunderwyrm ("Grammaw").

She has since heartily plunged into the war with the Garou of Gaia, personally slaying at least one pack on her own. She has little time for learning the more cryptic lore of the Wyrm; combat has always been and will always be her true love. Although many of the Black Spiral elders want her to produce offspring that will inherit her power (and several see themselves as the ideal sire), Zhyzhak ignores them. She heartily believes that she and her allies have power and potential enough to end the war *now*, and the hell with preparing for the next generation of combat! It is perhaps this impatience that gives the most consolation to her unlucky opponents; Zhyzhak delivers death and pain aplenty, but has no time to make it linger the way her erstwhile packmates prefer.

Pentex First Team #21

Led by Sergeant T.F. MacNeil, First Team #21 is one of Pentex's finest. Seasoned veterans and some of the meanest S.O.B.s to ever level a caern, members of First Team #21 are on many Garou's "most wanted" lists. Members of #21 are infamous for their team loyalty, much of which is attributed to MacNeal's powerful leadership.

Corinna

Breed: Homid
Auspice: Galliard
Tribe: Black Spiral Dancers
Nature/Demeanor: Deviant/Caregiver
Physical: Strength 2 (4/6/5/3), Dexterity 3 (3/4/5/5), Stamina 3 (5/6/6/5)
Social: Charisma 3, Manipulation 3 (2/0/0/0), Appearance 4 (3/0/4/4)
Mental: Perception 2, Intelligence 2, Wits 3
Talents: Alertness 2, Athletics 1, Brawl 3, Expression 3, Primal-Urge 1, Subterfuge 3

Corinna

Skills: Firearms 3, Melee 3, Repair 2, Stealth 3
Knowledges: Computer 1, Enigmas 2, Occult 1, Rituals 2
Backgrounds: Fetish 2, Resources 3
Gifts: (1) Bane Protector, Persuasion, Sense Wyrm; (2) Wyrm Hide
Rank: 2
Rage 5, Gnosis 3, Willpower 5
Rites: None
Fetishes: Blood Dagger

Image: A bewilderingly beautiful woman, Corinna looks like she just stepped off the screen of a rock video. Her hair is dark and slicked back; her eyes a pale, luminescent brown; and her skin a dark olive. She stands around 5'5" tall and has a slim build. Her Crinos form is manic; her fur is black and stringy; her ears, matted and torn.

Roleplaying Notes: Pretend you care about everyone. That way they'll let their defenses down. You derive enjoyment from inflicting misery on another creatures. You live for the moment, but have learned to savor the taste of revenge. You despise most other creatures; you don't even like your teammates, but you hate them less than you hate others.

History: Corinna was taken from her mother at a very young age and sold into slavery. There she was subjected to every type of demeaning and degrading activity imaginable. At the age of 15 she underwent her First Change and killed her masters and all the slaves around her. That's when the "kindly" Black Spirals arrived and showed her the natural order of things.

Corinna learned that she and her brethren had a lot of work to do to make the world habitable for their master the Wyrm. She took to it quite naturally and began wreaking havoc left and right. She soon caught the attention of Pentex, which retained her services on a formal level, and has been working for the company ever since. Corinna joined T.F. MacNeal's First Team five years ago and has been spreading her special flavor of goodwill ever since.

Ragnor the Terror

Willpower 4, Rage 3, Gnosis 3, Power 30
Charms: Airt Sense, Armor, Healing, Materialize (Power cost 13; Str 3, Dex 2, Sta 3, Brawl 3, Dodge 1, Bite: Str + 2, 7 Health Levels), Reform, Possession
Host Form:
• **Physical:** Strength 2, Dexterity 1, Stamina 4
• **Social:** Charisma 2, Manipulation 3, Appearance 1
• **Mental:** Perception 5, Intelligence 4, Wits 4

Ragnor the Terror

Image: Ragnor prefers to inhabit obese hosts. When he does materialize in Bane form, he appears as two disembodied glowing-orange eyes and a serpentine tongue.

Roleplaying Notes: You don't usually inhabit hosts for very long; they tend to break, and you have to find replacements. You love to consume and spoil that which is pure and enjoy inciting fear in others. However, your favorite thing of all is the look of terror on a host's face before you take his body over.

History: Ragnor the Terror, as he calls himself, has been around for centuries. He has lived many days in the physical world and prefers it to the Umbra.

Ragnor stumbled across T.F. during his journeys and was impressed by the man's calculating viciousness. The Bane initially inhabited one of T.F.'s First Team members, but has since found his own hosts and has been contributing to First Team #21's successes ever since.

Sybil

Breed: Iliad Fomor
Nature/Demeanor: Survivor/Predator
Physical: Strength 3 (8), Dexterity 3 (5), Stamina 3 (7)
Social: Charisma 2, Manipulation 3 (1), Appearance 3 (0)
Mental: Perception 2, Intelligence 2, Wits 3
Talents: Alertness 2, Athletics 4, Brawl 4, Intimidation 1, Streetwise 2, Subterfuge 1

Skills: Drive 3, Etiquette 2, Firearms 3, Melee 3, Security 2, Stealth 2
Knowledges: Bureaucracy 2, Investigation 2, Law 1
Backgrounds: Contacts 2, Resources 3
Powers: Body Barbs, Immunity to the Delirium, Mega Strength
Willpower 4
Equipment: Flak jacket, shotgun
Note: The numbers in parenthesis are Sybil's attributes when she is in fomor battle form.

Image: In Homid form, Sybil is a tall, strong, shapely blond in her late 20s. In fomor battle form, she is approximately eight feet tall, with gray skin that ripples over her sinewy muscles. Her mouth is easily twice as large as normal and full of sharp teeth. Her blond hair is replaced by long, spidery barbs.

Roleplaying Notes: You have been fully corrupted by Pentex and the Wyrm. You don't love what you do, but accept it as the way of things. You despise your weak Homid form and only assume it to move through mortal society. You constantly long for the thrill of combat; it's the only thing that silences the voices in your head.

History: At the age of 22, the 5'10", 228-pound Sybil Danson decided it was time to take charge of her life. She was tired of being overweight and resolved to make a difference. She joined the Total Body Fitness Clinic — a special gym that, through special dietary preparations, vitamin supplements

Sybil

and regular resistance training, guaranteed a stronger body within 30 days or your money back.

At first, Sybil's transformation seemed miraculous. She lost over 60 pounds and reduced her body fat to only 12%. The clinic fulfilled its promise, but went further than advertised. The Total Body Fitness Clinic was actually a front for Pentex's Project Iliad. After a month of enjoying her body's changes, Sybil underwent some more. She began having nightmares. Her body continued to transform. At first she thought she was simply exercising too much, but when she accidentally maimed her new boyfriend, she realized she had a problem. Unfortunately, her life as she knew it, like those of the others who had undergone the program, was over.

Sybil adapted to her circumstances better than most. At first she rebelled against the Pentex people who came to "help" her, but later realized that she couldn't undo what had happened and moved on with her life. After years of training and performing various odd jobs for Pentex, Sybil was recruited by T.F. MacNeil for First Team #21. The pay and vacation plan were excellent, but the job itself was hell. Sybil now tries to quiet the voices of guilt that murmur in the back of her mind.

T.F. MacNeil

Nature/Demeanor: Director/Director
Physical: Strength 3, Dexterity 4, Stamina 4
Social: Charisma 5, Manipulation 4, Appearance 2
Mental: Perception 3, Intelligence 4, Wits 5
Talents: Alertness 4, Athletics 3, Brawl 2, Dodge 3, Empathy 3, Intimidation 4, Streetwise 2
Skills: Drive 3, Etiquette 4, Firearms 5, Leadership 5, Melee 3, Stealth 3, Survival 4
Knowledges: Bureaucracy 4, Computers 3, Investigation 4, Law 3, Linguistics 4, Medicine 3, Occult 4, Politics 2, Science 1
Backgrounds: Allies 2, Contacts 4, Resources 5
Willpower 9
Equipment: 9 mm semi-auto pistol, flak jacket, silver ammo

Image: A grizzled combat veteran, MacNeil is tough-as-nails and looks it. He has a stern face that has never cracked a smile, he always wears sunglasses and he bears the scars of many battles. He is very intimidating, moreso than Garou expect from a "mere human."

Roleplaying Notes: You treat everyone on your team with equal respect. You know the value of loyalty and lead your team well. You have seen it all and, through sheer force of will and sound judgment, have overcome every obstacle you've ever faced.

History: T.F. MacNeil began his career in the U.S. Marines. He quickly rose through the ranks and became an officer. After Vietnam, he mustered out and hired out his skills to corporations and Third World countries. After nearly 10 years' freelancing, MacNeil accepted regular employment

T.F. MacNeil

with Pentex. The company offered him the resources he needed and sent him against opponents and into situations that he'd never dreamed of before. Thrilled by his new missions, MacNeil rose to the occasion every time.

MacNeil now commands one of Pentex's deadliest First Teams. His leadership skills are remarkable, and his tenacity is legendary. Pentex executives know that no matter where they send MacNeil, he and his team will come back with another success to report.

Special: T.F. MacNeil has a nearly insurmountable will. He can use all types of Fetish and Bane Fetish equipment. Furthermore, he is such an inspiration to his teammates that they each gain one point of Willpower before each battle.

Barnaby Shadrack

Nature/Demeanor: Autist/Director
Physical: Strength 3, Dexterity 2, Stamina 2
Social: Charisma 4, Manipulation 5, Appearance 4
Mental: Perception 3, Intelligence 5, Wits 4
Talents: Alertness 2, Dodge 2, Expression 4, Intimidation 5, Subterfuge 5
Skills: Drive 2, Etiquette 4, Firearms 4, Leadership 5
Knowledges: Computer 3, Investigation 2, Law 3, Linguistics 2, Occult 1, Politics 4, Science 3
Backgrounds: Allies 5, Contacts 5, Mentor (Robert Allred) 4, Resources 5

Barnaby Shadrack

Powers: Immunity to Delirium

Gnosis 1, Willpower 10

Equipment: Mini-Uzi submachine gun with three clips of silver bullets.

Image: Barnaby is a tall, thin, clean-shaven man with perfectly groomed black hair. His eyes are steel-gray, and his glare is intense. He never blinks when talking to others. Never. He wears a fine suit, whatever is in fashion at the moment, and has a Rolex. He always has a briefcase with him and hides an Uzi inside it. The Pentex Amazon staff have nicknamed him "Crow." The name stuck and is now practically a code word for the current Chief Regional Officer.

Roleplaying Notes: You wonder why other people have a hard time keeping their cool. You have no trouble whatsoever in keeping your emotions bottled up. You know that to show any kind of emotion — other than what you want to show, of course — is the ultimate sign of weakness.

History: Joseph Sheldan was one of the most feared corporate raiders on Wall Street before he took a high-powered job with Endron Oil. The tragic accident that took his life on a deep-sea derrick was well-publicized. Thus, Joseph was put to rest and Barnaby was born, a whole new identity for the hot-shot Pentex executive. Joseph...

er, Barnaby didn't care if his public life was gone. The raw power of his new position was enough to occupy him.

When his good friend and mentor, Robert Allred, relocated him to the Amazon to clean up one of Elliot Meiche's mistakes, he knew he was on a stepping stone to the Board. Chief Regional Officer — it sounded nice, but why stop there? Barnaby knows his job and his future are riding on his performance, so he's not about to let a bunch of furry animals on two legs get in the way. No, the Garou will simply have to step aside for his interests. Of course, Barnaby knew they wouldn't, and that gave him a chance to show a good kill ratio to his superiors. Why the ratio isn't as good as expected is beginning to trouble him.

Prentice Turner

Nature/Demeanor: Judge/ Director

Physical: Strength 2, Dexterity 2, Stamina 2

Social: Charisma 2 , Manipulation 4, Appearance 2

Mental: Perception 4, Intelligence 3, Wits 3

Talents: Alertness 1, Athletics 1, Brawl 2, Dodge 1, Expression 2, Instruction 3, Intimidation 1, Subterfuge 3

Skills: Drive 2, Etiquette 1, Firearms 2, Melee 1, Leadership (Military) 4

Knowledges: Computer 2, Investigation 1, Law 1, Politics 2

Backgrounds: Contacts 2, Allies 2, Resources 4

Willpower 6

Equipment: Fatigues, sidearm revolver, clipboard and important papers, aviator sunglasses

Image: Prentice is a skinny, pasty, tightly wound drill sergeant type. His hair is perpetually in a military jarhead cut, and he sleeps in his uniform khakis. The creases in his pants are so sharp that the men in his unit joke that Prentice cuts his chair when he sits down. Prentice has a face that would shatter if he smiled.

Roleplaying Notes: You are a morale officer for Pentex, and you love your job. You are responsible for making sure that your unit operates at peak efficiency, and you're damn well going to do it. A disciplined unit is a happy unit, after all, and a happy unit is the best in the field. Now you just have to convince your men to see happiness as you see happiness. You always follow orders to the letter, and if the spirit of those orders is somewhat different, well, then, someone up the chain isn't doing his job. Must be an unhappy guy.

History: As a child, Prentice Turner was everything his father didn't want. Hoping for an athletic football star, Edgar Turner instead saw the birth of a sickly wretch of a son toward whom he took an immediate dislike. Naturally, Prentice's childhood was a string of unpleasant events, ranging from being locked in the basement for a weekend to having to wear a dress when the neighbors came over for dinner. It was no

Prentice Turner

wonder that before his 15th birthday, Prentice had beaten his father to death with an ax handle.

Taken from his teary-eyed mother, Prentice was placed by the judicial system in a military school for boys. Now, instead of only his father, he had an entire staff of bureaucratic megalomaniacs hammering at his psyche. All tolled, Prentice learned to suffocate his emotions and maximize his efficiency, and he seemed ready to be reintroduced into society by graduation time. Pentex was ready with a job offer as Prentice left the gates of the facility; he was just what they needed. Recently, Prentice has been reassigned to the Pentex Amazon effort to rekindle the men's spirits. Constant war with the Garou and the local shapechangers has led to high occupational mortality, and Prentice is there to get the men back on track.

PENTEX

Fomori

Blossom

Breed: Odyssey Fomor
Nature/Demeanor: Survivor/Reveler
Physical: Strength 2, Dexterity 3, Stamina 3
Social: Charisma 4, Manipulation 3, Appearance 4
Mental: Perception 2, Intelligence 3, Wits 3
Talents: Dodge 1, Guile 2, Intimidation 2, Seduction 2, Streetwise 3, Subterfuge 2
Skills: Drive 2, Etiquette 2, Melee 1, Performance 2
Knowledges: Law 2, Occult 2
Backgrounds: Favors 3, Resources 2
Powers: Enhancement, Immunity to the Delirium, Mouth of the Wyrm, Succubus Veil
Willpower 4
Equipment: None

Image: Blossom is a very attractive woman who appears to be in her late teens or early 20s. She has long, thick, black hair and brown eyes. She dresses in tight clothing to accent her perfect figure. When she's in her battle form, her eyes glow a hellish red and barbed teeth emerge from between her lips.

Blossom

Roleplaying Notes: You are the ultimate seductress. You know what people want, how to give it to them, and how to keep them coming back for more. But you don't push it; you let them come to you. You know they will.

History: Blossom started working the streets at the tender age of 15, after leaving home for the last time. She soon became a favorite and was able to command nearly any sum. But then time began to catch up with Blossom, and her age began to show; customers moved on to younger, more attractive pursuits.

Desperate, Blossom began to use more cosmetics than she had before. When they proved useless, she turned to a new brand — Siren Cosmetics — that was guaranteed to attract members of the opposite sex. She entered a contest to win a free month's supply and was thrilled to win. She began using the cosmetics immediately and discovered that the ads were true. Blossom once again turned more tricks than any other girl on the street. In fact, she turned more than ever before.

Problem was, she had to start turning clients down; she would bring tricks home and they would want to stay. She also started to undergo strange changes. Her teeth became sharp and barbed. Most johns didn't seem to mind, so Blossom never really let it bother her.

What did concern her was her dwindling supply of Siren Cosmetics. Blossom contacted the manufacturer — she just *had* to have more. The company was more than happy to oblige, but at a price. At first, Blossom refused the demands. She would do a lot of things, but she had limits. Then her cosmetic supply ran out, and the company's demands didn't seem so unreasonable.

Blossom now works as an Enticer for Pentex. While it isn't exactly how she'd planned to spend her life, the money is fantastic and she always has a complete line of cosmetics.

Dr. Spencer

Breed: Odyssey Fomor
Nature/Demeanor: Visionary/Visionary
Physical: Strength 2, Dexterity 3, Stamina 2
Social: Charisma 2, Manipulation 3, Appearance 3
Mental: Perception 4, Intelligence 4, Wits 4
Talents: Alertness 2, Dodge 1, Expression 1
Skills: Animal Ken 4, Etiquette 2, Leadership 1
Knowledges: Computer 3, Enigmas 3, Investigation 2, Medicine 4, Occult 2, Psychology 4, Science 4
Backgrounds: Allies 3, Resources 2
Powers: Immunity to the Delirium, Prediction (Dr. Spencer can roll Wits + Enigmas at difficulty 8 to try to anticipate an enemy's next action. He is accurate if he succeeds, but gets a false message if he botches.)

Dr. Spencer

Sometimes they even defy his psychic abilities (which Project Odyssey has enhanced even further). Marcus has learned that even though he may be aware of a werewolf's possible actions, his is unable to predict exactly which will be carried out. Anticipating Garou thoughts has become his new calling.

Juicy Johnes

Breed: Iliad Fomor
Nature/Demeanor: Fanatic/Autist
Physical: Strength 1, Dexterity 3, Stamina 2
Social: Charisma 3, Manipulation 3, Appearance 2
Mental: Perception 4, Intelligence 2, Wits 4
Talents: Alertness 2, Dodge 2, Streetwise 2, Subterfuge 3
Skills: Drive 2, Firearms 3, Repair 3, Stealth 2, Survival 3
Knowledges: Computers 3, Law 1, Linguistics 1
Backgrounds: Contacts 3, Resources 2
Powers: Immunity to the Delirium, Plasmic Form (see below)
Willpower 3
Equipment: None
Special: Juicy's Plasmic Form is flawed. He cannot turn fully into plasma. He will only achieve complete plasmic state upon death, at which time he'll explode and coat whomever he's fighting. The affected person will be covered with gelatinous remains, causing her to lose 2 permanent Gnosis until she cleans up and purifies herself.

Willpower 3
Equipment: None

Image: Dr. Spencer is a thin, pale-skinned man with thinning, red hair and brown eyes. He dresses casually and almost always wears a blood-stained lab coat.

Roleplaying Notes: You are scientist, first and foremost. Nearly everything you do is approached with an analytical perspective. You find others' reactions to your statements and behavior fascinating.

History: As a boy, Marcus Spencer loved animals. He sat for hours studying almost every type he could find and enjoyed trying to influence and predict their behavior. As the years went by, he found that he had a gift for anticipating animal behavior. He went on to study animal psychology, and eventually Dr. Marcus Spencer became a leading animal behavior specialist. Although he enjoyed his work, he found it somewhat boring; latent psychic powers took all the thrill out of his efforts.

Then Dr. Spencer heard of Project Odyssey, or rather its backers heard of him and approached him with a job offer. They promised the opportunity to study a whole new species, one thought to be legendary. Marcus was skeptical, but since he had the distinct impression that this was his only opportunity, he joined Project Odyssey.

Marcus was surprised to learn that his employers' promises were genuine. The werewolves he now experiments on are indeed the most fascinating creatures he has ever encountered.

Juicy Johnes

Image: Juicy looks like a janitor or custodial engineer; he's somewhat plain and dopey looking. When he assumes plasmic battle form, his skin becomes thin and gelatinous.

Roleplaying Notes: You are a walking time bomb and know it. Your life is forfeit; your days are numbered. You live for the moment. Anyone could be the one to take you out. Yet, you don't hesitate to get in the face of any jerk who looks at you funny.

History: Juicy was a janitor for Cyadine Industrial Chemicals and Food Processing Inc. when he fell into a testing vat. The experimental substance within transformed him into a fomor, leaving him forever scarred.

Company scientists ran tests. His condition: irreversible and terminal. Juicy was then sedated and flown to Pentex's corporate headquarters in New York. The men in charge gave him a choice: be listed as the casualty of an industrial accident or work for them until his fateful day. Juicy realized that he was going to die, but didn't want to invite it right away. In exchange for his services, the magnanimous executives assured him that his young brother and sole benefactor would receive a generous trust fund.

Juicy recently accepted what he believes will be his final assignment: clean up the Amazon Jungle. Whether Pentex will make good on its promise remains to be seen.

Mr. Iguana

Breed: Iliad Fomor
Nature/Demeanor: Predator/Bravo
Physical: Strength 4 (8), Dexterity 3, Stamina 5 (8)
Social: Charisma 3, Manipulation 3 (0), Appearance 2 (0)
Mental: Perception 3, Intelligence 3, Wits 3
Talents: Alertness 2, Athletics 2, Brawl 2, Dodge 1, Intimidation 3, Subterfuge 1
Skills: Disguise 2, Drive 2, Etiquette 3, Firearms 3, Repair 3, Stealth 2, Survival 2
Knowledges: Investigation 2, Law 2, Medicine 1, Poisons 2
Backgrounds: Resources 5
Powers: Enhanced Strength, Eyes of the Wyrm, Hide of the Wyrm, Immunity to the Delirium, Stomach Pumper
Willpower 5
Equipment: Subdermal radio, 9mm pistol

Image: In his Homid form, Mr. Iguana is a plain, unassuming and utterly unnoticeable man. In his battle form, Mr. Iguana resembles a giant lizard, with horny frills jutting from his head and neck; a sharp, bony mouth; and haunting, reptilian eyes that emanate the hideousness of the Wyrm.

Roleplaying Notes: You never get upset. Sometimes unexpected things happen, but your job is to stay cool, take it in stride, and achieve your objective. Keep calm, and adjust your course of action appropriately. If some jerk starts acting like Charles Bronson, hit him in the nose with the butt of your gun and see what that does for his disposition.

Mr. Iguana

History: Very little is known about Mr. Iguana; outside Pentex, even less is known. In every chance meeting Mr. Iguana has with Garou, he operates with a grim resolve and a coolness under fire that makes others wonder just what goes on in his mind. Before finding himself in the employ of Pentex, Mr. Iguana was an industrial snoop and saboteur working for Vista-Abraxas Chemical Corporation. While on an operation that took him into an Endron Oil facility, he came across a Pentex First Team that recognized his prowess, captured him, and turned him over to their leaders.

The Pentex executives at Endron proceeded to debrief Mr. Iguana, explaining to him that he had managed to contract, through unknowing contact at the facility, a strange disease that turned its carrier into a lizardlike monstrosity. This was a lie, of course, as Pentex had truly dosed Mr. Iguana with a beta sample of Fomorol to create the same effects. They made Mr. Iguana an offer he couldn't refuse: Work for Pentex, and we'll have top scientists get to the cure. Don't work for us, and see ya later, lizard-boy.

Mr. Iguana accepted and has since undertaken hush-hush and sensitive Pentex projects, including long-range assassinations and silencing those who would sell their stories to the papers or the 11 o'clock news. He continues his work with cold efficiency, working in vain for a cure that he doesn't know will never come.

Technician #7

always come back for more. Get flustered often, even when things are going well, and go into your battle form as a way of attracting attention. Beep a lot.

History: Technician #7 knows nothing about his past, except that he probably went to Georgia Tech (he has a Yellow Jackets banner in his personal room at Pentex Laboratories) and loves rooting for his old team when games are on TV. Beyond that, his predominant interests are pain and drudgery.

He has been known to work 24 hours a day for weeks at a time, alone in his lab, even though he has a girlfriend, named Dee Dee, who is also a fomor working for Pentex. When he's not actually doing something, he falls asleep on the spot, often still standing, and is very hard to rouse; usually he only awakens after having been hit several times in the vitals, whereupon he instantly gets back to work. He is very fond of citrus fruit and enjoys Garou attacks on the lab. One day, if he can make time, he and DeeDee may marry. The very idea revolts his coworkers.

Wailer

Breed: Iliad Fomor
Nature/Demeanor: Conformist/Penitent
Physical: Strength 2, Dexterity 3, Stamina 3
Social: Charisma 1, Manipulation 3, Appearance 2
Mental: Perception 3, Intelligence 4, Wits 3

Technician #7

Breed: Iliad Fomor
Nature/Demeanor: Conformist/Masochist
Physical: Strength 2, Dexterity 3, Stamina 3
Social: Charisma 1, Manipulation 1, Appearance 1
Mental: Perception 2, Intelligence 4, Wits 2
Talents: Brawl 1, Dodge 2, Subterfuge 1
Skills: Drive 1, Firearms 2, Melee 1, Repair 3, Stealth 2
Knowledges: Computer 4, Enigmas 1, Medicine 1, Occult 3, Science 4
Backgrounds: Allies 2, Contacts 2, Resources 1
Powers: Extra Limbs, Immunity to the Delirium
Willpower 3
Equipment: None

Image: In his human form, Technician #7 is a frumpy lab worker of very skeletal build and spectrally white complexion. There is something frightening about his eyes. He doesn't speak; instead he makes strange beeping sounds that indicate his present emotional condition. When actual communication is needed, he will write messages in jagged, barely legible script. When he gets irritated, he literally bursts into his battle form, which is dark and squidlike, though still humanoid. He is known to eat large rodents during his coffee breaks.

Roleplaying Notes: Irritate those around you until they hit you. You like this. You are the perfect company man and

Wailer

Talents: Alertness 4, Brawl 1, Intimidation 2, Streetwise 3
Skills: Drive 2, Firearms 2, Security 1, Stealth 4
Knowledges: Computers (Hacking) 4, Investigation 2, Law 3, Science 4
Backgrounds: Contacts 1, Resources 3, Allies 2
Powers: Immunity to the Delirium, Roar of the Wyrm
Willpower 4
Equipment: Burned out cybernetic datajack, high-grade computer

Image: Plain, nondescript and lonely. Wailer has a flat face and long, uncombed hair. He dresses casually, in T-shirts and jeans; stands 6'2"; and weighs a mere 165 pounds.

Roleplaying Notes: Don't make eye contact; do what you're told. You get rewarded when you do what you're told. Your old life is just a dream to you now. When a confrontation is unavoidable — scream. When the nightmares of your past come back to you — scream. When the pressure gets too much — scream.

History: Wailer once went by the name Andy Waller, but he has since forgotten his first name. His shyness was legendary in college. Not content avoiding crowds, Andy turned loneliness into an exact science. He meticulously alienated himself from every possible friend, social group and club.

The one relationship that he did permit himself was with his computer, and it would be his undoing. Andy spent hours logged on, communicating with foreign databases and exploring the underside of the Internet. He subscribed to the most depraved and sadistic newsgroups and kept in touch with various online criminals. Of course, Pentex kept tabs on such forums, and Andy's activities signaled a flag on Pentex's search program.

The corporation invited Andy to contribute to a new research program that would let him tap directly into the Internet. Theoretically, he would be able to project his consciousness into the computer and manipulate it at the speed of thought. While the process seemed sound, the best scientists in the world couldn't pull it off, let alone the goons Pentex hired (budget cuts and all that). Andy became a liability and was scheduled for termination. However, the Iliad scientists decided to perform an experiment of their own. Andy died that day, and Wailer was born.

Wailer resembles Andy in many ways; not even his parents could tell the difference. He is as shy and socially awkward as ever. Wailer has no hobbies besides computing. The only friends he currently has are using him for his skills and only associate with him because they're ordered to by Pentex. The largest difference between Andy and Wailer lies in Wailer's ability to transform into a hideous, sharp-toothed, screaming monster that enjoys venting its frustrations on helpless victims.

Banes

Chirox the Unfeeling

History: Christopher Roxbury was a good social worker — some would say too good. He often found himself empathizing with his clients and was generally frustrated with a system he was part of yet could not change. The anger and frustration kept building until Christopher found himself able to do what he'd been trying to do all along — absorb the pain of others so they wouldn't have to suffer it. Of course, there was a price to pay for this gift, but to Christopher, now Chirox, it was worth it.

Chirox suffers the abuse of its allies without flinching. It is as alien a spirit as any Garou has ever met and performs its duties without hesitation or enthusiasm. Chirox simply does what Chirox must.

Dr. Pearvous Smithe, The Hunter

Willpower 6, Rage 5, Gnosis 5, Power 45

Charms: Airt Sense, Armor, Corruption, Materialize (Power cost 19, Str 4, Dex 5, Sta 3, Brawl 3, Dodge 3, Bite: Str + 1, Crush: Str + 2, 7 Health Levels), Possession, Tracking, Reform

Host Form:
- **Physical:** Strength 3, Dexterity 4, Stamina 3

Chirox the Unfeeling

Willpower 5, Rage 3, Gnosis 4, Power 30

Charms: Armor, Healing, Materialize (Power cost 15; Str 4, Dex 1, Sta 5, Brawl 2, Dodge 2, Punch: Str + 1, 8 Health Levels), Possession

Host Form:
- **Physical:** Strength 2, Dexterity 2, Stamina 8
- **Social:** Charisma 0, Manipulation 0, Appearance 0
- **Mental:** Perception 2, Intelligence 3, Wits 2

Image: Once a handsome young man, Chirox is now crippled, deformed and blind. He has also become destitute and looks it. He's thin from malnourishment, and his right arm and hand are curled toward his body. His head is permanently tilted to the right, as if his neck had broken and healed incorrectly. When freed from its host, Chirox is a large humanoid who appears to have been carved from onyx. Above its head floats an eerie onyx sphere that emanates a soft purple light.

Roleplaying Notes: Christopher Roxbury was your host's real name, or at least it used to be. Poor idiot. At least now he has a purpose. You don't maintain your physical form at all, caring little for its welfare. If you have to abandon it, too bad.

- **Social:** Charisma 3, Manipulation 4, Appearance 2
- **Mental:** Perception 4, Intelligence 3, Wits 4

Special: Dr. Smithe usually carries a shotgun and flak jacket. His skill in Firearms is 3.

Image: The host, Dr. Pearvous Smithe, is a rough-and-tumble, educated explorer. He is rugged looking, with long dark hair and a hairy, muscular build. The Bane that possesses Smithe is long, serpentine and silver and has rows of sharp teeth.

Roleplaying Notes: You are a consummate hunter, a predator through and through. As a man, you tracked, explored and hunted everything that ever walked or crawled. Now that you're possessed by the Wyrm, you're even more formidable.

History: Dr. Smithe was exploring the Amazon jungle, looking for the lost city of gold. What he found was an ancient Inca temple. After disarming all of the death traps that protected the temple's treasure, Smithe prepared to reap the rewards of his efforts. He didn't count on the temple's last line of defense though: the Bane that resided in a golden statue. When Smithe touched the statue, the Bane inhabited his body. Smithe, however, became a willing host, believing that the Bane offered him more knowledge and power than he had ever known before.

Smithe is partially correct. The Bane has made him more powerful. Unfortunately, it plans on leaving his body soon — destroying poor Dr. Smithe in the process.

Kitalid the Deceiver

Willpower 3, Rage 2, Gnosis 3, Power 30

Charms: Airt Sense, Materialize (Power Cost 13; Str 3, Dex 2, Sta 3, Brawl 3, Dodge 1, Bite: Str + 2, 7 Health Levels), Possession, Reform

Host Form:

- **Physical:** Strength 1, Dexterity 3, Stamina 1
- **Social:** Charisma 3 , Manipulation 3, Appearance 2
- **Mental:** Perception 2, Intelligence 2, Wits 2

Image: In its physical form, Kitalid infallibly possesses a cherubic and innocent little boy or girl. In its spirit form, Kitalid looks like a man-sized insectoid monstrosity with multiple heads. These heads may resemble animals, people, insects, mythic creatures, or any combination of these.

Roleplaying Notes: You are thoroughly vile, as are most Banes. You take great pleasure in corrupting the pure and innocent into tools of the Wyrm. You are not as wantonly destructive as some Banes, as you prefer to operate more subtly and treacherously. Having completely taken over your host body (kids are sooo easy...), phase two of your insidious plan is to corrupt all of your "friends" at school and on the playground.

History: Formed in one the stinking pits in the realm of Malfeas, Kitalid is a Bane spirit of treachery and deceit. Since time immemorial, it has corrupted the innocent, pure and often overlooked in its effort to serve its unholy masters. Generally, Kitalid first begins possession of the host body when the child's emotions are at the most pained

Kitalid the Deceiver

and raw state, like after a spanking or when they are grounded. Kitalid slips into the soul of the child, further entrenching itself with promises of getting more toys, having more friends and staying up later. Kitalid then goes to work, bent on spreading its influence among the friends of the possessed child. Only in the most dire of circumstances will Kitalid Materialize, because it destroys the host body and draws unwanted attention, but those who are unprepared for Kitalid's true form are seldom seen again.

Latonia the Temptress

Willpower 5, Rage 6, Gnosis 6, Power 45

Charms: Airt Sense, Blighted Touch, Corruption, Materialize (Power Cost 22; Str 5, Dex 4, Sta 4, Brawl 5, Dodge 3, Bite: Str + 1, Claw: Str + 3, 7 Health Levels), Possession, Reform

Host Form:

- **Physical:** Strength 2, Dexterity 3, Stamina 3
- **Social:** Charisma 4, Manipulation 5, Appearance 4
- **Mental:** Perception 3, Intelligence 2, Wits 3

Image: Latonia is a painfully attractive woman in her mid-20s with raven black hair and a seductively athletic build. When she appears in public, she wears promiscuous clothing, which may appear as skin-tight leather or revealingly cut velvet or satin. Away from the public eye, however, she wears only the uniform of the professional dominatrix. As a materialized spirit, Latonia sloughs off her skin and appears as an arguably reptilian humanoid with a

Latonia the Temptress

Shoragg

Willpower 3, Rage 5, Gnosis 3, Power 25

Charms: Blast Flame, Blighted Touch, Materialize (Power cost 15; Str 4, Dex 4, Sta 3, Brawl 2, Dodge 2, Bite: Str + 1, 7 Health Levels), Possession

Host Form:
- **Physical:** Strength 7, Dexterity 1, Stamina 3
- **Social:** Charisma 0, Manipulation 0, Appearance 3
- **Mental:** Perception 2, Intelligence 2, Wits 1

Image: In his horse form, Shoragg is a handsome, chestnut-brown horse, but has bright, bloodshot eyes. Shoragg's true form appears as an extremely emaciated humanoid with large jaws and teeth.

Roleplaying Notes: Wow, look at all the idiots who think Banes only possess people! If anyone deserves your tender attentions, they do. You take great delight in attacking those who try to "help" you. The simple truth is that you don't want to be helped; you like yourself just the way you are, thank you very much.

History: For several years, Shoragg's host worked as a trained horse on a popular television show. Eventually, abuse by trainers and actors grew too much for the poor beast, and he lashed out at any two-legs around. As he kicked and bit at the frightened humans, a gleeful Bane took the opportunity to slide into a new host body.

horrible mouth full of sharp teeth, clawlike talons at the ends of her hands and a prehensile tail.

Roleplaying Notes: Give men and women pleasure, because you live off their psychic emanations as a vampire does of blood. The more people you seduce, the more willing servants you may deliver to the Wyrm and your dark mistress, Empress Aliara. You yourself find pleasure in inflicting pain on others, though not necessarily killing them, and by receiving pain yourself.

History: Before her possession by the Bane that inhabits her soul, Latonia was a straight-laced nine-to-five paralegal consultant. After a series of unhealthy and unfulfilling relationships, her constantly faltering self-esteem opened her soul to the dark Bane spirit of the Countess of Desire, which began to contort Latonia's mind and warp it to its own evil whims.

Turning her host into a tool of hedonistic pleasure was only the first step in the Bane's agenda; now Latonia actively converts her customers into the service of the Wyrm with entreating promises of endless sensual pleasure and untold power. To her surprise, one of her customers actually turned out to be a Glass Walker Garou, and she is slowly, carefully and subtly culling him for the use of her superiors.

Shoragg

The relationship proved to work quite nicely. The horse was a pliable host, and the element of surprise continues to delight Shoragg. Since then, Shoragg has allowed himself to be ridden only by those whom *he* has chosen, and they have been few and far between.

Tsannik

Willpower 6, Rage 10, Gnosis 10, Power 60

Charms: Airt Sense, Materialize (Power cost 39; Str 8, Dex 5, Sta 7, Brawl 5, Dodge 3, Bite: Str + 2, Talon Rend: Str + 3, 10 Health Levels), Reform, Warp Reality

Host Form:
- **Physical:** Strength 3, Dexterity 3, Stamina 5
- **Social:** Charisma 3, Manipulation 4, Appearance 5
- **Mental:** Perception 3, Intelligence 4, Wits 3

Image: Tsannik is a man of slightly above-average height and build, with brown hair and dark eyes. He has impeccable taste in clothing, cars, women and men. He's good looking, and he knows it. His true form is a Nexus Crawler: a slimy, green thingie with horned protrusions and spindly legs; a long-ass tongue; and lots of mean-looking teeth.

Roleplaying Notes: You have power beyond imagining, and yet your master says you must exercise restraint, and you will — for now. You are always calm and collected, even reserved, but should anyone cross you, you have no problem with sharing your "true self."

Tsannik

History: Power. That's what Samuel Connor lived for. What else was there? With power came respect, and with respect came fear. Samuel learned that lesson early in life, from his father. His mother died when Samuel was an infant. Some say it was suicide to escape the abuses of her husband. Others say Samuel's father killed his wife in a fit of rage over an undercooked steak. At any rate, the boy quickly learned that little other than controlling others was worth having.

Young Samuel took that lesson to heart and applied it to every decision, every action, but it wasn't enough. He could never achieve enough power; he wanted to tap into the very essence of power itself before he could be satisfied, but exactly how to do that remained beyond him.

That is, true power eluded him until he found an old book tucked away in a bookstore. The owner told him that all other copies had been destroyed for the occult knowledge they contained and was reluctant to sell this last. Samuel, who by then was in his 20s and already had a reputation for being a shrewd, if ruthless, businessman and politician, was not to be dissuaded. In fact, the woman's reluctance to sell him the book only served to fuel his desire to have it.

That night, as Samuel wiped blood from the book's cover, he knew he had finally found the key that would grant him the power he deserved. Leafing through the pages, he settled on a formula that would bind into service one of the most powerful beings in existence, or so the book promised. The book wasn't wrong, nor was it entirely truthful.

Samuel watched, horribly fascinated, as the thing materialized before him. But his perverse glee turned to stark terror as it looked at him, smiled and happily ignored the mystic, protective boundary that he had so carefully constructed. Samuel, who now answers to Tsannik, finally understands what true power is. And he couldn't be happier.

Voragg the Unbound

Willpower 5, Rage 4, Gnosis 5, Power 40

Charms: Airt Sense, Armor, Blast Flame, Healing, Materialize (Power cost 14; Str 2, Dex 4, Sta 3, Brawl 2, Dodge 2, Bite: Str + 2, 7 Health Levels), Possession, Reform

Host Form:
- **Physical:** Strength 4, Dexterity 3, Stamina 4
- **Social:** Charisma 3, Manipulation 2, Appearance 4
- **Mental:** Perception 3, Intelligence 2, Wits 2

Image: Voragg inhabits large, physically powerful hosts. Construction workers, body builders and professional wrestlers all fall within his purview. His materialized Bane form is 2-1/2 feet tall, sinewy, black and demonic. His eyes are glowing red orbs, and his teeth are too numerous to count.

Roleplaying Notes: You believe yourself invincible, even though you're not. You anger quickly and resent nearly all forms of authority. You are hateful of Garou Theurges, especially Wendigo, and attack them on sight.

Voragg the Unbound

History: Voragg has served the Wyrm for hundreds of years. Unfortunately for him, he's spent most of that time locked in a spiritual prison deep beneath the Rocky Mountains. In the latter part of the 16th century, Voragg made trouble for a Wendigo tribe. The tribe called gathered its forces and defeated Voragg, leaving him bound in a rock.

Hector Fritz inadvertently freed Voragg while working a temp job for a construction company. Hector noticed strange markings on a rock that he had unearthed. Instead of calling his supervisor, who would have been forced to call in archeologists who would have put the project on hold, Hector jackhammered straight through the markings and the rock.

Free, Voragg instantly overwhelmed Hector's body and soul. He then proceeded to wreck the construction site and two nearby buildings. Voragg left town with his host, bent on making trouble in the world.

Voragg pays little attention to his master, the Eater-of-Souls. This suits the Eater, for Voragg is beneath his notice. If Voragg were ever to gain any real power or allies, the Eater-of-Souls might notice him. The Bane currently wanders California with a pack of fomori. Although he is nominal leader of the group, the fomori have designs on Voragg and his human puppet.

Seventh Generation

The Seventh Generation is a secret society dedicated to the service of the Defiler Wyrm. Their leaders are ancient and powerful, and many ranking members gain special magical abilities through their debased rites. Storytellers are free to give members of the Seventh Generation various abilities roughly equivalent to fomori powers or werewolf Gifts; Immunity to the Delirium is definitely in keeping with their practiced soldiers.

Johnson P. Donnovan

Caste: Business
Nature/Demeanor: Conniver/Competitor
Physical: Strength 3, Dexterity 3, Stamina 3
Social: Charisma 2, Manipulation 4, Appearance 4
Mental: Perception 2, Intelligence 3, Wits 3
Talents: Alertness 2, Dodge 2, Intimidation 2, Streetwise 3, Subterfuge 3
Skills: Drive 3, Etiquette 2, Firearms 3, Leadership 2
Knowledges: Law 2, Politics 2
Backgrounds: Contacts 3, Resources 4
Willpower 3
Equipment: Gold card

Image: Johnson is a short man of average build who smokes too much, drinks too much and really doesn't care if people approve of him. At least he is always well-dressed; he prefers silks and leather to cotton and polyesters.

Roleplaying Notes: You're a business man, a professional; act like one. Exude confidence in yourself and your abilities to make your customers happy. If they think a price is high, let them look elsewhere; you know they'll be back. They always are.

History: Johnson grew up in an average suburban family, but as the youngest and smallest of his siblings, he took more than his fair share of abuse. His size kept him from participating in what his father considered "manly" sports, which only served to alienate him further.

At school, Johnson adapted to yet another hostile environment, learning that being small and looking innocent had its advantages. Who, he realized, would suspect that nice Donnovan boy of stealing the final exam right off the teacher's desk? Before long Johnson became known as a source for almost any kind of illicit good. Sure, items came at a price, and sometimes prices were high, but he was the one taking all the risks. Besides, Donnovan provided the best.

Johnson entered the "business" world right after high school graduation and quickly moved up the ladder of success. His rise was so quick, in fact, that he was noticed and approached by an organization, the Seventh Generation, the depths of which he did not even begin to understand. At first, Johnson refused; his "acquisition" business was booming, and

Johnson P. Donnovan

he saw no reason to sell out to anyone. At least, that was how he felt until an event which became known among his peers as "The Chicken Head Incident." The complete fiasco really wasn't his doing, but the sharks Johnson swam with didn't care. They were quick to discredit him regardless of circumstances. After all, in the "business" world, anything that can be used to discredit the competition will be used: "If you can't take the heat, get out of the kitchen," as the adage goes.

That's a lesson Johnson had to learn the hard way, and as he slowly rebuilds his reputation, that's a lesson he teaches others. And now, with the assistance of the Seventh Generation, he's one hell of a teacher.

Lorenz Winkler

Caste: Medical
Nature/Demeanor: Deviant/Reveler
Physical: Strength 2, Dexterity 2, Stamina 2
Social: Charisma 3, Manipulation 5, Appearance 2
Mental: Perception 3, Intelligence 4, Wits 3
Talents: Alertness 2, Dodge 2, Empathy 2, Expression 3, Streetwise 3, Subterfuge 4

Lorenz Winkler

Winkler, with the help of new and powerful friends in the Seventh Generation, next accepted a high-paying position with a prominent HMO. In time he manipulated his way into its Washington, D.C., offices as a lobbyist against health care reform. Lorenz has been so successful in his lobbying, especially with the current crop of congressional freshmen, that the Seventh Generation has expanded his influence to include lobbying for the tobacco industry and other volatile, health-and-public-wealth-oriented special interests. He is often seen at right-wing fundraisers, a huge cigar in hand, cheerfully sharing detailed anecdotes of his private practice.

At heart, Lorenz Winkler has always been a corrupter. Now he has dedicated his "gift" not only to women in his care, but to the world.

Maximillian

Caste: Military
Nature/Demeanor: Competitor/Curmudgeon
Physical: Strength 4, Dexterity 3, Stamina 3
Social: Charisma 2, Manipulation 2, Appearance 2
Mental: Perception 3, Intelligence 2, Wits 3
Talents: Alertness 1, Athletics 2, Brawl 2, Dodge 1, Intimidation 1, Streetwise 1, Subterfuge 2
Skills: Drive 3, Firearms 3, Leadership 1, Melee 3, Repair 2, Stealth 2

Skills: Drive 2, Etiquette 4, Firearms 3, Leadership 1, Stealth 2
Knowledges: Computer 2, Law 2, Linguistics 1, Medicine 4, Occult 2, Politics 4, Science 3
Backgrounds: Allies 3, Contacts 4
Willpower 5
Equipment: Medical kit, derringer

Image: Lorenz Winkler is an aging, dapper-yet-smarmy man who never wears casual clothing. He clearly enjoys the trappings of wealth and power and possesses a snide wit that he uses to bludgeon those of lower station.

Roleplaying Notes: Leer at beautiful women, and lick your lips subconsciously. Pick on those who aren't up to snuff. Slap backs like a politician. Tell dirty jokes. Throw your money around like you make the stuff in your basement (you would, but fortunately don't have to). If someone offends you, send others to avenge the offense; there's no need to lower yourself to that level when there are low-born more suited to it.

History: Once a successful gynecologist in New York City, Dr. Lorenz Winkler was forced to retire by the American Society of Obstetrics and Gynecology under threat of full public disclosure of illicit practices (ones that would cast the entire profession in a bad light). A huge settlement was awarded to Lorenz's victims, none of whom will ever again be comfortable hearing the phrase, "Could you hop up on the table?"

Maximillian

Knowledges: Computer 2, Investigation 1, Law 1, Occult 2

Backgrounds: Contacts 2, Allies 2, Resources 2

Willpower 5

Equipment: 9mm pistol, kevlar vest, knife

Image: Maximillian is a brutish brick wall of a man with the body of a Russian weightlifter. He rarely ever wears anything other than his military uniform or his battle dress fatigues. The look in his eyes is one of pure malevolence. He keeps his hair close-cropped per the military standard.

Roleplaying Notes: Enough talking! Let's see some action! You are impatient, crude, misogynistic, and a little paranoid. Crack your knuckles, bristle, and glare a lot, and bark orders at others when you're in the field. Nothing anybody ever does is good enough in your opinion, and you wish they would just let you do it first so it gets done the right way.

History: Maximillian was introduced to the Seventh Generation by a superior in the United States Army. Singled out for his martial prowess, his effectiveness and his fearlessness, Max has quickly risen through the ranks by proving his worth in the field. His main inhibition, though, has been his powderkeg temper, which the General recognizes as a significant disadvantage.

Maximillian, of course, believes none of this and thinks that the General has it in for him. This subtle paranoia has colored his field assignments in the past, some of which are only now blowing over, like the time Max shot his second-in-command in the face, believing him to be a bureaucratic spy placed by his superior. The event was marginally overlooked due to the success of the assignment, but most of the Seventh Generation realize that Max sometimes skates on thin ice and request transfers from his division. In any case, few are as accurate with a pistol, as silent climbing fences, and as successful driving a flaming jeep through a police barricade as Maximillian.

Miles Kent

Caste: Government

Nature/Demeanor: Lone Wolf/Traditionalist

Physical: Strength 2, Dexterity 2, Stamina 2

Social: Charisma 2, Manipulation 4, Appearance 2

Mental: Perception 3, Intelligence 4, Wits 3

Talents: Alertness 2, Athletics 2, Brawl 3, Dodge 2, Intimidation 3, Streetwise 2, Subterfuge 3

Skills: Drive 3, Etiquette 2, Firearms 3, Leadership 3, Melee 1, Stealth 1

Knowledges: Computer 2, Investigation 4, Law 3, Linguistics 1, Occult 1, Politics 2

Backgrounds: Allies 1, Contacts 1, Resources 2

Willpower 5

Equipment: .45 automatic with silver rounds

Image: Miles is a man of slightly above-average looks and height, and he dresses fashionably yet conservatively. In low light, his Wyrm taint can be seen in his left eye, which is said to dimly glow with the fires of the pits of hell itself.

Miles Kent

Roleplaying Notes: You're Crockett from *Miami Vice*. You exude sexuality and are sure that every woman wants you, whether they know it or not. And you also know that the best places for them are the kitchen or the bedroom. However, you don't let any of this interfere with your sworn duty to protect the country from the slime that would drag Old Glory through the mud and call it freedom of expression. If you're willing to die for your country, then by God, so should everyone else; it was that attitude that made this country great and will make it great again.

History: Miles Kent was born in a small Arkansas farm town to a family that on its most progressive-thinking days could only be called traditional. The government, the country and the family were what he and his brothers were raised to respect and serve, generally in that order. (Miles did have a sister who no one speaks of openly. She defied her family and chose to go to college and get a career of her own; both of her parents have legally disowned her.) Upon graduation from high school, Miles entered the military and joined the military police.

His career with the military was somewhat brief, but distinguished; in the end, Miles chose to leave the military when the Soviet Union collapsed. He promptly joined the National Security Agency, where he could protect the country from the "liberal, commie weirdoes" who were trying to destroy it. (He personally feels that allowing women into the military was a mistake and that allowing homosexuals and lesbians to enlist has been an act tantamount to treason.)

Miles has pursued each of his assignments with a great deal of… enthusiasm, bordering on the cold-blooded and even brutal. It is a common belief that Miles would "sanction" his own mother if she tried to use a postage stamp twice. However, his unquestioning devotion to his job has led his superiors to often look the other way when it comes to Miles' conduct "in the interests of national security."

A short time after joining the NSA, Miles was approached by a representative from the Seventh Generation. Feeling that he was speaking with kindred spirits, Miles agreed to assist them with their efforts.

Miles' greatest talent and asset to the Seventh Generation in the War of the Apocalypse has been his ability to run interference for others when necessary. More than one agent of the Wyrm has eluded capture after a particularly grisly crime, usually murder, whenever Miles has gotten involved himself. It is expected that this talent will enable Miles to rise quickly through the ranks of the Seventh Generation.

Snickers

Caste: Snatcher
Nature/Demeanor: Predator/Bravo
Physical: Strength 4, Dexterity 2, Stamina 4
Social: Charisma 2, Manipulation 2, Appearance 2
Mental: Perception 3, Intelligence 4, Wits 3
Talents: Alertness 1, Athletics 3, Brawl 3, Dodge 3, Intimidation 4, Streetwise 4
Skills: Drive 2, Firearms 2, Melee 2, Stealth 3
Knowledges: Law 1, Occult 2
Backgrounds: None
Willpower 7
Equipment: None

Image: Snickers is an extremely large individual, standing better than six-and-a-half feet tall and weighing close to 300 pounds, all of it muscle. He has black hair that he never combs, has multiple piercings in each ear and usually wears clothing that best shows off his muscular physique.

Roleplaying Notes: Sick. Perverted. Twisted. That's what they call you, but you know better. You're an artist. When someone disappears, they know when you did it because you have style. The look on your victims' faces is such a rush: the fear, the horror, and then, when they realize that they won't be going home again, the terror. God, how you love it. How can you help but giggle and snicker in their terrified faces?

History: From childhood, Snickers always enjoyed frightening others. He would often trick neighborhood kids into hiding in "special spots," and then lock them in there for days. His tricks and abductions always looked like accidents, so no one caught on until Snickers got sloppy shortly after his 16th birthday. He could have sworn that little girl didn't know it was him, but she identified him by his unusual laughter. It was this laughter that earned him his nickname and landed him in a juvenile prison for five years.

Snickers

At 21, Snickers returned to the streets. Not much had changed for him, except that he'd met some new friends in prison, friends who promised to teach him how to avoid being caught again. But he had to promise to take whomever they asked him to. Snickers agreed, figuring that he could still grab who he wanted every once in a while. Besides, if his friends really could teach him some new tricks….

The Seventh Generation did teach him. Snickers was a fast learner, particularly when he realized the usefulness of his lessons. It's been almost 15 years since Snickers was released from prison. While the number of his abductions certainly hasn't decreased, Snickers has grown cocky again, and the chances of catching him have begun to increase.

The General

Caste: Military
Nature/Demeanor: Fanatic/Director
Physical: Strength 3, Dexterity 3, Stamina 4
Social: Charisma 5, Manipulation 5, Appearance 3
Mental: Perception 3, Intelligence 4, Wits 4
Talents: Alertness 3, Brawl 2, Empathy 1, Intimidation 4, Subterfuge 4
Skills: Drive 2, Etiquette 4, Firearms 5, Leadership 5, Survival 2
Knowledges: Computer 2, Law 4, Linguistics 3, Politics 5, Science 2
Backgrounds: Allies 4, Contacts 5, Resources 5

The General

Talents: Alertness 2, Brawl 2, Intimidation 3, Streetwise 4, Subterfuge 4

Skills: Drive 3, Firearms 2, Repair 2, Stealth 3, Survival 1

Knowledges: Investigation 3, Law 4, Occult 1

Backgrounds: Contacts 3, Resources 2

Willpower 3

Equipment: Cellular phone, corporate credit card, 9 mm semi-auto pistol

Image: A dirty-looking old man with Coke-bottle glasses and a ratty gray beard, Uncle Freddy usually wears a trench coat with a variety of drugs and candy stuffed in its pockets.

Roleplaying Notes: Everyone's a commodity. That's how you see it anyway. You have yet to meet someone who you couldn't drug and sell on the black market. You prefer children because they're naive and trusting, although anyone will do when push comes to shove.

History: Uncle Freddy never had a break. He was the youngest child of a family of five. He ran away at 15 and took to the streets. He got in with a bad crowd, and it made him everything he is today. Uncle Freddy has been in "business" since the mid-'70s. He makes his living kidnapping the weak and unsuspecting and selling them through an underground slave auction. He has always lived alone and has neither friends nor non-business associates. He doesn't know what the Wyrm is, but is an unwitting servant.

Willpower 9

Equipment: Silver ammo, submachine gun

Image: A polished, stern man, the General's exact age is unknown, although he appears to be in his late 50s. He wears a heavily starched military uniform with his rank and medals displayed proudly. His hair is dark gray, and his eyes are black.

Roleplaying Notes: You are a leader of men. When you say jump, you expect to hear "How high, Sir?" You have no patience for hippies, druggies, granola eatin' pansies, liberals, pop stars, radio personalities, check-out clerks, loose cannons and the homeless.

History: A career military man, the General has transcended command of the regular army. Now he heads up the warrior caste of the Seventh Generation. He leads mice and men alike as he relentlessly presses the agenda of the Seventh Generation.

The General rarely gets directly involved in operations, instead orchestrating events from afar. He has top-level government security clearance and thus has literally hundreds of law enforcement officials at his disposal, if not under his thumb.

Uncle Freddy

Caste: Snatcher

Nature/Demeanor: Deviant/Jester

Physical: Strength 2, Dexterity 3, Stamina 3

Social: Charisma 1, Manipulation 4, Appearance 2

Mental: Perception 3, Intelligence 2, Wits 4

Uncle Freddy

Vampires

For full details on the Count's statistics, see **Vampire: The Masquerade**.

Count Vladimir Rustovitch

Clan: Tzimisce
Generation: 6th
Embrace: A.D. 876
Nature: Fanatic
Demeanor: Traditionalist
Physical: Strength 6, Dexterity 5, Stamina 6
Social: Charisma 6, Manipulation 5, Appearance 5
Mental: Perception 5, Intelligence 5, Wits 4
Talents: Alertness 5, Athletics 3, Brawl 6, Dodge 5, Intimidation 6, Leadership 5, Subterfuge 3
Skills: Animal Ken (bats) 5, Body Alteration 5, Etiquette 4, Firearms 2, Melee 5, Stealth 4, Survival 3, Torture 5
Knowledges: Finance 4, Linguistics 7, Lupine Lore (Shadow Lords) 4, Medicine 3, Military Science 6, Occult 5, Politics 4, Sabbat Lore 4, Science 2, Seneschal (from **Vampire: The Dark Ages**) 5
Disciplines: Animalism 6, Auspex 6, Dominate 3, Fortitude 2, Potence 4, Presence 5, Protean 4, Thaumaturgy 3, Vicissitude 6
Discipline Notes: Rustovitch's extra level of Animalism allows him to extend his consciousness into a swarm of bats, thereby controlling the swarm like a communal puppet. His extra level of Auspex enables him to "see" in 360 degrees by means of sonar emissions, like a bat. His extra level of Vicissitude allows him to assume the batlike Chiropteran Marauder form, from **Vampire: The Dark Ages**.
Backgrounds: Influence 2, Resources 5, Retainers 5 (guardian *szlachta* ghouls, swarm of giant ghoul bats), Sabbat Status 4
Virtues: Callousness 4, Instincts 4, Morale 5
Path: Path of Honorable Accord 8
Willpower: 9

Image: Rustovitch is the embodiment of the Old World gentleman. He stands an even six feet, dresses immaculately in conservative suits and cravats and is perfectly manicured and groomed (courtesy of Vicissitude).

This, of course, is the Count's human form. When Rustovitch uses Vicissitude to assume the Chiropteran Marauder shape, he metamorphoses into a hideous, tusk-fanged bipedal bat.

Roleplaying Notes: Like many Tzimisce, you are a peculiar combination of nobility and evil. Indeed, you are

Count Vladimir Rustovitch

the archetypal Tzimisce: the embodiment of the term "vampire lord." You are unfailingly gracious to your friends and are a man of your word; unfortunately, you have very few friends. You are fond of your ghoul bats and often "converse" with them.

History: The man who would become Count Vladimir Rustovitch was born amid the Balkan crags during the bleakest times of the Dark Ages. Even before his Embrace the shadow of the Tzimisce vampire clan fell across him: the Rustovitch family was an offshoot of House Bratovitch, the Tzimisce's line of warrior-revenants.

Rustovitch demonstrated his mettle early on, fighting the Tzimisce's wars under the bat banner of his house. An adept soldier, Rustovitch proved a cunning tactician and a merciless foe. Within 10 years of assuming leadership of House Rustovitch, Vladimir had expanded his fiefdom from a rocky tuber-patch precariously guarded by earthen stockades to a vast tract dominated by a sprawling fortress.

This display of power impressed even the jaded Tzimisce, and in 876 the ancient Fiend Kosczecsyku elevated Rustovitch from revenant to full Tzimisce vampire. Rustovitch dutifully served his sire, but when Kosczecsyku fell to the Shadow Lords in 983, Rustovitch declared himself *voivode* and savagely put down all rival claimants to his sire's fiefdom. Most of his "brothers" were slain, but two — Mischa and Csikos — fled Castle Kosczecsyku into the werewolf-haunted pines surrounding the estate.

The next centuries were good: Rustovitch led successful campaigns against the Old Clan, the Shadow Lords, the Gangrel, the Ventrue and the newly formed Tremere. Even the Warlocks' Gargoyle servitors could not dislodge the *voivode* from his bat-haunted stronghold — now known as Castle Rustovitch. Rustovitch's fiefdom expanded and expanded again; he was acknowledged as *voivode* among *voivodes*, and the most beautiful women of Hungary were brought before him as food or brides-to-be.

Then, in 1313, Rustovitch was called to the Old Country's borders to assist in its defense against a massive Teutonic Knight invasion. Dutifully, Rustovitch went to the clan's aid. The invasion was easily — too easily — put down, and Rustovitch returned to his home. Or to what was left of it.

Vengeful Mischa and Csikos, conspiring with jealous rivals and the Shadow Lords, had sown their discord well. Rustovitch's bat banner had been torn down, and pieces of his stalwart guards lay strewn throughout the courtyard.

Baying Shadow Lords stalked through the halls, and all that remained of his brides — even little Elzbieta, his favorite — were tattered, bloody rags.

Rustovitch's wrathful frenzy on that night is still spoken of by Shadow Lords who wish to frighten unruly cubs. But there were too many foes, and all his allies had been slain. Filling a sack with dirt from his courtyard, the grieving Rustovitch fled his estate and hid amid the Carpathians. When the Sabbat formed, the bitter Rustovitch gladly rose against the traitorous *voivodes* who had engineered his downfall (and what he did to Mischa and Csikos, who were captured alive during the struggle, sends a shudder even up Tzimisce spines).

Now Rustovitch wanders the world, caring little on which side of the Atlantic he walks. Displaced and bereaved, the ancient vampire exists only for revenge against the Shadow Lords. He is a member of the Sabbat, but has less interest in the goals of his sect than in vengeance on the hated werewolves. Rustovitch is particularly interested in finding and capturing those Shadow Lords descended from his brides' killers, for he is aware of the concept of Past Lives, and he very much wishes to hear his Lupine victims scream in voices 700 years dead....

Abomination

Allonzo Montoya

Sire: Hansard
Generation: 8th
Embrace: 1894 (born 1847)
Apparent Age: Late 40s
Breed: Homid
Auspice: Philodox
Tribe: None (formerly Shadow Lord)
Clan: Malkavian
Nature/Demeanor: Masochist/Deviant
Physical: Strength 5 (7/9/8/6), Dexterity 3 (3/4/5/5), Stamina 5 (7/8/8/7)
Social: Charisma 1, Manipulation 4 (3/1/1/1), Appearance 2 (1/0/2/2)
Mental: Perception 4, Intelligence 3, Wits 4
Talents: Alertness 3, Brawl 2, Dodge 3, Empathy 2, Expression 1, Intimidation 3, Streetwise 1, Subterfuge 4
Skills: Animal Ken 1, Drive 2, Etiquette (Nobility) 4, Firearms 1, Melee 3, Leadership 2, Stealth 3, Survival (Urban) 5

Allonzo Montoya

Knowledges: Computer 1, Enigmas 3, Law 3, Linguistics (Romance) 5 (Greek, Italian, Spanish, French, Latin), Occult 3, Politics 2, Science 2
Backgrounds: Contacts 2, Generation 5, Resources 4, Totem 5
Gifts: (1) Aura of Confidence, Fatal Flaw, Resist Pain, Scent of Man; (2) King of the Beasts, Luna's Armor, Staredown; (3) Disquiet, Icy Chill of Despair; (4) Cocoon, Open Wounds
Disciplines: Animalism 2, Auspex 3, Dominate 2, Obfuscate 4, Serpentis 2
Blood Pool (Max. Per Turn): 15/3
Rank: None (formerly 4)
Rage 9, Gnosis 6, Willpower 9, Ego 5
Rites: (Death) Gathering for the Departed; (Mystic) Rite of Talisman Dedication, Rite of Binding
Fetishes: Bane Sword
Derangements: Delusions of Grandeur, Fantasy, Intellectualization, Perfection

Image: Montoya has a disquieting appearance. In his Homid form, his skin has a deathly pallor and is stretched tight over his prominent cheekbones. He has a hooked aquiline nose and a jutting lower jaw that signifies relation to nobility. His clothes look straight out of GQ magazine; the kind of couture that no one really wears, but set the styles for the season. Long white hair flows to the middle of his back, and a full beard and mustache give him a dignified look that reinforces his subtle air of odd majesty. In Crinos form, gray-white fur covers his body, combining to look like silver in the light of the moon. He is especially thin in his Crinos form. Lupus form sees Montoya thin and emaciated, though still bearing silvery-gray fur. Montoya rarely takes his Lupus form, as he knows that his vampiric metabolism takes its toll on him, making his wolf form utterly disturbing.

Roleplaying Notes: There is nothing redeemable about you; you are going to hell, and you had best make as many friends there as you can. Serve the Wyrm? Why not? It has been better to you than accursed Gaia or her mad sister. You are a brother to dragons and a companion to owls, after all. Indulge your desires, and inflict your whims on others. Why the hell not? You're damned if you do, and damned if you don't.

History: Damnation. Fear. Hate. Outcast. As if life wasn't troublesome enough. Montoya was Garou, a member of a dying race, duty-bound to pursue a futile war against an invincible foe. Though Montoya possessed supernatural healing powers, he still felt the pain every time a minion of the Wyrm tore his flesh and spilled his guts. Montoya learned the angst and frustration of devoting every waking

·hour to combating the Wyrm, only to discover that it had crept up behind him as he fought it from the front.

He felt the loss as his Kinfolk fell beneath the brutal slaughter of Banes in the caern's bawn. Montoya wept hot tears of fury as all of the other members of his pack were destroyed in a hopeless confrontation with an Urge-Wyrm. It was all a walk in the park compared to his Embrace. Unconscious in the lair of the Wyrm, he was dragged to the sanitarium haven of an old and very deranged vampire who took great pleasure in the irony of Montoya's position. Drop by drop he stole Montoya's blood and then gashed his wrist to pour it back into the fallen Garou's mouth. His limbs began to ache as the liquid fire poured through them. The torments of a thousand hells filled his mind and clouded his vision, and when Montoya finally regained consciousness, he was an Abomination, the bastard child of two alien worlds.

Montoya slew his sire without a second thought and ran blindly into the night that had become his eternal home. Since then, Montoya has learned what it is like to be spurned by everything he once held dear. His own people, the Garou, attack him on sight, and the vampires call Blood Hunts as Montoya sets foot in their towns. Even the poor simple mortals shun him, as Montoya is cold and they are but food to him. Through no fault of his own Montoya is damned, forever barred from all worlds and any salvation.